CW00732227

Glorify God in your Body

Human identity and flourishing in marriage, singleness and friendship

Commended by CEEC as a resource for the Living in Love and Faith project

Martin Davie

CEEC

Church of England Evangelical Council

Glorify God in your Body:
Human identity and flourishing in marriage, singleness and friendship

By Martin Davie

© CEEC 2018

web: www.ceec.info

email: info@ceec.info

CEEC

CEEC, c/o All Souls Church, 2 All Souls Place, London, W1B 3DA.

ISBN: 978-1-9993270-0-2

Published by Lost Coin Books on behalf of CEEC
Printed in the UK

Contents

Foreword   5

Introduction   7

PART I: A Christian approach to marriage, sex and family life

Chapter 1: Why ethics needs God   17
    Introduction
    Being true to ourselves
    The importance of flourishing
    The Sexual Revolution
    A Christian view of the 'i world'
    The purpose and shape of this study

Chapter 2: Doing the right thing   31
    How do I make decisions?
    How can I know what God wants?
    How can I know what the Christian faith is?
    What does the Christian faith say?
    Doing what we were made to do
    Doing what we were saved to do
    Doing what we are set free to doFree to love
    Grace, forgiveness, hope and patience

Chapter 3: Men, Women and Marriage in this world   45
    Human sex
    Sex in Genesis 1:26-31 and 5:1-2
    Sex in Genesis 2:18-25
    Sex in Matthew 19:3-6 and Mark 10:2-9

Chapter 4: Men and Women in the world to come   59
    The life of the world to come
    What does Jesus say about resurrection life?
    Will we still have sexed bodies?
    Will we be married?

Chapter 5: Marriage, singleness, and friendship (I)   69
    Two ways to live
    Marriage as instituted of God
    Equality in marriage
    Submission, love and honour
    Five objections to the view of marriage set out in this chapter
    Marriage as spiritual warfare
    The Christian view of marriage and modern approaches
       to relationships
    Appendix 1: Guidelines on male headship in marriage
    Appendix 2: Sex and shame in the Christian tradition

Chapter 6: Marriage, singleness, and friendship (II)   **95**
Everyone is doing it
Intentional singleness
Jesus' intentional singleness
Singleness misunderstood
Singleness and marriage as dual vocations
Everyone is called to friendship
The Church is called to friendship

PART II Challenges facing a Christian approach

Chapter 7: Intersex and Transgender   **111**
Recognizing reality
Might there be more than two sexes?
What causes physical sexual differentiation?
How many people are intersex?
Are people with the intersex a third type of human being?
How can people with intersex conditions live rightly before God? ..
What does transgender mean?
Why is the transgender phenomenon problematic?
How should Christians respond to transgender?
Appendix: The ordination of transgender people and services to
mark gender transition

Chapter 8: Sex outside marriage   **133**
Christianity's challenge to pagan sexual standards
What is wrong with sex outside marriage?
Why does it matter what we do with our bodies?
What does Jesus say about rejecting sexual immorality?
What does it mean to exercise chastity?
Why is chastity so difficult?
Prostitution
Pornography
Masturbation
Sexual surrogacy
Cohabitation
Same-sex sexual relationships
Responding rightly to those of us who are same-sex attracted
Living a life of love

Chapter 9: Divorce and re-marriage   **163**
The prevalence of divorce
Is the Church of England inconsistent on marriage?
How has the Church of England's position changed?
What does the Old Testament say?
What does Jesus say?
What does St Paul say?
How should Christians respond to divorce and re-marriage?

Chapter 10: Birth control and infertility treatment   181

Be fruitful and multiply
What did the Church traditionally teach about birth control?
When did Protestant teaching change?
Why does the Roman Catholic Church oppose contraception?
Is opposition to contraception theologically valid?
How should Christians assess different methods of birth control?
Forms of infertility treatment
Are Roman Catholic objections to fertility treatment valid?
What moral issues are raised by gestational surrogacy and in vitro fertilisation?
What about 'designer babies'?
What does all this mean in practice?

PART III CONCLUSION

Chapter 11: Conclusion—Glorify God in your body   199

Appendix 1: *St Andrews Day Statement*   207
Appendix 2: *St Matthias Day Statement*   213
Appendix 3: *Gospel, Church and Marriage*   219

Scripture index   228

FOREWORD

The Church of England is currently facing a navigational challenge unlike any she has experienced in living memory. On the one hand she is facing the new reality of a government redefinition of marriage—something unforeseen even at the height of the 1960s sexual revolution. On the other, she is witnessing within both a simultaneous rise in the use of experience as a hermeneutical tool and a divergent exegesis of Scripture on matters of sexual ethics.

This study is an invaluable signpost for such a precarious time. The Church of England Evangelical Council commends it as a resource in the discussions that will take place as part of the "Living in Love and Faith: Christian teaching and learning about human identity, sexuality and marriage" project—but it will also be a gift on a much wider scale. Its genius is in its scope – and the way in which the author (supported by a team of evangelical theologians) brings together a robust exploration of an apostolic understanding of Scripture with a pastoral consideration of key life issues.

It is worth emphasizing further what this book is and is not. This book seriously engages with the pastoral and ethical issues of our time and is written with knowledge of and appreciation for scientific study and sociological consideration. But it is not intended as a contribution to the biographical narrative that is dominating much of the current church debate around human sexuality. Rather, it is a substantial and robust apologetic for a classic biblical understanding around issues of identity, sexuality and gender—an understanding that is held to by the vast majority of Anglicans throughout the world.

We commend this book for study in the Church of England: by those preparing resources as part of the "Living in Love and Faith" project, by those who teach and preach in our parish churches, for young people and students wrestling with the realities of a society that appears to have lost its historic and Christian ethical moorings and for any wishing to dig deeper into Scripture regarding sexual ethics.

We echo Paul's plea that Christians everywhere should glorify God with their bodies (1 Corinthians 6:20)—and we pray that this book might enable us to hear God's voice in Scripture afresh on these important matters, thereby knowing His perfect will for our flourishing in both soul and body.

The Rt Rev'd Julian Henderson (CEEC president)
The Rev'd Hugh Palmer (CEEC chair)
Mr Stephen Hofmeyr (CEEC secretary)
The Rev'd George Curry (CEEC treasurer)
The Rev'd John Dunnett (CEEC Working Group)
The Rev'd Rachel Marszalek (CEEC Working Group)
Mrs Amanda Robbie (CEEC Working Group)
The Rev'd Robert Slipper (CEEC Working Group chair)
Mrs Alison Wynne (CEEC Working Group)

INTRODUCTION

Should I make love to a sex robot? This is probably not a question many people will have asked themselves, but advances in animatronics mean that this issue is now on the moral horizon.[1] Whether we are asking this or another more traditional question to do with marriage, sex and family life, our culture's prevailing moral framework is based on the importance of being true to ourselves and the importance of flourishing. This is how we approach questions today like 'Should I get married or stay single?', 'Is it right to have sex outside marriage?' and 'Is it right for someone who has been divorced to re-marry?'

Being true to ourselves

According to the prevailing narrative in our society, in the Western world at least we are being set free. The dominant voices in our culture tell a positive and inspiring story about how people are being set free from the chains of traditional morality so that they can live as the unique individuals they are. Glynn Harrison helpfully summarizes it as follows:

> For centuries, traditional morality had us—all of us—in its suffocating grip. Year after year the same old rules, chained in the past, heaped shame on ordinary men and women (and boys and girls) whose only crime was being different. Enemies of the human spirit, these bankrupt ideologies befriended bigots and encouraged the spiteful. They nurtured a seedbed of hypocrisy and offered safe havens to perpetrators of abuse.

> No more. Change is here. We are breaking free from the shackles of bigotry and removing ourselves from under the dead hand of tradition. Our time has come. A time to be ourselves. A time to be who we truly are. A time to

---

1   See David Levy, *Love and Sex with Robots: The Evolution of Human-Robot Relationships*, New York: Harper Collins, 2008 and John Danaher and Neil McArthur (eds.), *Robot Sex: Social and Ethical Implications*, Cambridge: MIT Press, 2017.

celebrate love wherever we find it. A time for the human spirit to flourish once again.[2]

This story reflects an emphasis on individualism and personal authenticity which characterizes what has been called the 'i world.'[3] This means that our dominant cultural assumptions prioritize the individual. In particular, it is up to individuals to discover for themselves who they truly are and then to live their lives according to that discovery. As Jonathan Grant puts it:

> Modern authenticity encourages us to create our own beliefs and morality, the only rule being that they must resonate with who we feel we really are. The worst thing that we can do is to conform to some moral code that is imposed on us from outside—by society, our parents, the church, or whoever else. It is deemed to be self-evident that any such imposition would undermine our unique identity…. The authentic self believes that personal meaning must be found within ourselves or must resonate with our one-of-a-kind personality.[4]

The importance of flourishing

Central to this story is the belief that it is good when human beings flourish as the unique individuals they are. The purpose of society and its institutions is to encourage this flourishing, which is understood in terms of achieving the maximum possible physical and psychological well-being for the individual between their birth and the time they cease to exist at death. Moreover, in our late capitalist consumer culture free choice by the individual from a potentially endless range of options, not just in goods and services, but also in lifestyles and in personal relationships, is seen as the way in which flourishing can best be achieved. Life is seen as a vast shopping centre, or online shopping site, and we flourish when we are free to choose whatever we want from everything that is on offer.[5]

Sexual activity, which is often identified with love, is seen as an integral part of human flourishing, so in line with the contemporary emphasis on free choice it is held that each individual should have the freedom to engage in sexual activity with whomsoever they wish and in the way that they want, provided that such

---

2 Glynn Harrison, *A Better Story*, London: IVP, 2016, Kindle edition, Loc.787-797.
3 See Dale Kuehne, *Sex and the iWorld*, Grand Rapids: Baker Academic, 2009,
4 Jonathan Grant, *Divine Sex*, Grand Rapids: Brazos Press, 2015, p.30.
5 For a more detailed discussion of the influence of a consumer culture on sexual ethics see Grant, *op. cit.* Chapter 4. It is an interesting historical irony that although the attack on traditional family structures and traditional sexual morality has roots in the writing of Marx and Engels and has been supported by those with a Marxist agenda, it can be argued that it has actually been the triumph of a capitalist consumer culture that has done most to undermine the traditional family and traditional sexual ethics.

activity is not imposed on other individuals without their consent.

In addition our sexual identities (seen in terms of both who we desire to have sex with and whether we identify ourselves as male, female, or in some other way) are seen as integral to who we are (which is why they are protected categories under the Equality Act of 2010).[6] There is a continuing debate about the extent to which our sexual identities are fixed or fluid, are innate or chosen, but the prevailing view in our culture is that people should be free to accept and act upon whatever form of sexual identity they find most authentic. This, it is held, is what will best enable them to flourish.

The Sexual Revolution

The Sexual Revolution across the Western world since the 1960s has resulted from a combination of these 'i world' emphases: the importance of individuals being true to themselves, the importance of free choice, and the importance of sexual activity and identity for human flourishing. The revolution has had three stages.

The first stage of the revolution, with its slogan of 'free love', was about giving people the freedom to have sexual intercourse as and when they wanted. It de-coupled sex from marriage and the procreation of children both ideologically and though the provision of contraception and access to abortion and it liberalized divorce laws so as to allow people to be true to themselves by more easily walking away from unhappy marriages and entering into new relationships. The second stage, 'gay liberation', was about allowing people who are sexually attracted to members of their own sex to enjoy the same sexual freedom as all other people without legal sanction or social stigma. The third stage, which we are now in, is about allowing people to define and live out their own sexual identity, whether male, female, or other, regardless of the biological sex with which they were born.

These three stages of the revolution have gained the backing of the media, the political establishment (and therefore the law), the education system and big business. Now the emphases of the 'i-world' and the developments of the Sexual Revolution are together a central part of the governing ideology of the United Kingdom. It is understood as being just, tolerant, loving and liberating. Those groups and individuals who object to this ideology (including religious bodies) are therefore widely regarded as immoral because they are construed as being anti-freedom and anti-love. [7]

---

6   See Jenelle Williams, *The End of Sexual Identity*, Downers Grove: IVP Academic, 2011.
7   For an overview of the history of the sexual revolution see Gabriele Kuby, *The Global Sexual Revolution*, Kettering OH: Angelico Press, 2015.

A Christian view of the 'i world'

The world view of the 'i world' is consonant with many aspects of the Christian faith and has been welcomed by many Christians on that basis. Christianity too holds that each individual is unique, that they should be true to who they really are and they should have the opportunity to flourish in every aspect of their being. Christianity also says that our sexual identities are central to who we are and that sexual activity is a good and important part of human experience. However, Christianity would go on to say that the positive insights of the 'i world' need to be understood in relation to what the Christian story tells us about God, God's activity, and the fact that death is not the end of the human story but merely the beginning of a new chapter in it.

The reason each person is unique, according to the Christian story, is that each individual is a special creation of the God who created and sustains the universe as a whole. This God has created human beings as male and female to be in a loving relationship with him, to reflect his character and to care for each other and for the world that he has made. Consequently, being true to ourselves means being true to the person God has made us to be and choosing to live in the way that he has designed us to live. This is sometimes seen as inimical to human autonomy, but, as Richard Bauckham points out, the very opposite is true:

> God's law is not the will of another, in the ordinary sense in which this would be true of the will of another creature, but, as the law of the Creator and his creation, also the law of our own being, in conforming to which we become most truly ourselves.[8]

The Christian faith further tells us that the intrusion of evil into God's good creation and into our individual lives means that we have become unable to know properly our true, God given, identities and to live as we are meant to live. However, God has dealt with this situation by sending his Son Jesus Christ to reveal who we truly are and to give us a new start in which we receive supernatural strength through God's Spirit to begin to live in accordance with God's will. Those who live in this way will truly flourish, even if they face acute challenges and hardship. After they die they will be resurrected at the end of time to live with God forever in a new creation from which all evil will have been banished and in which they will find true fulfilment beyond our present capacity to imagine.

---

8   Richard Bauckham, *God and the Crisis of Freedom*, Louisville and London: Westminster John Knox Press, 2002, p.208.

The purpose and shape of this study

This study, which has been written with the assistance of a representative group of Evangelical theologians, is intended as a contribution to the discussions that are taking place, and will take place, in the Church of England in relation to the House of Bishops' Living in Love and Faith project on 'humanity identity, sexuality and marriage.[9] It explores a Christian approach to human identity, marriage, sex and family life, in the light of the overall Christian worldview that has just been described. It considers the challenges to this approach arising from the Sexual Revolution and from technological developments in the fields of birth control and infertility treatment and looks at how Christians should respond to these challenges. The study is in three parts:

Part I, 'A Christian approach to marriage, sex and family life,' consists of six chapters. It explains why the existence of the soul and belief in the existence of right and wrong point us to the existence of an infinitely wise and good creator God (chapter 1). It explores how we can know this God and what it means to live rightly before him (chapter 2). It considers God's original creation of sex and marriage and what human existence will be like in the world to come when we shall still be men and women but marriage as we know it will be no more (chapters 3 and 4). Finally, in the light of the preceding chapters, it looks at the Christian understanding of marriage and singleness as the two vocations to which God calls men and women in this world and suggests that friendship is the basic pattern of Christian relationship which undergirds these two vocations (chapters 5 and 6).

Part II, 'Challenges facing a Christian approach,' consists of four chapters. It looks at the challenge to traditional Christian anthropology posed by intersex and transgender (chapter 7). It considers sex outside marriage and same-sex relationships (chapter 8). It explores the issues of divorce and re-marriage (chapter 9). Finally it looks at birth control and infertility treatment (chapter 10). All four chapters address both the theological and pastoral issues which these topics raise.

Part III, 'Conclusion,' summarizes the argument developed in the study through a series of seventeen questions and answers about what it means to live in accordance with God's will and therefore, as St Paul says (1 Corinthians 6 :20) to 'glorify God in your body.'

Three appendices contain three previous statements from the Church of England Evangelical Council covering some of the issues covered in this study.

---

9   For details of the Living in Love and Faith project see https://www.churchofengland.org/about/leadership-and-governance/general-synod/bishops/living-love-and-faith

PART I

A Christian approach to marriage, sex and family life

CHAPTER 1

Why ethics needs God

'The fear of the Lord is the beginning of wisdom, and the knowledge of the Holy One is insight' (Proverbs 9:10).

A very good place to start

In *The Sound of Music* Maria begins to instruct her charges about music with the words,

> Let's start at the very beginning
> A very good place to start.[10]

We are concerned in this study with difficult and pastorally sensitive questions about how we glorify God in our bodies. They are deeply personal and sometimes urgent and painful questions for many of us, and the fact that it is a conversation about the personal experiences of real people must be borne in mind throughout. We want to explore these questions in the context of the Christian story and so, in the spirit of Maria's words, we shall start this study 'at the very beginning' by looking at some basic questions about what it means to be human and how this points to our relationship with God. This will help us when it comes to questions about marriage, sex and family life.

If you are unfamiliar with the philosophy of religion and theories of ethics you may find this chapter a bit hard going and be tempted to skip it and move on to the discussion of specific ethical issues in the later chapters of this study. Please resist this temptation. This chapter lays the foundation for what is said in these later chapters and so you need to have got to grips with what it says to understand them properly.

---

10 *The Sound of Music,* 'Maria and the Children—Do-Re-Mi Lyrics' at http://www.lyricsonde-mand.com/soundtracks/s/thesoundofmusiclyrics/do-re-milyrics.html.

Being human

The purpose of this study is to consider how Christians should think and act in relation to issues to do with sex, marriage and family life.

Being a Christian necessarily involves being a human being. There are not, and cannot be, Christian dogs, fish, or sandwich makers, since being a Christian involves a commitment to God that only a human being can make. It follows that if we want to understand how Christians should think and act in relation to these matters, we need to understand what it means to be human in the first place.

Down through the centuries the Christian tradition has taught that human beings are what is known as a 'psychosomatic unity' of bodies and souls. That means that all humans are both a material body and an immaterial soul.[11] This view is based on the Bible[12] and the insights of the Greek philosophers Plato[13] and Aristotle.[14] It was taught by the Early Church Fathers[15] and by the theologians of the Middle Ages,[16] and it continued to be taught by mainstream Protestant theologians during the Reformation. Martin Luther, for example, in his *Small Catechism* (1529), explains that the Creedal statement 'I believe in God, the Father almighty, Maker of heaven and earth' means 'I believe that God has created me and all that exists, that he has given me and still sustains my body and soul.'[17]

The Anglican tradition agrees that human beings consist of bodies and souls. We can see this, for example, in the words of the Holy Communion service in *The Book of Common Prayer*. The Minister gives people the bread and wine so that Christ's body and blood may 'preserve thy body and soul unto everlasting life.' The people 'offer and present unto thee, O Lord, ourselves, our souls and bodies' and pray 'that through thy most mighty protection, both here and ever, we may be preserved in both body and soul.' Likewise, in the Burial Service a distinction is made between the soul of the departed 'which it hath pleased Almighty God of his great mercy to take unto himself' and their body which is committed to the

---

11 Some Christians have preferred to say that human beings consist of body, soul and spirit in line with 1 Thessalonians 5:23, but the idea that human beings are 'dichotomous' creatures consisting of body and soul has been more common.
12 For example, Genesis 2:7, Psalm 103:1-2, Matthew 10:28, John 12:27 and 2 Corinthians 5:1-10.
13 Plato, *The Republic*, Book IV.
14 Aristotle, *On the Soul*.
15 This Patristic teaching is summarized in Chapter XII of St John of Damascus, *Exposition of the Orthodox Faith*.
16 The classic Medieval statement is found in St Thomas Aquinas, *Summa Theologica*, Part 1, Questions 75-76.
17 Martin Luther, Small Catechism, in Mark Noll (ed), *Confessions and Catechisms of the Reformation*, Vancouver: Regent College Publishing, 1991, p. 68.

ground, 'earth to earth, ashes, dust to dust.'

So, 'who am I?' The Christian tradition says that I am a human being, a single self, a psychosomatic unity consisting of a body and a soul. I am a material body, including a material brain, but that is not all I am. I am also an immaterial, conscious, rational, soul that is aware of God, other people, and the world in general, a mind that acts in and through my body in the light of this awareness.

One day my material body will die, but my soul will survive that death, and because disembodiment is not its proper state God will re-unite my soul with a resurrected body in the general resurrection of the dead at the end of time.

Although there are reports of out-of-body experiences, for the most part everything that we do as human beings takes place by means of the soul and the body acting together. For example, these words you are reading exist because a soul, by means of a body, was aware of the words and instructed a body to type them on the computer through the operation of a brain, an arm and a hand.[18]

How can I act morally?

The fact that human beings have souls as well as material bodies is what enables them to act in a moral fashion. To act morally is to freely choose to do something in response to a sense of moral obligation. In the case of purely material entities there is no element of choice. Thus a stone hurled at someone's head has no choice in whether or not it will hit them. If the physical forces impelling it to move mean that it will hit that person then it will hit them.

If we hold that a human being is a purely material entity the same point would apply. We would have to take a determinist view of human activity and say that all our thoughts and intentions, and the acts that flow from them, are controlled by physical forces in a way not chosen by us and that we therefore have no freedom of the will and consequently no more freedom over our actions than a flung stone has.

If determinism were true it would be difficult to make sense of moral obli-

---

18 There are Christians who would take what is known as a 'physicalist' position and who would argue that rather than having an immaterial soul human beings are purely physical creatures who nevertheless have the capacity to think, choose and relate to God (for this position see Nancey Murphy, *Bodies and Souls, or Spirited Bodies?*, Cambridge: CUP, 2006. This is a minority position within the history of the Christian tradition and its critics would say that it is not demanded by the findings of neuroscience, that it is unable to account satisfactorily for the biblical references to the soul, and that it is unable to explain how a purely physical creature can think rationally, choose freely and have a conscious self that survives the death of the body.

gation and responsibility. As J. P. Moreland notes, 'If I 'ought' to do something, it seems to be necessary to suppose that I can do it, that I could have done otherwise and that I am in control of my actions. No one would say that I ought to jump to the top of a fifty foot building and save a baby, or that I ought to stop the American Civil War in this present year, because I do not have the ability to do either.'[19] Since human morality, presupposing freedom to choose and act on what we choose, does exist,[20] the only reasonable explanation is that, as the Christian tradition has affirmed, humans have souls as well as material bodies.

Now, if human beings have souls, how can we explain their existence? As C S Lewis notes, it does not make sense to say that conscious rational minds are the product of an irrational material universe (what Lewis calls 'Nature'). Rather, they must be 'supernatural' entities originating in a supernatural rational mind outside of Nature; and this is what the Christian tradition calls 'God'. 'Human minds, then, are not the only supernatural entities that exist,' writes Lewis. 'They do not come from nowhere. Each has come into Nature from Supernature: each has its tap root in an eternal, self-existent, rational Being, whom we call God. Each is an offshoot, or spearhead, or incursion of that Supernatural reality into Nature.'[21] We

---

19 J P Moreland, *The Soul, how we know it's real and why it matters*, Chicago: Moody Publishers, 2014, Kindle Edition, pp.128-129.

20 In the history of Christian theology there has been a debate about the extent of the freedom of choice possessed by human beings after the Fall (see, for example, E. Gordon Rupp and Philip S. Watson (eds.) *Luther and Erasmus: Free Will and Salvation*, Philadelphia: Westminster Press, 1969). The witness of the Bible and of our everyday human experience indicate that the correct answer to this debate is to say that fallen human beings do possess freedom of choice in matters to do with their day to day lives in this world (including matters to do with marriage, sex and family life). However, they are not free to relate rightly to God, and thus be saved, without the supernatural assistance of the Holy Spirit. This is the position taken by Article XVIII of the Lutheran Augsburg Confession of 1530 and by the Church of England's Necessary Doctrine and Erudition for Every Christian Man of 1543. The former declares: 'It is also taught among us that man possesses some measure of free will which enables him to live an outwardly honourable life and to make choices among the things that reason comprehends. But without the grace, help, and activity of the Holy Spirit man is not capable of making himself acceptable to God, of fearing God and believing in God with his whole heart, or of expelling evil lusts from his heart. This is accomplished by the Holy Spirit, who is given through the Word of God, for Paul says in 1 Corinthians 2:14. 'natural man does not receive the gifts of the Spirit of God.' (Text in Mark A Noll (ed.), *Confessions and Catechisms of the Reformation*, Vancouver: Regent College Publishing, 2004, p.93).
The latter states: 'And so likewise although there remain a certain freedom of the will in those things which do pertain unto the desires and works of this present life (cf. Augsburg Confess., XVIII), yet to perform spiritual and heavenly things free will of itself is insufficient: and therefore the power of man's free will, being thus wounded and decayed, hath need of a physician to heal it, and an help to repair it; that it may receive light and strength whereby it may see, and have power to do those godly and spiritual things, which before the fall of Adam it was able and might have done.' (Text in W H Griffith Thomas, *The Principles of Theology*, London: Church Book Room Press, 1951, p.177.)

21 C S Lewis, *Miracles*, Glasgow: Fontana, 1985, p. 32. For a further explanation and defence of Lewis' argument see Peter S Williams, *C.S.Lewis v The New Atheists*, Milton Keynes, Paternoster, 2013, ch.4.

can thus say that ethics requires the existence of souls and the existence of souls in turn requires the existence of God.

As noted above, when a human being does something, it takes place because the soul and body are acting together. This is true of marriage, sex and family life: getting married, engaging in sexual intercourse, and begetting and raising children are all activities which necessarily involve the action of embodied souls. If either the soul or the body were absent they could not take place. We have just seen that the existence of our souls allow us to act morally, and this raises an ethical question: what does it mean for embodied souls to act rightly in the contexts of marriage, sex and family life?

As we all know, many different answers are given to this question both in the Church and in wider society. People disagree, for instance, about whether people should have sex before they are married, whether it is right for people of the same sex to get married, what it means to say someone belongs to a particular sex, and about what kinds of fertility treatment are ethically acceptable for couples who have difficulty conceiving naturally. Before we can consider what it means for Christians to act rightly in these specific situations, we need to know what it means to act rightly in general.

How do I know what is right?

Authenticity is highly valued in our culture. It is generally held that people should be free to choose to act in whatever way seems to be most authentic to them. However, our culture also continues to hold that there is a real distinction between actions that are right and actions that are wrong. For example, the recent rise of the #Me Too movement stemming from the tweet by Alyssa Milano 'if all the women who have been sexually harassed or assaulted wrote 'Me Too.' as a status we might get some idea of the magnitude of the problem,' is based on the belief that it is wrong for women to be sexually harassed by film producers, politicians, or anyone else with power, and that is right to protest against this and stop it happening in future.[22]

Christianity would agree with the belief that there is a real distinction between right and wrong actions. Mugging old ladies is wrong. So is defrauding bank customers of their life savings. But helping old ladies across the road or giving to those in need is right, because the former are against God's will and the latter

---

22 See Nadia Khomami, '# Me Too: how a hash tag became a rallying cry against sexual harassment,' *The Guardian*, 20 October 2017 at https://www.theguardian.com/world/2017/oct/20/women-worldwide-use-hashtag-metoo-against-sexual-harassment

are in accordance with it. What God says goes, or to quote David Baggett and Jerry Walls, 'God's commands dictate what is moral.'[23] This is known as Divine Command Theory, and this is how Christians have traditionally understood what constitutes an action as right or wrong.

Divine Command Theory does not entail the belief that there is somewhere a detailed list of divine commands that can be directly applied to each and every situation that human beings face. Those who have held to the various forms of Divine Command Theory have generally acknowledged the complexity of discerning God's will and applying it to particular circumstances.[24] What Divine Command Theory in all its forms does involve, however, is the belief that what God wills determines what is good and therefore what should be done and what God opposes determines what is evil and therefore should not be done. Thus God wills that we should honour our parents (Exodus 20:12) and so that is what we should do, whereas he opposes killing the innocent (Exodus 20:13) and therefore this is what we should not do. [25]

However, in spite of the central place of Divine Command Theory in Christian ethics (and also in Jewish and Muslim ethics), in recent centuries there has been an increasing revolt against Divine Command Theory on the basis you do not need to believe in God to know and do what is right. There are two distinct issues raised by this challenge to God's place in morality:

1. Is it necessary to believe in God in order to act in a moral fashion?

2. Do we need to believe in God in order to make sense of the idea of moral obligation?

In response to the first question, the answer is clearly 'No.' Plenty of people who reject belief in God do behave in a moral fashion; for example, being faithful to their spouses, kind to their children and generous to those in need. But this is not surprising from a Christian perspective, since all human beings can access what God commands through creation, conscience and often, at least in the West, a residual influence of Christian teaching. They can still know what is moral and be inclined to act morally despite their disbelief in God himself.

---

23 David Baggett and Jerry Walls, *Good God—the theistic foundations of morality*, New York: OUP, 2011, p.32.

24 For a good example of the acknowledgement of the complexity involved see Richard Hooker, *The Laws of Ecclesiastical Polity, Book I*, Oxford: OUP, 1841.

25 For introductions to Divine Command Theory see Baggett and Wells, op,cit, Ch.6, Paul Helm (ed) *Divine Commands and Morality*, Oxford: OUP, 1981 and Robert Adams *Finite and Infinite Goods: A Framework for Ethics*. Oxford: OUP, 2002.

In response to the second question, the answer is 'Yes.' This is because although there are a variety of secular theories of ethics, any view of ethics that denies the existence of God and his law fails to provide a strong and coherent basis for affirming that some actions are moral while others are not, and that we are therefore obliged to do some things and not do others. The atheist Richard Dawkins, in a famous passage in his book *River Out of Eden*, declares:

> The universe we observe has precisely the properties we should expect if there is, at bottom, no design, no purpose, no evil and no good, nothing but blind, pitiless indifference. As that unhappy poet A.E. Housman put it:
>
> > 'For Nature, heartless, witless
> > Nature will neither know nor care.'
>
> DNA neither knows nor cares
> DNA just is.
> And we dance to its music.[26]

If this view of the universe is accepted then there is no coherent basis for any form of moral judgement. God does not exist, the universe does not know or care about morality, and so there is no transcendent moral authority to which we can appeal when we want to decide what is right and what is wrong.[27]

In the absence of a transcendent moral authority and an objective standard of good or evil, we are left with the arbitrary choice of the individual or the state. The Yale law professor Arthur Leff makes this point in his celebrated paper 'Unspeakable Ethics, Unnatural Law', helpfully summarised by Andy Bannister as follows:

> [Leff] points out that any moral claims (e.g. 'You ought to help old ladies across the road'; 'You ought not to poke badgers with a stick'; 'Generosity is good'; 'Paris Hilton is bad')—are authority claims, and to any authority claim we can respond like the school bully or the town drunk and cry, 'Yeah? Sez who?' In the absence of God, says Leff, there are but two options: you can turn every individual person into a little godlet, able to decide good and evil for themselves. But then who evaluates between them when there are clashes

---

26 Richard Dawkins, *River Out of Eden: A Darwinian View of Life*, New York: Basic Books, 1995, p.133.
27 It is sometimes suggested that there is a third option between theism and atheistic materialism, which is belief in some form of spiritual power or 'life force' at work in the universe, but as C S Lewis points out in *Mere Christianity* we have to ask proponents of this view whether this power or life force is 'something with a mind or not.' If it does have a mind then we are back to theism. If it does not, then it is difficult to see how it could have a will or purpose for the universe which could be the foundation for ethics (C S Lewis, *Mere Christianity*, Glasgow: Fount, 1984, pp.33-34). We would be back to blind indifference.

between godlet claims? Alternatively, you can turn the state into God and let it determine good and evil, but then might becomes right and you have sheer, naked brutality (and what's wrong with government-sponsored brutality, if the state is the only moral authority?). In short, if you try this latter route, morality becomes meaningless. If you go down the former route, morality becomes impossible. And in either case, whenever another godlet, or the state, tells you that anything is good, right, or the Proper Thing To Do, you can look them squarely in the eye and sneer: 'Really, sez who?' Leff ends his essay by pointing out that there is only one solution to this—and that would be if goodness were something bigger than us, something outside us. Only then could ethics, morality, and law actually work.'[28]

Sez who? God says!

The reason that ethics, morality, and law do actually work, according to the Bible and Christian theism, is that God does exist. He is not absent. There is a transcendent source of moral authority outside of us. This means we can answer the 'sez who?' question by replying 'God says.' Divine Command Theory thus not only makes sense, but is in fact the *only* theory of ethics that ultimately makes sense. There have been, and are, many ethical theories that seek to explain what it means to make morally good decisions, but none of them apart from Divine Command Theory provide a rationally satisfactory answer to the basic questions of how we can be confident that there really is a distinction between good and evil that is not just an arbitrary human invention and on what basis we can know the difference between the two.[29]

The appeal to God's will as the source of moral authority is often challenged on the basis of what is known as the 'Euthyphro dilemma.' The Euthyphro dilemma is so called because it is first formulated in Plato's dialogue *Euthyphro* in which Euthyphro and Socrates discuss whether Euthyphro would be right, or 'pious,' to denounce and prosecute his father for having unjustly caused the death of a servant. In the course of their discussion Euthyphro affirms that 'the pious is what all the gods love, and the opposite, what all the gods hate is the impious.'[30] In response Socrates then poses the question 'Is the pious loved by the gods because it

---

28 Andy Bannister, *The Atheist Who Didn't Exist*, Oxford and Grand Rapids: Monarch, 2015, Kindle edition, chapter 8, quoting Arthur A Leff, 'Unspeakable Ethics, Unnatural Law', *Duke Law Journal*, Vol.6, 1979, p.1249. Leff's full essay can be found online at http://bit.ly/leff.

29 For a comprehensive review of secular theories of ethics and their limitations see David Baggett and Jerry Walls, *God & Cosmos—Moral Truth and Human Meaning*, New York: OUP, 2016.

30 Euthyphro 9e in G M A Grube and John M Cooper, *The Trial and Death of Socrates*, Indianapolis/Cambridge, 2000, p.11.

is pious, or is it pious because it is loved by the gods?'[31]

As Louise Anthony notes:

Translated into contemporary terms, the question Socrates is asking is that: Are morally good actions morally good simply in virtue of God's favouring them? Or does God favour them because they are—independently of his favouring them—morally good?[32]

If we want to say that God is the source of moral authority, we seem to be left with two problematic alternatives. Either we could go down the 'voluntarist' route with the medieval theologian William of Ockham and say whatever God willed would be right even if, for example, he were to command us to torture children for fun; or we could go for the second option and say that right and wrong are independent of, and antecedent to, God, which would mean God is no longer the source of moral authority. We have a dilemma: either morality is arbitrary or God is unnecessary. However, many theologians have pointed out that this dilemma is a false one. God can avoid being morally arbitrary without referring to an external standard because, as Richard Hooker explains, 'The being of God is a kind of law to his working: for that perfection which God is, giveth perfection to that he doth.'[33]

God's perfection means he is able to provide his own perfect standard, which is not arbitrary. Human beings need external moral standards because we lack wisdom to know what is right and the goodness to desire to do it. But, as Article I of the *Thirty Nine Articles* states, God is of 'infinite…wisdom and goodness.' He does not require any external guidance or motivation. In his infinite wisdom he knows what the right things to do is and in his infinite goodness he desires it and acts upon it.

The reason God would never command us to torture children for fun is not because he follows an external standard of right and wrong, but because he only wills things that are in accordance with his nature, and his nature is perfectly wise and good. Torturing children for fun would be neither wise nor good and therefore God would not will it. Thus, in response to Socrates' question to Euthyphro we can say that good actions are favoured by God because they are in accordance with his own perfect wisdom and goodness.

---

31 Euthyphro 10 a in *ibid*, p.11.
32 Louise Anthony, 'Atheism as Perfect Piety' in Robert K Garcia and Nathan L King (eds), *Is Goodness without God Good Enough?*, Lanham: Rowman & Littlefield, 2009, p.71.
33 Richard Hooker, *The Laws of Ecclesiastical Polity*, Book I.III.2,

As Baggett and Wells note, it is because God is perfectly wise and good and is also all powerful that he rightfully possesses supreme moral authority and therefore provides the secure transcendent basis for ethics to which we can appeal in response to the challenge 'sez who?':

> God has supreme power, knowledge, and goodness and all of these underwrite his moral authority. He created us and this world and stamped us with his image, and has the power to hold us fully accountable for our actions. Since he has perfect knowledge of us, he understands perfectly what is good for us and our flourishing. Moreover, since he is perfectly good he desires our well-being and does everything short of overriding our freedom to promote it. In view of his nature as a perfect being, there are no grounds for doubting his authority. There can be no blindsidedness, no bias, no imperfect understanding, no possibility of misuse of power, or having obtained it wrongly. If all rational witholdings are blocked we ought to accept God as an authority. And part of what is involved in that is accepting his commands, unless we have good reason to do otherwise; but again, with a perfect being, there cannot possibly be good reasons to do otherwise.[34]

What we know and how we know it

In order to conclude that God is in fact wise and good, wouldn't we already need to know what wisdom and goodness looked like? That is, could we be in a position to judge that God is the ultimate moral authority unless we had antecedent knowledge of wisdom and goodness? And, if we did already know what these looked like, wouldn't we have an independent basis for deciding right and wrong without reference to God?

Imagine someone who has never been to San Francisco and does not even know that the city really exists. He has, however, read about it in books without knowing its name and he has seen pictures of it in photographs and films, again without it ever being identified. He has knowledge of the city even though he does not know it at first hand and doesn't even know that he knows about it.

We must not confuse how we know about things (epistemology) with the nature of things (ontology). The man in our example has learnt about San Francisco and has knowledge of it second hand. This is possible because the city really exists. The existence of a real city is necessary as the explanation for his knowledge about it. In the same way, we might learn about wisdom and goodness from somewhere else rather than directly from God, but the reality of God's perfect wisdom and

---

34 Baggett and Wells, *Good God* p.123.

goodness is still necessary as the explanation of us knowing about it. Without God's existence there would be nothing for us to know.

Christian theology says that humans do have the capacity to recognize wisdom and goodness. We are creatures made in God's image and likeness (Genesis 1:26-27) having the law of God written in our hearts (Romans 2:14-15) and living in a world created by God that points to what he is like (Psalm 19:1, Romans 1:20). But the very reason we have this capacity in the first place is because God himself is wise and good. The existence of his wisdom and goodness are what make our knowledge of wisdom and goodness possible.

What about evil?

Humans not only have a capacity to recognize what is good, but also what is not good. Their recognition of the presence of evil in the world raises a further objection to belief in the existence of a perfectly wise, good and powerful God as the basis for ethics, namely that such a belief is undercut by the existence of evil. The argument goes that if such a God existed he would not permit the existence of evil. Evil, however, exists. It follows that God does not exist. As David Hume puts it:

> Is God willing to prevent evil but unable to do so? Then he is not omnipotent.
> Is God able to prevent evil, but unwilling to do so? Then he is malevolent (or at least less than perfectly good). If God is both willing and able to prevent evil, then why is there evil in the world.[35]

C S Lewis wrestled with his own experiences of evil including the death of his mother from cancer and his experience on the Western Front during the First World War, but he points out, in a celebrated passage from *Mere Christianity*, that the problem with this objection to God is that it cuts off the very branch it is sitting on:

> My argument against God was that the universe appeared so cruel and unjust. But how had I got this idea of just and unjust? A man does not call a line crooked unless he has some idea of a straight line. What was I comparing this universe with when I called it unjust? If the whole show was bad and senseless from A to Z, so to speak, why did I, who supposed to be part of the show find myself in such violent rejection against it? A man feels wet when he falls into water, because man is not a water animal: a fish would not feel wet. Of course I could have given up my idea of justice by saying it was nothing but a private

---

35 David Hume, *Dialogues Concerning Natural Religion*, Harmondsworth: Penguin, 1990.

idea of my own. But if I did that, then my argument against God collapsed too—for the argument depended on saying that the world really was unjust, not simply that it did not happen to please my fancies. Thus in the very act of trying to prove that God did not exist—in other words that the whole of reality was senseless—I found I was forced to assume that one part of reality—namely, my idea of justice—was full of sense. Consequently atheism turns out to be too simple.[36]

In other words, to be outraged by evil we have to have a sense of justice and the only thing that makes sense of our sense of justice is if a wise and good God exists as its source. Hence to object to evil we have to posit God.

Oliver O'Donovan writes that the problem of evil is 'the problem of the inscrutability of providence in the light of the moral order.'[37] To put it another way, why does a good and wise God act in a way that appears to violate the sense of justice he has placed in our minds? This problem is raised in the Book of Job and our response must be to accept the message of Job that, as finite human beings, we are never going to be able to understand fully in this world why God acts as he does (see Job 38:1-42:6). We know enough, however, to make it rational to believe that God is wise and good. As our experience of God grows we begin to see more clearly how God has been at work for good even in those areas of life where his actions seemed at first to make no sense at all. A good analogy here is our experience of first of all trusting our parents because they are our parents even when they do things that we do not understand and then gradually coming to comprehend the reasons for their actions as we grow older. [38]

The fear of the Lord is the beginning of wisdom

What we have seen in this chapter is that human beings are creatures who consist of both souls and bodies. It is because they have both that they are able to act ethically. In order to make sense of both the existence of souls and the existence of a moral standard against which human actions can be assessed, we need to believe that there is an infinitely wise and good God and that acting rightly means acting in accordance with what he wills.

It is for this reason that the writer of Proverbs declares that 'The fear of the

---

36 C S Lewis, *Mere Christianity*, pp.41-42.
37 Oliver O'Donovan, *Resurrection and Moral Order*, Leicester: Apollos, 1994, p. 44.
38 Helpful studies on evil and the providence of God include Austen Farrer, *Love Almighty and Ills Unlimited*, Glasgow: Fontana, 1966, C S Lewis, *The Problem of Pain*, Glasgow: Collins, 1978 and Vernon White, *The Fall of a Sparrow*, Exeter: Paternoster 1985.

Lord is the beginning of wisdom, and the knowledge of the Holy One is insight' (Proverbs 9:10). Given God's existence, fearing him (in the sense of acknowledging and reverencing him) and knowing and obeying his commands, has to be the basis for moral wisdom and insight and thus the proper starting point for thinking about matters to do with sex, marriage and family life.

Questions for discussion

1. Why is it important for ethics that humans have souls?

2. Why does belief in the existence of God enable us to make sense of the idea of moral obligation?

3. Why is the will of God the proper foundation for ethical behavior?

CHAPTER 2

Doing the right thing

'Thy word is a lamp to my feet and a light to my path' (Psalm 119:105).

How do I make decisions?

Imagine parenting a small child. All kinds of decisions have to be made. You might have to stop them drinking bleach or jumping from an upstairs window. You might choose to take them swimming or to the cinema. You might decide it is time they had a bath or went to bed. In each case the voice of reason tells you, respectively, what you must do, what you may do, or what is the best thing to do out of the possible options.

As human beings we can make free moral decisions about how to act because, as we saw in the last chapter, we have conscious rational souls. When we make a decision, says Richard Hooker, 'the natural measure whereby to judge our doings, is the sentence of Reason, determining and setting down what is good to be done.' Reason tells us what is 'either mandatory, shewing what must be done; or else permissive, declaring only what may be done; or thirdly admonitory, opening what is the most convenient for us to do.'[39] The challenge we face as decision makers, then, is to distinguish between what we must do, what we may do, and what is the best thing to do, and then to decide what is the right thing to do in each case.

Reason needs information about reality in order to help us make decisions. Only when we know that drinking bleach is harmful can our reason tell us to stop a child downing a bottle. We need to know that swimming lessons are beneficial for our reason to suggest we take a child to the pool. Bath and bedtimes are reasonable because we know why children need them. Information is necessary to make a reasonable decision, and the ultimate reality and final point of reference when making reasonable decisions is the will of God.

We saw in Chapter One that the moral authority of God is, in the end, the only

---

39 Hooker, *The Laws of Ecclesiastical Polity*, Book I, viii. 8.

rational basis for saying that doing some things is better than doing others. The ultimate reason why I should not let my child drink bleach (or any other kind of poisonous substance) is because God wills that children should flourish rather than be harmed, and he has given adult human beings the responsibility for ensuring that this is the case.

How can I know what God wants?

Suppose you saw a parent endangering their child by allowing them to leap dangerously from a first floor window, perhaps to test their ability to fly. You challenge the parent, and the parent retorts, 'sez who?' How might you respond? The final answer has to be not simply 'sez me' or 'sez society' or 'sez the law', but 'sez God.' We might be wrong about the matter, as might society, or the law, but because of God's infinite wisdom and goodness there is no possibility that *he* might be wrong. It is only from God's authority that there can be no possible appeal; but how do we as human beings know what the creator of the universe wants from us in any given situation?

Various religions and theistic philosophies give different answers to this question, but the Christian tradition says there are two ways we may come to know what God is like and what his will is for human beings. Firstly, from our innate sense of what is right and wrong (that is, the law God has written in our hearts and in the world he has made) and secondly, from the Christian faith.

The first way, by itself, is insufficient. This is because, as humans, we have abused our freedom by turning our innate knowledge of God into idolatry. The benefits of that knowledge are thus undermined. This is what St Paul talks about in Romans 1:19-23:

> For what can be known about God is plain to them, because God has shown it to them. Ever since the creation of the world his invisible nature, namely, his eternal power and deity, has been clearly perceived in the things that have been made. So they are without excuse; for although they knew God they did not honour him as God or give thanks to him, but they became futile in their thinking and their senseless minds were darkened. Claiming to be wise, they became fools, and exchanged the glory of the immortal God for images resembling mortal man or birds or animals or reptiles.

As Tom Wright explains, idolatry means we stop honouring God's rule in the way we live our lives:

> Human beings were made to know, worship, love and serve the creator

God. That always was and always will be the way to healthy and fruitful human living. It demands, of course, a certain kind of humility: a willingness to let God be God, to celebrate and honour him as such, and acknowledge his power in and over the world. Paul affirms that human beings have not lost this sense of God's power and deity, but he declares that they have chosen to suppress this truth, instead of honouring God and giving him thanks.[40]

Something else fills the gap when we suppress true knowledge of God; we fill the void with gods of our own imagination. As John Calvin notes, we are very good at creating gods to suit ourselves: 'Like water gushing forth from a large and copious spring, immense crowds of gods have issued forth from the human mind, every man giving himself full license, and devising some form of divinity, to meet his own views.'[41]

In the Western world we don't come across many people who worship stone or wooden statues and images like our ancestors did. Christianity has changed our culture. Our idols look different; we worship gods like money, sex, power, and technology, all of them usurping the place that rightly belongs to God.[42]

And where does idolatry take us? St Paul says that the corruption of human thinking leads to the corruption of human behaviour. God respects our choice to turn our backs on him. He allows us to reap what we sow, and Paul says the harvest is immoral behaviour. Remember from chapter one that immoral behaviour means behaviour contrary to God's standards. Paul can think of many examples:

And since they did not see fit to acknowledge God, God gave them up to a base mind and to improper conduct. They were filled with all manner of wickedness, evil, covetousness, malice. Full of envy, murder, strife, deceit, malignity, they are gossips, slanderers, haters of God, insolent, haughty, boastful, inventors of evil, disobedient to parents, foolish, faithless, heartless, ruthless. (Romans 1:28-31)

Now, because God is infinitely good, he does not want us to remain trapped in our ignorance of what he is really like and what he really wants. He has, therefore, given us a second way to get to know him and his will: the Christian faith.

---

40 Tom Wright, *Paul for Everyone—Romans Part 1: Chapters 1-8*, London: SPCK: 2004, p.16.
41 John Calvin, *Institutes of the Christian Religion*, Bk 1:V:13, Grand Rapids: Eerdmans, 1975, Vol 1, pp.59-60.
42 For this point see Timothy Keller, *Counterfeit Gods*, London: Hodder and Stoughton, 2010 and Bob Goudzwaard, *Idols of Our Time*, Downers Grove: Inter-Varsity Press, 1984.

How can I know what the Christian faith is?

The Christian faith is the message which Jesus gave to the Apostles and which he commanded them to pass on. It is the same message which has been taught, believed and confessed by orthodox Christians ever since.[43] If we want to access this message, the Church of England gives us helpful directions in its Canon Law, where the words 'doctrine' and 'the faith' refer to the Christian faith as the Church of England has received it. Canon A5 states that:

> The doctrine of the Church of England is grounded in the Holy Scriptures, and in such teaching of the Fathers and Councils of the Church as are agreeable to the said Scriptures. In particular such doctrine is to be found in the Thirty-nine Articles of Religion, the Book of Common Prayer, and the Ordinal.

Canon C15 states that the Church of England:

> ... professes the faith uniquely revealed in the Holy Scriptures and set forth in the catholic creeds, which faith the church is called upon to proclaim afresh in each generation. Led by the Holy Spirit, it has born witness to Christian truth in its historic formularies, the Thirty-nine Articles of Religion, the Book of Common Prayer and the Ordering of Bishops, Priests and Deacons.

In other words, we can learn the Christian faith through the Scriptures, the teaching of the Early Church, and the witness of the Church of England's three historic formularies. These three sources do not possess the same authority.

The Holy Scriptures are the primary source of our knowledge of God and his will because they contain the Apostolic message in words inspired by God himself (2 Timothy 3:16, 2 Peter 1:24).[44] The Church of England recognises the thirty-nine books of the Old Testament and the twenty-seven books of the New Testament as Scripture.

The major Christian writers of the early centuries of the Church such as St Irenaeus, St Athanasius and St Augustine (referred to as the 'Fathers'), the great orthodox councils of this period such as the Councils of Nicaea, Second Constantinople and Chalcedon, and the Apostles, Nicene and Athanasian Creeds (which also emerged out of this period) are a secondary source for our knowledge of God

---

43 It is this message that is referred to in New Testament passages such as Acts 2:42, Romans 6:17 and Jude 3 which talk about the 'teaching of the apostles,' 'the standard of teaching to which you were committed' and 'the faith once delivered to the saints' and which formed the basis of what came to be known in the early Church as the 'rule of faith.'

44 For the primary importance of Scripture for our knowledge of God see J I Packer, *Fundamentalism and the Word of God*, Grand Rapids: Eerdmans, 1982, N T Wright, *Scripture and the Authority of God*, London: SPCK 2005 and Timothy Ward, *Words of Life*, Nottingham, Inter-Varsity Press, 2009.

because they teach us how to understand properly the faith to which the Scriptures bear witness. [45]

The three historic formularies of the Church of England are the Thirty-Nine Articles of 1571, the *Book of Common Prayer* and the *Ordinal* of 1662. These are a tertiary source for our knowledge of God because they give theological and liturgical expression to the faith witnessed to by the Scriptures and then by the Early Church.

What does the Christian faith say?

Knowing how to access the Christian faith is an important start, but we then have to move on to explore what the content of the Christian faith is and how it provides a framework for determining how we should behave. The Catechism in the *Book of Common Prayer* gives us a useful summary. It is based on the Apostles Creed and uses a question and answer format:

Catechist. Rehearse the Articles of thy Belief.

Answer. I believe in God the Father Almighty, Maker of heaven and earth:

And in Jesus Christ his only Son our Lord, Who was conceived by the Holy Ghost, Born of the Virgin Mary, Suffered under Pontius Pilate, Was crucified, dead, and buried: He descended into hell; The third day he rose again from the dead; He ascended into heaven, And sitteth at the right hand of God the Father Almighty; From thence he shall come to judge the quick and the dead.

I believe in the Holy Ghost; The holy Catholick Church; The Communion of Saints; The Forgiveness of sins; The Resurrection of the body, And the life everlasting. Amen.

Question. What dost thou chiefly learn in these Articles of thy Belief?

Answer. First, I learn to believe in God the Father, who hath made me, and all the world.
Secondly, in God the Son, who hath redeemed me, and all mankind.
Thirdly, in God the Holy Ghost, who sanctifieth me, and all the elect people of God.

These are the basics of Christian faith in the triune God. Notice how big a contrast there is with the materialist worldview of an atheist philosopher like Bertrand Russell. In his 'Litany of despair' he said we must accept

---

45 For a helpful overview of how the Bible, the Creeds and the Historic Formularies bear a convergent testimony to the Christian Faith see W H Griffith Thomas, *The Catholic Faith*, London: Church Book Room Press, 1960.

...that man is the product of causes which had no prevision of the end they were achieving; that his origin, his growth, his hopes and fears, his loves and his beliefs are but the outcomes of accidental collocations of atoms; that no fire, no heroism, no intensity of thought and feeling, can preserve an individual life beyond the grave; that all the labours of the ages, all the devotion, all the inspiration, all the noonday brightness of human genius, are destined to extinction in the vast death of the solar system, and that the whole temple of man's achievement must inevitably be buried beneath the debris of a universe in ruins—all these things, if not quite beyond dispute, are yet so nearly certain that no philosophy which rejects them can hope to stand. Only within the scaffolding of these truths, only in the firm foundation of unyielding despair, can the soul's habitation henceforth be safely built.[46]

What Russell calls 'truths' are in fact lies demonstrating ignorance of God. The Christian faith tells us the truth about who God is and what God does, and when we know these things we learn what it means to act rightly before him.

Doing what we were made to do

Bertrand Russell believed that humans exist by chance and without purpose, but the Christian faith tells us that God is the Father 'who hath made me, and all the world.' This rules out ancient heresies about creation being the product of incompetent or malevolent demi-gods. It also rules out Russell's claim that creation is a pointless accident.

We saw in chapter one that God is infinitely wise. The Christian faith teaches that creation exists as a result of that wisdom. In the words of the Psalmist, 'O Lord, how manifold are thy works! In wisdom thou hast made them all' (Psalm 104:24). We also saw that God is infinitely good, so the things he creates are good. That is why at the end of the creation account we are told that 'God saw everything that he had made, and behold, it was very good' (Genesis 1:31). This truth is reiterated in the New Testament in 1 Timothy 4:4 where we are told that 'everything created by God is good, and nothing is to be rejected if received with thanksgiving.'

But what about evil and sin? If everything that exists comes from God, what is the nature of evil? Kallistos Ware states the Christian answer: 'Since all created things are intrinsically good, sin or evil as such is not a 'thing,' not an existent being or substance.'[47] In other words, evil and sin exist only as the absence or the perversion of the good which God created.

---

46 Bertrand Russell, *Mysticism and Logic*, New York: Barnes and Noble 1917, pp.47-48.
47 Kallistos Ware, *The Orthodox Way*, London and Oxford: Mowbrays, 1979, p. 59.

If all of creation is good then the nature of evil is 'nothingness'. This does not mean that evil is not real, explains Karl Barth, but its reality consists in its being 'that which God does not will.' Evil is what God has overcome through Jesus and will one day banish from his eternal kingdom.[48] For this reason Christians can neither affirm it nor compromise with it.' Christians may only say 'no' to that to which God says 'no'. Goodness is negated and perverted when fallen angels or human beings misuse free will to affirm or compromise with evil.

Having created the world God 'rested from all his work which he had done in creation' (Genesis 2:3). God preserves what he has made and acts to bring it to the goal he intends for it, but he does not change it or create it afresh. Thus Karl Barth says, 'It is part of the history of creation that God completed His work and confronted it as a completed totality.'[49] This means that there is a created order 'which neither the terrors of chance nor the ingenuity of art can overthrow.'[50] As we shall see in chapter four below, the Christian faith holds that there will be a world to come in which human beings will live in a way that transcends their life in this world. However, this transcendent life will be a fulfilment rather than a negation of God's action in creation.

Living rightly, therefore, means living in the light of the unchanging order that God has established. This in turn means that Christian ethics are not idiosyncratic house rules that apply to Christians but not to anyone else. As Oliver O'Donovan explains, the doctrine of creation tells us that

> The order of things that God has made is there. It is objective, and mankind has a place within it. Christian ethics, therefore, has an objective reference because it is concerned with man's life in accordance with this order. The summons to live in it is addressed to all mankind, because the good news that we may live in it is addressed to all mankind. Thus Christian moral judgements in principle address every man.[51]

Doing what we were saved to do

The second lie put forward by Russell which is nailed by the Christian faith is that humankind and all of the rest of creation is on a one way ride to extinction. The affirmation that God the Son 'hath redeemed me and all mankind' declares that this is not so.

48 Karl Barth, *Church Dogmatics III.3.4*, London & New York, T&T Clark, 2004.
49 Karl Barth, *Church Dogmatics, III.1*, London & New York, 2004, p.222.
50 O'Donovan, *Resurrection and Moral Order*, p. 61.
51 *Ibid*, p.17.

The image of redemption is that of rescue, and the Christian faith teaches that the created order became in need of rescue because the abuse of their God given freedom by humans and fallen angels meant that creation became subject to the power of sin and therefore subject to death.

However, the resurrection of Jesus Christ from the dead tells us that this rescue which creation required has in fact occurred. God has stood by his creation (us included) and not simply let it die. In the words of O'Donovan:

> The resurrection carries with it the promise that 'all shall be made alive' (1 Cor. 15:22). The raising of Christ is representative, not in the way that a symbol is representative, expressing a reality which has an independent and prior standing, but in the way that a national leader is representative when he brings about for the whole of his people whatever it is, peace or war, that he effects on their behalf. And so this central proclamation directs us back also to the message of the incarnation, by which we learn how, through the unique presence of God to his creation, the whole created order is taken up into the fate of this particular representative man at this particular moment in history, on whose one fate turns the redemption of all. And it directs us forward to the end of history when that particular and representative fate is universalized in the resurrection of mankind from the dead. Each in his own order: Christ the first fruits, then at his coming those who belong to Christ' (15:23). The sign that God has stood by his created order implies that this created order, with mankind in its proper place within it, is to be totally restored at last.[52]

'Christian ethics' is thus 'resurrection ethics' in the sense that it is concerned with living out the new life that Christ has achieved for us by his resurrection. This new life is the foretaste of that renewal of the whole of creation that will take place at the end of time (Romans 8:18-25).

On the first Good Friday Christ died on the cross in an act of divine judgement that put to death our old sinful natures and this took place in order that we might receive instead a wholly new life through his resurrection (Romans 6:6-11). As Calvin puts it:

> .... our old man is destroyed by the death of Christ, so that His resurrection may restore our righteousness, and make us new creatures. And since Christ has been given to us for life, why should we die with Him, if not to rise to a

---

52 *Ibid*, p.15.

better life? Christ, therefore, puts to death what is mortal in us in order that He may truly restore us to life.[53]

As a consequence, the Christian life, a life of holiness to which all human beings are summoned, is a life marked by mortification and vivification. 'As mortification, holiness is the laying aside of that which has been put to death at the cross of the Son of God; as vivification, holiness is the living out of that which has been made alive in the Son's resurrection.'[54]

Doing what we are set free to do

Living a holy life is not something we can do in our own strength. We need the power of God the Holy Spirit 'who sanctifieth me, and all the elect people of God.' What Christ did for us becomes effective in us as the Spirit, given by God to all baptized believers (Acts 2:28, 1 Corinthians 12:13), sets us free from the power of sin and death (Romans 8:1-11). Through the Spirit we are set free, but this freedom is not what the contemporary world thinks of when it talks about freedom.

John Webster highlights two different understandings of what it means to be 'free'. One is freedom from my created identity; the other is freedom to be what I was created to be:

> Modern accounts of freedom identify freedom as unfettered liberty for self-creation, and therefore contrast freedom and nature: freedom is the antithesis of the given, a move over and against any sense that I have a determinate identity. Evangelical freedom, by contrast, does not envisage being human as an utterly original making of life and history. Rather to be human is to live and act in conformity to the given truth (nature) of what I am—a creature of grace, a reconciled sinner and caught up in the movement of the ways and works of God in which I am pointed to a perfection to be revealed in the last times.[55]

The Spirit gives us freedom to respond to the call to 'glorify God in your body' (1 Corinthians 6:20). St Paul says we have a choice: either we continue to live a life marked by the 'works of the flesh' which characterized our old fallen nature (the one Christ died to destroy) or we 'walk by the Spirit' and produce the 'fruit of the Spirit' (virtues which manifest the new life which Christ rose to give to us):

> But I say, walk by the Spirit, and do not gratify the desires of the flesh. For the desires of the flesh are against the Spirit, and the desires of the Spirit

53 John Calvin *Epistles of Paul the Apostle to the Romans and to the Thessalonians* Edinburgh: The Saint Andrew Press, 1961 pp.122-3.
54 John Webster, *Holiness*, London: SCM, 2003, p.88.
55 *Ibid*, p.94.

are against the flesh; for these are opposed to each other, to prevent you from doing what you would. But if you are led by the Spirit you are not under the law. Now the works of the flesh are plain: fornication, impurity, licentiousness, idolatry, sorcery, enmity, strife, jealousy, anger, selfishness, dissension, party spirit, envy, drunkenness, carousing, and the like. I warn you, as I warned you before, that those who do such things shall not inherit the kingdom of God. But the fruit of the Spirit is love, joy, peace, patience, kindness, goodness, faithfulness, gentleness, self-control; against such there is no law. And those who belong to Christ Jesus have crucified the flesh with its passions and desires. (Galatians 5:16-24)

Free to love

As St Paul indicates by his mention of love in this passage, a key part of what it means to walk by the Spirit is to love. The two great commandments set down for us in Scripture, which Jesus said epitomise the whole of what God requires of us as his creatures, is that we should 'love God with all our heart, soul, mind and strength' and love our neighbours as ourselves (Deuteronomy 6:4-5, Leviticus 19:18, Mark 12:29-31).

As O' Donovan notes, what is meant by love is 'the appropriate pattern of free response to objective reality.'[56] To love God is to freely respond to the reality of God's wisdom and goodness by living in the way he summons us to live. To love our neighbours is to freely respond to who they are as creatures made by God with particular needs which God calls us to discern and fulfil to the greatest extent that we can.

Love and reason thus go together. It is our reason, attentive to the reality that God has called into being, which shows us what it means to love in any given situation. To return to the example we began with of parenting a child, to love them involves using our reason to discover their needs and the best way to meet them. This means that we will not let them drink bleach, and that our decisions about swimming lessons and bedtimes will be shaped by what is best for their welfare and happiness. Sometimes this may well mean saying 'no' to what they want to do, not because we are being mean or cruel, but because our reason, working on the basis of who they are, shows us that what they want will not ultimately be good for them.

---

56 O'Donovan, *op.cit.* p. 25.

Grace, forgiveness, hope and patience

In this chapter we have looked at the account given by the Christian faith about who God is, what God has done and what it means for human beings to live rightly before him. What lies at the heart of this account is the grace of God.

The grace of God is the love of God shown to those who have done nothing to deserve it. We see this grace at work in the way that God has created us out of nothing when he had no obligation to do so and in the way that he bestowed new life on us through Christ and the Spirit when through our rebellion against him we had fallen under the power of sin and death.

Living the Christian life means living in the light of this double grace. As we have seen, it means being set free to live a life of love for God and neighbour that reflects the truth about who we are as the people God has created and on whom he has bestowed new life, so that we might live with God forever in a restored creation and thus fulfil the purpose for which we were made.[57]

The fact that we have received the grace of God does not mean that we can henceforth live the way we are called to live without any difficulty. On the contrary, the Bible and the mainstream Christian tradition following the Bible, both insist that the Christian path is a difficult one, but that God will give us what we need to live it successfully.

The reason why the Christian path is difficult is because although the devil and his angels have been decisively defeated through Christ's death and resurrection this does not mean that their activity is at an end. On the contrary, as the book of Revelation makes clear, they continue to wage war 'on those who keep the commandments of God and bear testimony to Jesus' (Revelation 12:17). This assault on God's people takes the two forms of persecution and temptation, both of which are intended to lead Christians away from trusting and obeying God.[58]

These assaults by the devil, plus the continuing influence of our old fallen natures (which makes us want to obey the temptation which the devil lays before us), means that Christians will continue to sin for the whole of their lives on earth. As St John tells us, 'If we say we have no sin we deceive ourselves and the truth is not in us' (1 John 1:8). However, St John goes on to say that God has provided a remedy for this situation: 'If we confess our sins, he is faithful and just, and will forgive our sins and cleanse us from all unrighteousness.'

---

57 This is what the first question of the *Westminster Shorter Catechism* has in mind when it famously declares that 'Man's chief end is to glorify God, and to enjoy him forever.'
58 See C S Lewis, *The Screwtape Letters*, London: Harper Collins 1998,

Because this is the case, the mainstream Christian tradition has insisted that the Christian life is what Grant calls an 'oscillating narrative'.[59] It is not a smooth path of ever increasing holiness in which everything goes in the way we desire. It is a journey full of ups and downs, of sorrows and disappointments, in which we constantly let God down and constantly have to turn back to receive his forgiveness and seek his strength to do better in future.

That is why down the centuries Anglicans have prayed at Morning and Evening Prayer:

> Almighty and most merciful Father, We have erred, and strayed from thy ways like lost sheep, We have followed too much the devices and desires of our own hearts, We have offended against thy holy laws, We have left undone those things which we ought to have done, And we have done those things which we ought not to have done, And there is no health in us: But thou, O Lord, have mercy upon us miserable offenders; Spare thou them, O God, which confess their faults, Restore thou them that are penitent, According to thy promises declared unto mankind in Christ Jesu our Lord: And grant, O most merciful Father, for his sake, That we may hereafter live a godly, righteous, and sober life, To the glory of thy holy Name. Amen.[60]

As St Paul notes in Romans 8:25, living through all the ups and downs of the Christian life involves hope and patience: 'But if we hope for what we do not see, we wait for it with patience.' We do yet see, in the sense of presently experience, the total and complete victory over sin which God has promised us. However, on the basis of what God has done through Christ we confidently hope that this victory will one day happen and that we shall participate in it.

Because we have this hope we are able to be patient in the face of our current difficulties in the conviction that, as Paul puts it elsewhere, 'this slight momentary affliction is preparing for us an eternal weight of glory beyond comparison' (2 Corinthians 4:17). What will be, will make our present afflictions worthwhile.

To summarize where we have got to, what we have seen is that to live rightly before God involves responding to his grace shown in our creation and redemption. We do this by living a life characterized by the twin virtues of patience and hope in the face of the assaults of the devil and continuing influence of our fallen nature. We have to confess our sins before God and to seek his help to live in the

---

59 Grant, *op.cit.* p.200.
60 *Book of Common Prayer*, General Confession at Morning and Evening Prayer.

way he created us to live by loving him and our neighbours in the power of the Spirit as we journey through this world towards our life in the new creation.

What we will explore in this study, as it proceeds, is what it means to live in this way in relation to the areas of sex, marriage and family life. We shall begin in the next chapter by considering the reality of God's creation of human beings as male and female and how this forms the foundation for a Christian understanding of marriage.

Questions for discussion

1. How can we know what God wants?

2. How does a Christian view of human existence differ from that put forward in Bertrand Russell's 'Litany of Despair?'

3. Why does living rightly before God involve grace, forgiveness, hope and patience?

CHAPTER 3

Men, Women and Marriage in this world

'From the beginning of creation, 'God made them male and female''
(Mark 10:6)

Human Sex

In the last chapter we saw that to love involves attentiveness to the reality of the object of our love. It follows that if we are to love our fellow human beings we have to be attentive to the reality of their humanity. We need to use our reason to help us understand who they truly are and how we should behave as a result.

Everyone is unique. God does not make clones when he knits people together in their mothers' wombs (Psalm 139:13). Even identical twins are different from each other in a variety of ways. They are not absolutely identical, which is why we can learn to tell them apart if we get to know a pair.

Although no two human beings are the same, we do have certain things in common. These shared characteristics allow us to recognise each other as being part of one single human race. For instance, all humans have bodies and souls, as we saw in chapter one, and our bodies have common features, like heads, feet, hearts, and toenails, but with differences that allow us to tell one human being from another. Some have red hair while others are blonde; some people have blue eyes while others have brown eyes; and some people are tall while others are short. The most significant difference among human beings is that they differ in their sex.

There is a lot of confusion in contemporary discussion between 'gender' and 'sex'. The two terms are used as synonyms and 'gender' is sometimes used in place of 'sex'. However, there is an important distinction: sex is the biological reality that is experienced and expressed, whereas gender is the way this biological reality is experienced and expressed by individuals in particular social contexts.

Further confusion is caused by the fact that 'sex' is itself used with two different meanings. Sex is commonly used as a shorthand term for sexual intercourse as when, for example, concern is expressed about 'teenage sex.' However, sex is also, and more properly, used to describe the bodily distinction that exists between men and women.

Mountains do not possess sex. There are no male mountains or female mountains. Similarly there are no male or female mobile phones. It would make no sense to say 'this phone is male.' There are many things in the world that do not have sex in the proper sense of the term. There are, however, many things that do have sex. For example, it makes sense to talk about male and female plants, male and female birds, and male and female dogs. What distinguishes male from female in all such cases is the existence of biological differences that are oriented to sexual reproduction. Thus in dogs there are distinct biological characteristics that allow male and female dogs to mate with one another so that female dogs can then give birth to offspring and there can continue to be dogs on the planet.

Like other animals, human beings do possess sex. When we look at human beings, says Christopher Tollefsen, we find that

> … our identity as animal organisms is the foundation of our existence as selves. But fundamental to our existence as this animal is our sex. We are male or female organisms in virtue of having a root capacity for reproductive function, even when that capacity is immature or damaged. In human beings, as is the case with many other organisms, that function is one to be performed jointly with another human being; unlike the digestive function, no individual human being suffices for its performance.

> Accordingly, reproductive function in human beings is distributed across the two sexes, which are identified by their having the root capacity for one or the other of the two general structural and behavioural patterns involved in human reproduction. In male humans, this capacity is constituted by the structures necessary for the production of male gametes and the performance of the male sex act, insemination. In females, the capacity is constituted by the structures necessary for the production of oocytes and the performance of the female sex act, the reception of semen in a manner disposed to conception.[61]

There are various other physical and psychological differences between men and

---

61 Christopher Tollefsen, 'Sex identity,' *Public Discourse*, 12 July 2015, text at http://www.the-publicdiscourse.com/2015/07/15306/

women,[62] but they are all characteristics of human beings who are fundamentally differentiated by the fact that their bodies are ordered towards the performance of different roles in sexual reproduction and in the nurture of children once they have been born.[63]

Both Christian and non-Christian thinkers agree on sexual differentiation amongst human beings along these lines, but they would offer different explanations as to its ultimate cause. The atheist evolutionary biologist Lewis Wolpert sets out the differences between men and women in his book *Why Can't a Woman Be More Like a Man?*[64] He suggests that sexual differentiation is simply the result of evolutionary processes; blind physical forces which had no awareness of what they were doing.

Christians, on the other hand—whether creationists, or those who accept the theory of evolution—would say that human beings are male and female, ultimately, because God wills it to be so.[65] They would base this view on creation in general (that God 'hath made me, and all the world') and specifically on the fact that the creation of human beings as male and female is taught in Genesis (Genesis 1:26-31, 2:18-25, and 5:1-2) and is reaffirmed by Jesus himself in the Gospels (Matthew 19:3-6, Mark 10:2-9). We will look at what each of these passages has to say.

---

62 See for example, Richard A Lippa, *Gender, Nature and Nurture*, 2ed, London: Routledge, 2005.

63 It is true that transgender activists would deny that a person's biology is the correct basis for classifying them as male or female. Thus in a recent American court case Dr Deanna Adkins from the Duke University Medical School testified that gender identity is 'the only medically supported determinant of sex.' In her view 'It is counter to medical science to use chromosomes, hormones, internal reproductive organs, external genitalia, or secondary sex characteristics to override gender identity for purposes of classifying someone as male or female.' To put it simply, according to Dr Adkins who people identify as being is the only thing that truly distinguishes them as male or female. This is clearly untrue. Someone with male biology may identify as a woman, but unlike someone with female biology he will be liable to get prostate cancer, will never have a period and will never be able to bear a baby. The basic biological differences between men and women are clear and ineradicable.

64 Lewis Wolpert, *Why Can't a Woman Be More Like a Man?*, London: Faber & Faber, 2014.

65 As the Church of England Doctrine Commission report *Being Human* (London: CHP 2003 p. 84) notes: 'There is sometimes a tendency to see evolution as an alternative to the purposes of God. However, ever since Darwin's *Origin of Species*, many Christians have seen evolution as the way in which God has achieved his creative purposes. Though evolution builds on random mutations, it has led to an increasing capacity for processing of complex information, and to consciousness. The result has been creatures who are capable of receiving God's self-revelation and grace, and we believe that it was God's intention that such creatures should evolve. Human sexuality, which goes beyond the capacity for procreation, is one aspect of those distinctive human qualities that can be used for the fulfilment of God's purposes.'

Sex in Genesis 1:26-31 and 5:1-2

Genesis 1:26-31 forms the climax of the account the six days of creation in Genesis 1. It runs as follows:

²⁶ Then God said, "Let us make man in our image, after our likeness; and let them have dominion over the fish of the sea, and over the birds of the air, and over the cattle, and over all the earth, and over every creeping thing that creeps upon the earth." ²⁷ So God created man in his own image, in the image of God he created him; male and female he created them. ²⁸ And God blessed them, and God said to them, "Be fruitful and multiply, and fill the earth and subdue it; and have dominion over the fish of the sea and over the birds of the air and over every living thing that moves upon the earth." ²⁹ And God said, "Behold, I have given you every plant yielding seed which is upon the face of all the earth, and every tree with seed in its fruit; you shall have them for food. ³⁰ And to every beast of the earth, and to every bird of the air, and to everything that creeps on the earth, everything that has the breath of life, I have given every green plant for food." And it was so. ³¹ And God saw everything that he had made, and behold, it was very good. And there was evening and there was morning, a sixth day.

Genesis 5:1-2 introduces the story of Adam's descendants by recapitulating the teaching of Genesis 1:26-31:

¹This is the book of the generations of Adam. When God created man, he made him in the likeness of God. ² Male and female he created them, and he blessed them and named them Man when they were created.

These two parallel accounts make six key points about God's creation of human beings.

First, we learn that human beings do not exist by chance. God, who created the universe in general, also decided to create human beings in particular and, as we noted in the last chapter, everything that God creates is 'very good' (Genesis 1:31), including the human race.

Secondly, we learn that God created human beings as male and female from the beginning. Although some Jewish and Christian writers have argued that the primal 'man' of Genesis 1:26-27 and 5:1 was an androgynous being (with the division of humanity into male and female being a later, and not necessarily beneficial, development)[66] this is not what these verses actually teach. The Hebrew words used here (*ha' adam*) mean 'humanity', just as 'Man' has traditionally done in English. 'The plural in v.27 ('he created them'),' according to Gerhard von Rad, 'is intentionally contrasted with the singular ('him') and prevents one from assuming the creation of an originally androgynous man' (the same in 5:1).[67] These verses are clear that, when God created the human race, he made human beings male and female. The sexual distinction is fundamental to what it means to be human.[68] Karl Barth concludes that 'we cannot say man without having to say male and female. Man exists in this differentiation, in this duality.'[69]

Thirdly, we learn that it is as male and female that human beings are the image and likeness of God. There has been much debate down the centuries as to what exactly it means for human beings to bear God's image and likeness. However, in recent years there has been a growing recognition of the connection between the creation of human beings in God's image and likeness in Genesis 1:26 and 27 and the vocation given to them in verses 26 and 28 to rule over the world that God has made. Thus Craig Bartholomew and Michael Goheen write:

> In Genesis 1:26, God says, 'Let us make man in our image….and let them rule… over all the earth.' He then says to the human beings he has created, 'Be fruitful and increase in number; fill the earth and subdue it. Rule…' (1:28). From this it should be clear that the fundamental similarity between God and humanity is humankind's unique vocation, its calling or commissioning by God himself. Under God, humanity is to rule over the non-human parts of creation on land and in sea and air, much as God is the supreme Ruler over all.
>
> In God's kingdom, which he has set up by creating it, the special role he has assigned to humanity is that we should serve as his 'under-kings', vice regents or

---

66 For the origins and development of this idea see Werner Neuer, *Man and Woman in Christian perspective*, Wheaton: Crossway 1991, pp.62-63. For a contemporary example see the commentary on Genesis 1:26-27 by Michael Carden in Deryn Guest, Robert E Goss, Mona West and Thomas Bodache (eds.), *The Queer Bible Commentary*, London: SCM, 2006, pp.26-27.

67 Gerhard Von Rad, *Genesis*, London: SCM, 1966, p.60.

68 In his book *Trans-Gendered* (Cleveland: The Pilgrim Press 2003) the American writer Justin Tanis argues that the Genesis account 'even while differentiating between elements of creation, still leaves space for 'in between' things: dusk, dawn, intersexed persons. God blesses all these parts of creation calling them good' (p.59). However, the examples he gives of in-between things, such as dawn, dusk or the sea shore, are actually examples of names for times or places at the edge of things (dawn or dusk at the beginning or end of the day, and the sea shore at the end of the land) they do not describe mixed things. Furthermore in the Bible there are no examples of mixed human beings. Human beings are exclusively either male or female.

69 Karl Barth, *Church Dogmatics III/2*, London and New York: T&T Clark, 2004, p.289.

stewards. We are to rule over the creation so that God's reputation is enhanced within his cosmic kingdom.[70]

If this is what it means for humans to be in God's image, what gives them the capacity to exercise royal rule? Matthew Levering, drawing on St Thomas Aquinas, argues it is 'the right embodied exercise of the powers that sustain our communion with God and each other—namely the powers of knowing and loving.'[71] In other words, as embodied souls, humans have the capacity to know and love God, each other, and creation as a whole; therefore we can fulfil our God given vocation to exercise God's rule.

Men and women have this capacity and vocation on an equal basis. Both are created with the capacity to know and love and rule over the world on God's behalf; but they are called to do so together as two indispensable halves of the human race. Barth is correct to say it is as male and female that humans exist in the image of God.[72] As Richard Davidson puts it, 'the *mode* of human existence in the divine image is that of male and female together.'[73]

In the words of the 2013 report from the Church of England's Faith and Order Commission, *Men and Women in Marriage*:

> In God's image we bring spiritual creativity to our natural endowment without denying it or overthrowing it. As male and female we have a foundation for growth, cultural development, moral responsibility, intellectual and practical fulfilment, and for the end to which God summons us individually and together, worship and fellowship with himself.[74]

Fourthly, we learn that there is an analogy between the existence of human beings as male and female and the life of God himself. In 1:26 God says, in the plural, 'Let us make man in our image, after our likeness.' Davidson explains that

> ...there have been many attempts to account for this use of the plural, but the explanation that appears most consonant with both the immediate context and the analogy of Scripture identifies the usage as a plural of fullness. The 'let us' as a plural of fullness 'supposes that there is within the divine Being the

---

70 Craig Bartholomew and Michael Goheen, *The Drama of Scripture*, London: SPCK, 2006, pp.14-15.
71 Matthew Levering, *Engaging the Doctrine of Creation*, Grand Rapids: Baker Academic, 2017, p.190.
72 This is a point that Barth makes in his exposition of the doctrine of creation in *Church Dogmatics* III.1-3.
73 Richard Davidson, *Flame of Yahweh, Sexuality in the Old Testament*, Peabody: Hendrickson, 2007, p.4).
74 *Faith and Order Commission, Men and Women in Marriage*, London: CHP, 2013.

distinction of personalities' and expresses 'an intra-divine deliberation among 'persons' within the divine being.'[75]

The use of the plural with reference to God's creation of humans as male and female points to a correspondence or analogy 'between this mark of the divine being, namely that it includes and I and a Thou, and the being of man, male and female.'[76] We know from elsewhere in the Bible that God exists as 'I and Thou' in the eternal relationship between the Father, the Son and the Holy Spirit, who are alike but also different. What Genesis 1:26 suggests is that the Triune God decided to create humans to exist in relationships with other humans who are alike but also different. The primary form of this analogy is the relationship between men and women.[77]

Fifthly, we learn that part of the human vocation to live as those made in God's image and likeness is obedience to the divine command in Genesis 1:28: 'Be fruitful and multiply, and fill the earth and subdue it; and have dominion over the fish of the sea and over the birds of the air and over every living thing that moves upon the earth.' This command to be fruitful and multiply is the culmination of a series of divine commands beginning with 'Let there be light' (Genesis 1:3). These commands bring about the world and its population with a variety of different kinds of creatures. Finally God invites his human creatures, male and female, to participate in his work of creation as his image bearers by producing lots of new image bearers, those created for relationship with one another and with God. As Dennis Hollinger puts it, 'When we bring children into the world through sexual union we reflect and share in God's creative work.'[78]

This brings us to the **sixth** and final thing that we learn from these verses: to be male and female in God's image involves having male and female bodies. Being male and female is not just about having a particular kind of consciousness derived from our immaterial soul. The soul is what allows us, like the angels, to have conscious personal relationships with each other and with God, but in order to share in God's work of creation and to obey his mandate to be 'fruitful and multi-

---

75 Davidson, op.cit, p.40, quoting Gerhard Hasel, 'The Meaning of 'Let Us' in Gen 1:26,' *Andrews University Seminary Studies*, 13 (1975), p.64.

76 Barth, Church *Dogmatics*, III.1, London and New York: T & T Clark, 2004, p.196.

77 The objection is frequently raised at this point that the relationship that exists between the persons of the Trinity is not the same as the relationship between two human persons. This is true, but the objection ignores the fact that analogy always involve dissimilarity as well as similarity. The point is not that the relationship between the persons of the Trinity and the relationship between two human beings are identical, but that there is a likeness between them in that in both cases there is a personal relationship involving both alikeness and difference.

78 Dennis P Hollinger, *The Meaning of Sex*, Grand Rapids: Baker Academic, 2009. p.149.

ply' human beings also need to have sexed bodies designed for both sexual inter-course and procreation. From a scientific perspective, we have sexed bodies right down to the depths of our being, and the distinction between the kinds of bodies we have is an inseparable part of what it means to be created as male or female.

Sex in Genesis 2:18-25

The details of what it means for God's people to live rightly in the place God provided and in obedience to his will are set out in Genesis 2:4-25, which com-plements the first account of creation. Verses 18-25 describe why and how God created the first woman to exist alongside the first man:

> [18] Then the LORD God said, "It is not good that the man should be alone; I will make him a helper fit for him." [19] So out of the ground the LORD God formed every beast of the field and every bird of the air, and brought them to the man to see what he would call them; and whatever the man called every living creature, that was its name. [20] The man gave names to all cattle, and to the birds of the air, and to every beast of the field; but for the man there was not found a helper fit for him. [21] So the LORD God caused a deep sleep to fall upon the man, and while he slept took one of his ribs and closed up its place with flesh; [22] and the rib which the LORD God had taken from the man he made into a woman and brought her to the man. [23] Then the man said,
>
> "This at last is bone of my bones
>   and flesh of my flesh;
>   she shall be called Woman, because she was taken out of Man."
>
> [24] Therefore a man leaves his father and his mother and cleaves to his wife, and they become one flesh. [25] And the man and his wife were both naked, and were not ashamed.'

This passage, like Genesis 1:26-31 and 5:1-2, contains a number of key points. **First of all**, humanity has always been sexually differentiated. Just as it is suggest-ed that humanity is originally androgynous in Genesis 1, so also it is suggested that here in Genesis 2 the 'man' is an androgynous being until the point that God creates the first woman. Only then does the man become male.[79] However, this reading misrepresents what the text says. As Davidson explains:

According to 2:7-8, 15-16, what God creates before woman is called ha adam,

---

79 See Carden, op.cit, p.28 and Phyllis Trible, *God and the Rhetoric of Sexuality*, Philadelphia: Fortress Press, 1978, p.80.

'the man,' better translated as 'the human.' After the creation of woman, this creature is denoted by the same term (vv 22-23). Nothing has changed in the makeup of 'the human' during his sleep except the loss of a rib. There is no hint in the text of an originally bisexual or sexually undifferentiated being split into two different sexes. The androgynous interpretation suggests that human beings are not intrinsically sexual, a view which contradicts the anthropology of Gen 1-2. According to the biblical text ha adam, 'the human' formed before woman was not originally androgynous but was 'created in anticipation of the future.' He was created with those sexual drives towards union with his counterpart. This becomes apparent in the first human's encounter with the animals, which dramatically pointed up his need of 'a helper as his partner' (vv.18-20). Such a need is satisfied when he is introduced to woman and he fully realizes his sexuality vis-à-vis his sexual complement.[80]

To put it another way, the 'man' is always a man, but only truly realizes what it is to be male when he wakes from his sleep and encounters the first female.

Davidson's reading of the text is supported by 1 Corinthians 11:8-9 and 1 Timothy 2:11-14, both of which use Adam as the name for a male individual who is created before the female Eve. However, it should also be noted that even if one reads the text as saying that Adam was orignally androgynous the theological message is still the same. The creative action of God has resulted in the fact that human beings exist in two sexes, male and female, and are to fulfil their God given vocation within this context

Secondly, men and women can only fulfil this God given vocation together. We saw in Genesis 1 and 5 that exercising dominion as God's image-bearers requires both men and women. So here, in Genesis 2, the man has been placed in the Garden of Eden to 'till and keep it' (Genesis 2:15), but it is 'not good that the man should be alone' (Genesis 2:18) as he carries out this task. He needs an appropriate helper, and this need is reciprocal. It is not as if a woman would have done just fine on her own. Rather, the man is representative; the point is that men and women need each other.

Thirdly, the reason that men and women are fit helpers for each other is that they share an equal humanity. The text says that the man needs 'a helper fit for him.' The Hebrew word translated 'fit for' (*kenegdo*) 'is unusual,' says Ian Paul, 'and has the sense of 'equal but opposite'; it is the kind of phrase you might use

---

80 Davidson, op.cit. pp.20-21. See also Richard Hess, 'Splitting the Adam: The usage of 'adam' in Genesis 1-V' in J A Emerton (ed.), *Studies in the Pentateuch*, Leiden: E J Brill, 1990, pp.1-15.

to describe the opposite bank of a river, combining both the sense of equality but difference and distinctiveness.'[81] The animals are not fit helpers because they are not human, so God creates one by making another human being who is equal in that she shares a common humanity ('bone of my bones and flesh of my flesh', v. 23); but she is also different in that she is a woman rather than another man. She is the helper the man needs because at last 'he has an egalitarian partner, a soul mate.'[82]

Fourthly, while, as St Paul notes in 1 Corinthians 8 and 1 Timothy 2:13, Adam has a priority in relation to Eve in that he existed first and she was created from him, the emphasis in Genesis 2 is not on his priority, but on the equality between the man and the woman flowing from their shared humanity. In the words of Geoffrey Bromiley.

> The male has a certain priority in this relation, for the woman is taken from the man and not the other way round. Yet priority is not the point of the story. The equal humanity which is needed for full companionship takes precedence. As in the Trinity the Father, as the fount of deity, has a certain precedence over the Son and the Spirit, yet all are equally God in eternal interrelation, so it is with man and woman in the fellowship which God has purposed and created.[83]

Fifthly, we learn that God's creation of human beings as male and female is the origin of marriage. In Genesis 2:24 the narrator makes a comment: 'Therefore a man leaves his father and his mother and cleaves to his wife, and they become one flesh.' The narrator indicates that God's bringing together of the first man and woman is the origin of the social institution of marriage. Human beings in subsequent generations come together in the same way as the first couple in the garden did. Furthermore, as Robert Lawton observes, the word translated 'leaves' in the RSV actually means 'shall leave'. Consequently, the verse expresses 'a description of divine intention rather than a habitually observed fact'.[84] Genesis 2:24 is saying that God ordained marriage as the ongoing expression of his creation of human beings as male and female.

Sixthly, Genesis 2 sets out the characteristics of the marriage relationship ordained by God:

- *It is a relationship outside the family circle.* The basis of marriage is that 'a

---

81 Ian Paul, *Same-Sex Unions: The Key Texts*, Cambridge: Grove Books, 2014, p.8.
82 Davidson, op.cit. p. 29.
83 Geoffrey Bromiley, *God and Marriage*, Grand Rapids: Eerdmans, 1980, p. 3.
84 Robert B Lawton, 'Genesis 2:24: Trite or Tragic?', *The Journal of Biblical Literature*, 105, 1986, p.98.

man leaves his father and mother.' The Old Testament mentions incestuous relationships from Genesis 19:30-38 onwards, but such relationships are always regarded a manifestations of human fallenness rather than being as in accordance with God's intention.

- *It is a relationship that has to be freely chosen.* Just as in the Genesis story the divinely matched relationship with the woman 'has to be recognised and affirmed by man himself',[85] so in all subsequent generations men and women have to freely affirm that they want to enter into a marital relationship with this other human being. In the words of Pope John Paul II, 'The choice is what establishes the conjugal covenant between the persons, who become one flesh only based on this choice.'[86]

- *It is an exclusive relationship between one man and one woman.* Genesis mentions polygamy from the time of Lamech onwards (Genesis 4:19), but its existence is contrary to the nature of marriage as ordained by God. In Genesis 2 it is one man and one woman who are to enter into marriage.

- *It is a sexual relationship.* 'The unity about which Genesis 2:24 speaks ('and the two will become one flesh') is without doubt the unity that is expressed and realized in the conjugal act.'[87] Furthermore, as Davidson observes (using 'clinging' in place of the RSV's 'cleaves'): 'this one flesh union follows the 'clinging.' Thus the Edenic blueprint for sexual relationships underscores that the one flesh union of sexual intercourse belongs within the context of the marriage covenant.'[88]

- *It is a permanent relationship.* The Hebrew word *dabaq* translated in 'cleaves' in the RSV is a word that is used in the Old Testament for the permanent bond between Israel and God (Deuteronomy 10:20, Joshua 22:5, 2 Kings 18:6). Its use in Genesis 2:24 'implies a devotion and an unbreakable faith between humans; it connotes a permanent attraction which transcends genital union, to which it, nevertheless, gives meaning.'[89]

- Finally, in the wider context of Genesis 1 – 5, the marital relationship established in Genesis 2:24 is *a relationship that is ordered towards procreation.* Genesis 2:24 is silent about the begetting of children, thus making the point

---

85 Barth, *Church Dogmatics* III/2, p. 291.
86 John Paul II, *Man and Women He Created Them*, Boston: Pauline Books and Media, 2006, p.168.
87 Ibid, p.167.
88 Davidson, op.cit. p.46.
89 Raymond E Collins, 'The Bible and Sexuality,' *Biblical Theology Bulletin*, 7, 1977, p.153.

that the relationship between men and women in marriage has value in and of itself. However, it is through the marriage between the first humans established by God in Genesis 2 that the command to human beings to 'be fruitful and multiply' in Genesis 1:28 begins to find fulfilment as Adam and Eve produce children as the fruit of their union (Genesis 4:1, 2, 25 and 5:3). This, says Genesis, is how God established it to be. To quote Hollinger: 'God's design is that humans enter the world through the most intimate, loving relationship on earth—the one flesh covenant of marriage.'[90]

Seventhly, we are told in Genesis 2:25 that 'the man and his wife were naked and were not ashamed.' This statement is the equivalent of the declaration in Genesis 1:31 that God saw everything that he had made and it was 'very good.' Shame and the desire to hide are the result of the guilt caused by sin (Genesis 3:7-11). By contrast, in Genesis 2:25 everything is as God means it to be, hence it is good, hence there is no cause for shame. Marriage, and sex within marriage, are not something shameful. They are good.

Sex in Matthew 19:3-6 and Mark 10:2-9

Jesus is 'Emmanuel—God with us' (Matthew 1:23), the creator God made flesh. This means that these verses from the Gospels record the creator himself talking about his own work of creation. This is what he had to say:

> [3] And Pharisees came up to him and tested him by asking, "Is it lawful to divorce one's wife for any cause?" [4] He answered, "Have you not read that he who made them from the beginning made them male and female, [5] and said, 'For this reason a man shall leave his father and mother and be joined to his wife, and the two shall become one flesh'? [6] So they are no longer two but one flesh. What therefore God has joined together, let not man put asunder." (Matthew 19:3-6)

> [2] And Pharisees came up and in order to test him asked, "Is it lawful for a man to divorce his wife?" [3] He answered them, "What did Moses command you?" [4] They said, "Moses allowed a man to write a certificate of divorce, and to put her away." [5] But Jesus said to them, "For your hardness of heart he wrote you this commandment. [6] But from the beginning of creation, 'God made them male and female.' [7] 'For this reason a man shall leave his father and mother and be joined to his wife, [8] and the two shall

---

90 Hollinger, op.cit. p;.102.

become one flesh.' So they are no longer two but one flesh. ⁹ What there-fore God has joined together, let not man put asunder." (Mark 10:2-9)

These two accounts are very similar, albeit not identical, and what they tell us, says Robert Gagnon, is that 'Jesus understood the stories about the creation of humans in Genesis 1 and 2 not merely as descriptive but also as texts that supplied a prescriptive model for subsequent human sexual behaviour.'[91] Jesus affirms that the dimorphic pattern of human existence as male and female, and the form of marriage based upon it, come with God's own authority. God has established and constituted them as the pattern within which he calls human beings to live in this world.

Being attentive to who we really are, created male and female, informs rea-soned decision making about how to love God and one another in this world. As we noted in the Introduction, our contemporary culture tells us that we should live in a way that is true to who we are. The Bible and the Christian faith would agree with this, but they would add that who we are is people created as male and female in God's image and likeness and called to live in the light of God's institu-tion of marriage and his command to be fruitful and multiply. To love God and other people is to relate to them appropriately in the light of this reality.

Elsewhere in his teaching Jesus explains that things will not be entirely the same in the next world, and so in the next chapter we will look at men and women in the world to come.

Questions for discussion

1. According to the Christian faith, why do human beings come in two sexes?

2. What is the relationship between being male and female and being made in the image and likeness of God?

3. How is marriage rooted in God's creation of the human race?

---

91 Robert Gagnon, 'Sexuality', in Kevin Vanhoozer (ed.), *Dictionary for Theological Interpreta-tion of the Bible*, Grand Rapids: Baker Academic, p.740.

CHAPTER 4

Men and Women in the world to come

'For in the resurrection, they neither marry, nor are given in marriage, but are like angels in heaven' (Matthew 22:30).

The life of the world to come

Sexual differentiation and marriage are key features of human existence in this world. In the last chapter we saw that the human race exists as a species divided into two sexes, male and female. The differences between the sexes are rooted in bodies designed to play different roles in the procreation and nurture of children. We also learned in Genesis and in Jesus' teaching that the division of humanity into two sexes is not a cosmic accident but the result of God's creation of human beings in his image and likeness. Finally, we found that God's creation of human beings is the origin of marriage. God has appointed marriage as the context for male and female human beings to join together in sexual union and fulfil his command to 'be fruitful and multiply.'

However, the Christian faith does not limit our view to this world alone. We are looking for life in the next world. In the Apostles Creed Christians confess their faith in 'the resurrection of the body, and the life everlasting.' In the Nicene Creed they likewise declare, 'I look for the resurrection of the dead, and the life of the world to come.' These words point to the truth that the end of our lives in this present world will not be the end of our individual stories nor that of the human race.

At the end of time God will fulfil the process of universal renewal he began with Christ's resurrection (see chapter two). This will involve bringing back to embodied existence those who have died. Moreover, God will grant a life of eternal blessing in a restored created order to those who belong to his people—a 'new heaven and a new earth' (Isaiah 65:17, Revelation 21:1) where 'the redeemed of

God will live in resurrected bodies within a renewed creation, from which sin and its effects have been expunged.'[92] This raises the question of what life will be like in the renewed creation. What place, if any, will there be for sexual differentiation and marriage in the world to come?

What does Jesus say about resurrection life?

Jesus spoke about what life will be like after the resurrection in a discussion with the Sadducees, a Jewish group that did not believe in life after death. They claimed that it was not taught in the Books of Moses (i.e., the first five books of the Bible). Jesus' discussion with them is recorded in the Gospel of Matthew as follows:

> [23] The same day Sadducees came to him, who say that there is no resurrection; and they asked him a question, [24] saying, "Teacher, Moses said, 'If a man dies, having no children, his brother must marry the widow, and raise up children for his brother.' [25] Now there were seven brothers among us; the first married, and died, and having no children left his wife to his brother. [26] So too the second and third, down to the seventh. [27] After them all, the woman died. [28] In the resurrection, therefore, to which of the seven will she be wife? For they all had her."
>
> [29] But Jesus answered them, "You are wrong, because you know neither the scriptures nor the power of God. [30] For in the resurrection they neither marry nor are given in marriage, but are like angels in heaven. [31] And as for the resurrection of the dead, have you not read what was said to you by God, [32] 'I am the God of Abraham, and the God of Isaac, and the God of Jacob'? He is not God of the dead, but of the living." [33] And when the crowd heard it, they were astonished at his teaching. (Matthew 22:23-33)

In this passage, as in the parallel passages in Mark 12:18-17 and Luke 20:27-40, the Sadducees try to undermine the credibility of belief in the resurrection of the dead with an argument from scripture: in Deuteronomy 25:5-6 the command is given that a brother should marry his dead brother's wife in order to raise up an heir for his dead brother. The Sadducees tell a story in which this happens to one woman seven times. Then they ask, 'whose wife will she be in the resurrection?'

The point of their question is that life after death appears to be incompatible with the law given by God through Moses. If Jesus advocates belief in life after death he must be rejecting this law. Jesus' response is twofold.

First, Jesus cuts to the heart of their objection by pointing out their misunder-

---

92 Bartholomew and Goheen, op.cit. p.165.

standing of the reality about God. In Exodus 3:6 God is called 'The God of Abraham and the God of Isaac and the God of Jacob,' so Jesus counters 'he is not God of the dead, but of the living.' God still wills to be the Patriarchs' God even though they have long since died. He keeps their souls alive and will one day resurrect them to full bodily life again. Jesus suggests that what is true of the Patriarchs is also true of all other people as well. The hope of resurrection is reasonable and well founded.[93]

Secondly, Jesus meets the Sadducees' hypothetical objection to the idea of resurrection. He says they should not assume that life after the resurrection will be just the same as life on earth now. It will not. Asking who will be married to whom is like asking about the fourth side of a triangle, because in the resurrection people will neither get married nor be given in marriage, but they will be like the angels.

Will we still have sexed bodies?

To be like the angels does not mean that humans will no longer be male and female in the world to come. This possibility was ruled out in the Early Church by St Augustine and St Jerome, among others, on the basis of Jesus' reply to the Sadducees.

'Will women retain their sex in the resurrection body?' is one of the questions addressed by Augustine in his book *The City of God*. Some people thought that women would turn into men:

> Because of these sayings, 'Until we reach the perfection of manhood, the stature of the full maturity of Christ,' (Ephesians 4:13) and 'Being shaped into the likeness of God's Son' (Romans 8:29) some people suppose that women will not keep their sex at the resurrection; but, they say, will rise again as men, since God made men out of clay, and woman out of man.[94]

Augustine rejects this argument because

> [God] who established the two sexes will restore them both. And indeed, Jesus was questioned by the Sadducees, who denied the resurrection; and they asked to which of seven brothers a wife would belong, to whom they had all been married (since each of them wished to produce descendants for his dead predecessor, according to the Law's instructions); and Jesus replied, 'You are on the wrong track, because you do not understand the Scriptures, or the power of God' And though he might have said, 'the women you are asking about will

---

93 For the details of how Jesus' argument works in its first century context see N T Wright, *The Resurrection of the Son of God*, London: SPCK, 2003, pp.423-427.

94 St Augustine, *The City of God*, Bk. XXII:17, Harmondsworth: Penguin, 1981, p.1057.

not be a woman, she will be a man,' he did not say this. What he said was this. 'For in the resurrected life men and women do not marry; they are like the angels of God in heaven.' That is, they are like them in immortality and felicity, not in body; nor are they like them in their resurrection, since the angels, being unable to die, need no resurrection. Thus Christ denies the existence of marriage in the resurrected life; he does not deny the existence of women in heaven. If he had foreknown that there would be no female sex in that life he could quickly and easily have disposed of the Sadducees' question by saying as much, whereas in fact he expressly stated that there would be both sexes when he said 'they are not married' referring to women, and 'they do not marry wives' referring to men. It follows that there will be in that life those who in this normally marry, and those who are taken in marriage, but they will not do so in heaven.[95]

St Jerome wrote a letter to a woman named Eustochium, consoling her after the death of her mother Paula. Jerome recalls various incidents in Paula's life, including the time Paula became troubled by some questions raised by 'a certain cunning knave':

> Will there be a distinction of sexes in the next world? Or will there be no such distinction? If the distinction continues, there will be wedlock and sexual intercourse and procreation of children. If however, it does not continue, the bodies that will rise again will not be the same.[96]

Jerome then recounts how he refuted him:

> As the fellow had tried to deceive Paula, I at her request went to him, and by asking him a few questions involved him in a dilemma. 'Do you believe', said I, 'that there will be a resurrection of the dead or do you disbelieve?' He replied, 'I believe.' I went on: 'Will the bodies that rise again be the same or different?' He said, 'The same.' Then I asked: 'What of their sex? Will that remain unaltered or will it be changed?' At this question he became silent and swayed his head this way and that as a serpent does to avoid being struck. Accordingly I continued, 'As you have nothing to say I will answer for you and will draw the conclusion from your premises. If the woman shall not rise again as a woman nor the man as a man, there will be no resurrection of the dead. For the body is made up of sex and members. But if there shall be no sex and no members what will become of the resurrection of the body, which cannot exist without

95 Ibid, p.1058.
96 Jerome, Letter CVIII, in *The Nicene and Post-Nicene Fathers*, 2nd Series, Vol.6, Edinburgh and Grand Rapids: T&T Clark/Eerdmans, 1996, pp.207-8.

sex and members? And if there shall be no resurrection of the body, there can be no resurrection of the dead. But as to your objection taken from marriage, that, if the members shall remain the same, marriage must inevitably be allowed; it is disposed of by the Saviour's words: 'ye do err not knowing the scriptures nor the power of God. For in the resurrection they neither marry nor are given in marriage but are as the angels.' When it is said that they neither marry nor are given in marriage, the distinction of sex is shewn to persist. For no one says of things which have no capacity for marriage such as a stick or a stone that they neither marry nor are given in marriage; but this may well be said of those who while they can marry yet abstain from doing so by their own virtue and by the grace of Christ. But if you cavil at this and say, how shall we in that case be like the angels with whom there is neither male nor female, hear my answer in brief as follows. What the Lord promises to us is not the nature of angels but their mode of life and their bliss.'[97]

Augustine and Jerome make two key points in these extracts:

1. Jesus' argument requires the existence of both men and women in heaven because, if there were not, then the issue of marriage would simply not arise.

2. The very concept of the resurrection of the dead involves the resurrection of the body. This must mean that people will be resurrected as men or women, since the bodies that God will raise up are either male bodies or female bodies.

But what about St Paul's teaching that God's people will have a 'spiritual body' at the resurrection (1 Corinthians 15:44)? If our resurrection body will be spiritual, it is suggested, then the issue of its sex no longer arises since the distinction between the sexes is something that only exists in the case of material bodies. However, this suggestion misunderstands Paul. The idea that our present physical, sexed bodies will be replaced by a new non-material form of existence is, explains Tom Wright, 'exactly what St Paul is *not* saying.' Paul does not conceive of the spiritual body in opposition to materiality. Rather, he contrasts

....a body animated by one type of life and a body animated by another type. The difference between them is found, if you like, on what the two bodies run on. The present body is animated by the normal life which all humans share. The word Paul uses for this often means 'soul;' he means it in the sense of the ordinary life-force on which we all depend in this present body, the ordinary energy that keeps us breathing and our blood circulating. But the body that we

---

97 Ibid, p.208.

shall be given in the resurrection is to be animated by God's own spirit. This is what Paul says in a simpler passage, Romans 8:10-11: the spirit of Jesus the Messiah dwells within you at the moment, and God will give life to your mortal bodies through this spirit who lives inside you.[98]

What all this means, in short, is that our physical bodies are an eternal part of our existence. In the world to come we shall have the same physical bodies that we have now. The difference is that they will be animated by the Spirit and will be, therefore, imperishable and immortal (1 Corinthians 15:52-54). If, due to the form of our embodiment, we are men in this life, we shall be men in the next life; and if we are women now we shall be women then.

We need only look at Jesus to see that this is true. Jesus, in his humanity, is the 'first fruits' of the new form of post-resurrection human existence (1 Corinthians 15:23). Jesus was a male human being with a male body, and it was this same male body that was raised from death (Luke 24:36-42), which subsequently ascended into heaven, and which will return to earth when Jesus comes in glory (Acts 1:9-11). What happened with Jesus will also happen with us. We shall be men and women for eternity.

The reason is simple. *We* are that particular male or female compound of body and soul that God called into existence, and it is as a male or female compound of body and soul that God calls us to inhabit eternity. As C S Lewis insists:

> ....it is not humanity in the abstract that is to be saved, but you—you, the individual reader, John Stubbs or Janet Smith. Blessed and fortunate creature, your eyes shall behold Him and not another's. All that you are, sins apart, is destined, if you will let God have His good way, to utter satisfaction.[99]

Will we be married?

Being like the angels means that there will be no marriage and therefore no sex and no procreation in the world to come. To quote Pope John Paul II,

> ....marriage—the union in which, as Genesis says, 'the man will...unite with his wife and the two will be one flesh (Genesis 2:24), a union proper to man from the 'beginning'—belongs exclusively 'to this world.' Marriage and procreation do not constitute man's eschatological future. In the resurrection they lose, so to speak, their raison d'etre. That 'other world' about which Luke speaks (Luke 20:35) means the definitive fulfilment of the human race, the

---

98 Tom Wright, *Paul for Everyone - 1 Corinthians*, London: SPCK, 2003, p.221.
99 C S Lewis, *The Problem of Pain*, Glasgow: Fount, 1978, p. 135.

quantative closure of that circle of beings created in the image and likeness of God in order that, multiplying through the conjugal 'unity of the body' of men and women, they should subdue the earth to themselves.[100]

The point here is that marriage, and sexual intercourse within marriage leading to procreation, are necessary features of life in this world in order to fulfil the divine mandate to 'be fruitful and multiply' given in Genesis 1:28. However, when God lowers the curtain on this world and raises it on the world to come that mandate will have been fulfilled. The number of people God wills to inhabit his eternal kingdom will have been brought into existence and because there will be no death their number will not diminish. Hence there will be no need for procreative sex, hence there will be no more need for one flesh unions, and hence there will be no more marriage.

The abolition of marriage and sexual intercourse might seem strange in light of C.S. Lewis's principle that everything good about our lives in this world is destined for 'utter satisfaction' in the world to come. In his science fiction novel *Voyage to Venus*, the rationalist McPhee is scornful: 'So you think you're going to have guts and palate forever in a world where there'll be no eating, and genital organs in a world without copulation? Man you'll have a grand time of it!'[101]

Lewis himself responds to this issue in his book *Miracles*:

The letter and the spirit of scripture, and all of Christianity, forbid us to suppose that the life in the New Creation will be a sexual life; and this reduces our imaginations to the withering alternative either of bodies which are hardly recognisable as human bodies at all or else of a perpetual fast. As regards the fast, I think our present outlook might be that of a small boy who, on being told that the sexual act was the highest bodily pleasure should immediately ask whether you ate chocolates at the same time. On receiving the answer 'No,' he might regard absence of chocolates as the chief characteristic of sexuality. In vain would you tell him that the reason why lovers in their carnal raptures don't think about chocolates is that they have something better to think of. The boy knows chocolate: he does not know the positive thing that excludes it. We are in the same position. We know the sexual life; we do not know, except in glimpses, the other thing which, in Heaven, will leave no room for it. Hence where fullness awaits us we anticipate fasting.[102]

So what is that 'positive thing,' that 'fullness,' which Lewis says we should antici-

---

100 John Paul II, op.cit. p.387.
101 C S Lewis, *Voyage to Venus*, London: Pan, 1953, p.27. '
102 Lewis, *Miracles*, pp.163-164.

pate? What will one day exclude our thoughts of marriage and sexual activity as sexual activity currently excludes our thoughts of chocolate?

The answer is 'marriage.' In the next world another form of marriage will replace and fulfil marriage and sexual activity as we experience them in this world. We are told this in the Bible. In the Old Testament human marriages are repeatedly used as pictures of God's relationship with his people (e.g., Isaiah 54:6, Ezekiel 16:8, Hosea 2:19-20). Then, in the New Testament, Jesus' relationship with his Church is compared to that of a bridegroom and his bride (e.g., John 3:27-30, 2 Corinthians 11:2, Ephesians 5:21-33). Finally, we are told to expect the 'marriage of the Lamb' at the end of time, that is, the marriage between God and humanity that will endure for eternity (Revelation 19:6-9, 21:2 & 9). This eternal marriage is the 'fullness' to which marriage and sexual activity in this world point. As Peter Kreeft writes:

> The last event in human history, according to the Bible, at the end of the Apocalypse, is a wedding between the Lamb and His Bride, His Church. And the centre of sex, and its greatest thrill, is the intimacy of intercourse, the almost mystical overcoming of separateness and egotism, the identification with the other, in body and mind, the fact that the beloved allows you into his or her 'holy of holies.' This is a natural icon, image, shadow, prophecy, appetizer and foretaste of that infinite and unimaginable ecstasy of Heaven that we were all made for. We are hardwired for becoming one with God; that's why we are so thrilled at becoming one with each other. That's why self-forgetfulness, the transcendence of egotism, and the loss of control, in sexual orgasm is so mysteriously fulfilling. It's not just the purely physical sensation; it's the mystical meaning. The higher animals experience the same physical pleasure (watch dogs!), but they don't write mystical romantic love poems about it, and they wouldn't write them even if they could write.
>
> Animal sex is only a remote image of human romance, and human romance is a remote image of Heavenly ecstasy. The earthly intimacy with the beloved is a tiny, distant spark of the bonfire that is the Heavenly intimacy with God. Sex is a faint image of the Beatific Vision.[103]

In heaven, in other words, sexual activity as we know it in this world will become redundant because the transcendent reality of communion with God to which it points us will have arrived. The caterpillar will have turned into the butterfly.

---

103 Peter Kreeft, *The Philosophy of Jesus*, South Bend: St Augustine's Press, 2007, pp.131-132.

In the previous chapter we saw that God, who exists in an eternal communion of love, created human beings as male and female so that they too might enter into relationship with each other and with him. The purpose of existing as an embodied male or female human being is that capacity for relationship. Human beings are embodied creatures made for communion. What this means is that marriage and procreation are not essential to the meaning of embodiment. As John Paul II explains,

> Marriage and procreation do not definitively determine the original and fundamental meaning of being a body, nor of being, as a body, male and female. Marriage and procreation only give concrete reality to that meaning in the dimensions of history. The resurrection indicates the closure of the historical dimension. And so it is that the words 'when they rise from the dead, they will take neither wife nor husband' (Mark 12:25) not only express clearly what meaning the human body will not have in the 'future world,' but allow us also to deduce that the 'spousal' meaning of the body in the resurrection will perfectly correspond both to the fact that man as male-female is a person, created in the 'image and likeness of God,' and to the fact that this image is realized in the communion of persons.[104]

The communion of persons in the world to come will not just be 'the flight of the alone to the alone,' in the words of Plotinus, the Neoplatonic philosopher. It will not be a solitary communion between God and individual male and female human beings. Life in the next world will be a communal life, hence the image of the holy city in Revelation 21 and 22. We will simultaneously be in perfect communion with God and all of God's people. This means that, while there will be no desire for sex (in the sense of sexual intercourse) in the world to come, there will be sexual desire. Sexual desire is the desire for intimate communion with another human being and ultimately with God and in the world to come that desire will be both eternally felt and eternally satisfied.[105]

Some married people feel uncomfortable about this dimension of the Christian hope because they think it threatens their unique relationship with their spouse. 'What will become of my special relationship with Janet or John if marriage is no more and we will be in relationship with God and all the rest of God's people?' The answer is that our limited time, energy and love in this world means that our relationship with X can be in competition with our relationship with Y, but in the next world we will be freed from the constraints of this world. We will

---

104 John Paul II, op.cit. p.399.
105 For this distinction between 'desire for sex' and 'sexual desire' see Grant, op.cit. pp.97-98.

learn to love as God loves,[106] and so will have the capacity to love God and all of his people perfectly without diminishing our capacity to love a particular individual perfectly too. We will not love our spouse less, but God and everyone else (including our spouse) infinitely more.

A final point is that Christian belief in the resurrection life challenges us on how we live this life now. The Bible and the Christian tradition teach us that the nature of our life in the world to come will depend on how we live in our bodies in this world (e.g., Matthew 25:1-36, 2 Corinthians 5:10, Revelation 20:11-15). This means we should live in light of the way God has made us, in such a way that we shall live with God and his people forever. As we saw in the Introduction, our contemporary culture emphasizes the need for each individual to have the opportunity to flourish. The Bible and the Christian faith agree, but they would add that just as the relationship between an engaged couple achieves its full flourishing when they are married, so also human beings will only ever achieve their full flourishing in the life of the world to come. It follows that to live well in this world means to live in such a way that means we shall experience this full flourishing in the life to come.

In the next two chapters we will begin to consider what living in this way means by exploring marriage, singleness, and friendship as forms of Christian discipleship.

Questions for discussion

1. How did Jesus respond to the Sadducees' question about the resurrection?

2. Will we have sexed bodies in the world to come?

3. Is it correct to say that there will be no marriage in the world to come?

---

106 See 1 John 3:2 'we shall be like him, for we shall see him as he is.'

CHAPTER 5

Marriage, singleness, and friendship (I)

'Be subject to one another out of reverence for Christ'
(Ephesians 5:21).

Two ways to live

One really important question confronts all of us as human beings: how can I live now so that, in the next world, I will be married to God and literally live 'happily ever after'? The basic answer as to what will determine our eternal destiny is how we have responded, or failed to respond, to God in this world.

So far in this study we have seen that human beings are male and female embodied souls who at the moment live in this world, but who will one day live forever in the world that is to come. In *The City of God* St Augustine talks about the characteristics of two human communities, or 'cities,' which will endure for eternity: 'We see then that the two cities were created by two kinds of love: the earthly city was created by self-love reaching the point of contempt for God, the Heavenly City by the love of God carried as far as contempt of self.'[107] Whether we are members of the heavenly city or the earthly city will decide whether we spend eternity married to God in his kingdom or whether we are cut off from God and all that is good forever and suffer an eternity of pain and loss.

C S Lewis makes the same point in *The Great Divorce*: 'There are only two kinds of people in the end: those who say to God, "Thy will be done," and those to whom God says, in the end, "*Thy* will be done."'[108] Those who put love for God at the centre of our lives—even when it means saying 'no' to self—and say to God 'Thy will be done' (Matthew 6:10) will be truly happy with God for ever. If, however, we give priority to self-love and say 'no' to God and his will for our lives

---

107 Augustine, *The City of God*, Bk. XIV:28 , p.593.
108 C S Lewis, *The Great Divorce*, Glasgow: Fontana, 1972, pp.66-67.

then one day God will ratify our decision; we will find ourselves in the eternal alienation from God we have chosen.[109]

As we saw at the end of chapter two, the continuing assaults of the devil and the continuing influence of our old fallen natures means that in this life none of us will ever be completely free from sin. Even if we are Christians, we will continue to be people who rebel against God and who at best obey him imperfectly, which is why we need to constantly turn to God in confession and repentance, seeking and receiving his forgiveness for the past and strength for the future.

However, this truth does not negate the basic point made by St Augustine and by Lewis. There is a binary division between those who will spend eternity with God and those who will not and this division is between those whose fundamental desire and intention is to do God's will (however much they may continue to fail in practice) and those whose fundamental desire is to go their own way.

Our need to be people who say to yes to God and his will ties in with what we saw when we looked at the shape of the Christian life at the end of chapter two. We saw that we are called to live out the new life of holiness that Christ has achieved for us by means of his death and resurrection through 'mortification' and 'vivification' and through using our Spirit enabled freedom to reject the 'works of the flesh' and to produce 'the fruit of the Spirit.'

If we look at what this means more closely we find that 'mortification' means dying to the old life in we which said 'no' to God and 'vivification' means living a new kind of life in which we say 'yes' to God in a life marked by obedience to what God requires of us (see Romans 6:1-18). Likewise rejecting the 'works of the flesh' means saying 'no' to a life of sin and producing the fruit of the Spirit means saying 'yes' to living the kind of holy life for which God created us and to which he calls us (see Galatians 5:13-24).

What all this means is that to live as a Christian means putting love for God at the centre of our lives by saying 'yes' to what God asks of us. As we do this we respond to God in a way that means that at the resurrection we shall be married to God and live happily forever in his kingdom.[110]

---

109 For a more detailed exposition of this point see *The Great Divorce* throughout and also Jerry L Walls, *Heaven: The Logic of Eternal Joy*, New York: OUP, 2002 and *Hell: The Logic of Damnation*, Notre Dame: University of Notre Dame Press, 1992.

110 Someone may object that this means we are saved by works rather than by faith. However, this is to fail to understand the meaning of faith. According to the New Testament the faith which saves us is a living faith which manifests itself in good works, that is, actions which conform to what God requires (see James 2:14-26). As the homily 'A short declaration of the true lively and Christian faith' in the First book of Homilies puts it: 'If these fruits do not follow, we do but mock with God, deceive ourselves, and also other men. Well may we bear the name

With this in mind, we are going to explore what putting love for God at the centre of our lives means in relation to three ways of living: marriage, singleness, and friendship as the overarching way of life that links them.

Marriage as instituted of God

In 2013 the *Washington Post* published an article proposing a new form of marriage which the author called a 'wedlease.' In a classic example of how our consumer culture is shaping our view of relationships, the author argues that we should have marriage leases in the same way as we have leases on our apartments.

> Here's how a marital lease could work: Two people commit themselves to marriage for a period of years—one year, five years, 10 years, whatever term suits them. The marital lease could be renewed at the end of the term however many times a couple likes. It could end up lasting a lifetime if the relationship is good and worth continuing. But if the relationship is bad, the couple could go their separate ways at the end of the term. The messiness of divorce is avoided and the end can be as simple as vacating a rental unit.[111]

From a Christian perspective the fundamental objection to this proposal is its underlying assumption that marriage is something that human beings have the power to change (in this case by making marriage a temporary rather than a lifetime commitment). What this assumption ignores is the fact that human beings do not have the power to change what marriage is because they did not create it, any more than they created other important aspects of their existence such as the laws of physics.

Marriage is not a human invention any more than the fact we are male and female is a human invention. It is, as the *Book of Common Prayer* marriage service puts it, a form of life 'instituted of God.' It is one of the things ordained by God at creation for the good of the human race; as such, it will remain unchanged until life in this world comes to an end. Oliver O'Donovan makes the point well:

> Jesus taught (as Saint Matthew reports) that 'he who made them from the beginning made them male and female, and said, "For this reason a man shall leave his father and mother and be joined to his wife, and the two shall become

---

of Christian men, but we do lack the true faith that doth belong thereunto. For true faith doth ever bring forth good works; as St James saith, Show me thy faith by thy deeds (James 2.18). Thy deeds and works must be an open testimonial of thy faith; otherwise thy faith, being without good works, is but the devil's faith, the faith of the wicked, a phantasy of faith, and not a true Christian faith' (I Robinson, *The Homilies*, Bishopstone: Brynmill/Preservation Press, 2006, pp.33-34).

111 Paul Rampell, 'A high divorce rate means it's time to try 'wedleases',' *Washington Post*, 4 August, 2013 cited in Todd Wilson, *Mere Sexuality*, Grand Rapids: Zondervan, 2017, p. 86.

one flesh "' (w). In attempting to understand him Christians have classically believed that in the ordinance of marriage there was given an end for human relationships, a teleological structure which was a fact of creation and therefore not negotiable. The dimorphic organization of human sexuality, the particular attraction of two adults of the opposite sex and of different parents, the setting up of a home distinct from the parental home and the uniting of their shared life (from which Jesus concluded the unnaturalness of divorce): these form a pattern of human fulfilment which serves the wider end of enabling procreation to occur in a context of affection and loyalty. Whatever happens in history, Christians have wished to say, this is what marriage really is. Particular cultures may have distorted it; individuals may fall short of it. It is to their cost in either case; for it reasserts itself as God's creative intention for human relationships on earth; and it will be with us, in one form or another, as our natural good until (but not after) the kingdom of God shall appear.[112]

In chapter three we noted that the form of marriage established by God at creation has six characteristics:

- it is a relationship outside the family circle;

- it is a relationship which has to be freely chosen;

- it is an exclusive relationship between one man and one woman;

- it is a sexual relationship;

- it is a permanent relationship;

- it is a relationship that is ordered towards procreation.

Consequently, there are certain forms of relationship that go against this divinely ordained form of marriage.

First, any form of incestuous marriage is forbidden. That is why the Church of England, like other churches, has lists of those family members people may not marry (the 'Laws of Kindred and Affinity' in the *Book of Common Prayer* and Canon B.31).

Secondly, any form of forced marriage is excluded.[113] If people are forced into a relationship against their will then a valid marriage cannot exist. Marriage liturgies express this principle with the section of the liturgy in which the couple

---

112 O'Donovan, op.cit. p. 69
113 This does not exclude the possibility of an arranged marriage provided this involves genuinely free consent.

both give their consent to the marriage.[114] It is because consent is required that people may not marry those below 'the age of consent' who are too young to give it. The principle of consent would not rule out marriage for people with learning difficulties unless it was the case that their particular form of learning difficulty made the giving of consent impossible because they were unable to understand what marriage involved. This would need to be assessed on a case-by-case basis.

Thirdly, the exclusive nature of marriage rules out more than one marital partner on either side, or any sexual relationship with anyone other than one's husband or wife. It also means that there can be no re-marriage unless a previous marriage has come to an end (an issue we shall look at when we consider divorce and re-marriage in chapter 9). In addition, the fact that this exclusive relationship is between a man and women rules out marriage between two people of the same sex (an issue to which we shall return in chapter 8).

Fourthly, the sexual nature of marriage means that people may not marry unless they are willing and able to engage in sexual intercourse with a member of the opposite sex (hence Jesus' comments about eunuchs not entering into marriage in Matthew 19:10-12). Full sexual intercourse is understood as meaning the coming together of the penis and vagina to achieve the one-flesh union that makes possible the procreation of children, with other forms of sexual activity being seen as preparatory or ancillary to this act.

However, a man or a woman who was incapable of full sexual intercourse for reasons of injury or disability could still arguably be married if they adhered to God's intention for marriage by desiring such intercourse if it were to become possible, and by being willing to engage in such forms of sexual activity as were possible.

We must also be clear that sexual activity between a man and a woman in marriage involves two people who have the inherent dignity of being made in the image and likeness of God. This dignity must always be respected. For this reason

---

114 In the *Book of Common Prayer* marriage service, for example, consent is given in the following words:
'If no impediment be alleged, then shall the Curate say unto the Man,
N. wilt thou have this woman to thy wedded wife, to live together after God's ordinance in the holy estate of Matrimony? Wilt thou love her, comfort her, honour, and keep her, in sickness and in health; and, forsaking all other, keep thee only unto her, so long as ye both shall live? The Man shall answer, I will.
Then shall the Priest say unto the Woman,
N. wilt thou have this man to thy wedded husband, to live together after God's ordinance in the holy estate of Matrimony? Wilt thou obey him, and serve him, love, honour, and keep him, in sickness and in health; and, forsaking all other, keep thee only unto him, so long as ye both shall live? The Woman shall answer, I will.'

it is wrong to engage in violence or humiliation (whether physical or psycholog-ical) in the context of sexual activity within marriage just as much as outside it. This rules out both marital rape and all forms of sado-masochistic sexual activity, such as those popularised in *Fifty Shades of Grey* and its numerous imitators.

Fifthly, the permanent nature of marriage means that people cannot rightly enter into marriage if they do not intend their marriage to be life-long (which is why the 'wedlease' approach to marriage is a non-starter). The exchange of vows in the marriage liturgy is designed to allow the couple to express this intention to remain married 'till death us do part'.[115] Since this intention is needed, the ex-istence of a pre-nuptial agreement specifying what would happen to the couple's assets in the case of divorce would be questionable from a Christian perspective. It would seem to imply that the couple were already entertaining the prospect that their marriage might not last. If it did indicate that they were not seriously committed to their marriage being life-long then, arguably, this would invalidate the marriage from a Christian point of view, turning it instead into a form of temporary cohabitation.

Sixthly, the procreative nature of marriage excludes a form of relationship that necessarily rules out the procreation of children. This might be taken to mean that childless couples, or those incapable of having children, are not truly married, but this does not follow. The key questions about childless marriages are (a) whether their form of relationship is one that would have led to children being born in the absence of accidental factors such as age or infirmity, and (b) whether the couple would welcome any children granted to them by God as a result of their union? If the answer to both questions was 'yes' then a childless marriage would fall within the scope God's intentions for marriage. The couple would be seeking to live as God has ordained. That is why in the Bible the childless marriages of Abram and Sarai (Genesis 12:2, 18:11) and Zechariah and Elizabeth (Luke 1:7) are still de-scribed as marriages. [116]

---

115 That is why in the *Book of Common Prayer* marriage service the vows exchanged by the couple are as follows:
'I N. take thee N. to my wedded wife, to have and to hold from this day forward, for better for worse, for richer for poorer, in sickness and in health, to love and to cherish, till death us do part, according to God's holy ordinance; and thereto I plight thee my troth.'
'I N. take thee N. to my wedded husband, to have and to hold from this day forward, for better for worse, for richer for poorer, in sickness and in health, to love, cherish, and to obey, till death us do part, according to God's holy ordinance; and thereto I give thee my troth.'

116 As the Church of England report *Personal Origins* (London: CHP 1996, p.66) notes, it is pas-torally important to stress to couples who are unable to have children that their lack of children does not call into question the validity of their marriage. 'In the face of feelings of inadequacy and of marital stress it is important to reassure couples that childlessness is not, according to Anglican belief, a threat to the integrity of marriage. A marriage in which there are no children is not in any sense made invalid or reduced to some second-class status.

Equality in marriage

In chapter three we noted that the relationship between the man and the woman in Genesis 2, which constitutes the basis for all subsequent marriages, is a relationship between two people who are equal because they possess a shared humanity. Eve is the fit companion for Adam because although she is different from him in being female rather than male she is equal to him as another human being made in the image and likeness of God.

In line with what is said in Genesis, the account of Christian marriage contained in the New Testament is also marked by equality between men and women.

First, the New Testament tells us that a Christian marriage is a marriage between two people who have the same standing before God. For example, Galatians 3:28-29 declares: 'There is neither Jew nor Greek, there is neither slave nor free, there is neither male nor female; for you are all one in Christ Jesus. And if you are Christ's, then you are Abraham's offspring, heirs according to promise.'

These verses are often read as if St Paul were saying that the difference between men and women established at creation has been done away with amongst Christians. However, that is not his point. These verses are not about sexual identity, but about spiritual identity. Paul means that anyone who has faith in Jesus and is baptised is a member of the family of God regardless of their race, social standing, or sex. Christian men and women are still men and women, but they both have equal standing before God, both as those originally made in God's image and likeness and as the recipients of the blessing promised to Abraham and delivered through Christ.

Secondly, in Christian marriage the same standard of sexual conduct is required of both parties. As Larry Hurtado notes in his book *Destroyer of the gods*, a 'double standard in sexual practice was fully in force' at the time the New Testament was written. This double standard meant that

> ....wives were generally held to one standard of behaviour, strict marital chastity, and husbands to quite another one. Men, husbands included, were allowed considerably more freedom to have sex with other women, particularly women deemed not to possess status and honour. So, although sex with the wives of other men or with freeborn virgins was not approved, other kinds of sexual activities were openly tolerated, and even encouraged.[117]

The New Testament tells men that this is no longer the case. The requirement for

---

Children are a blessing on marriage. They are not essential to it.'
117 Larry Hurtado, *Destroyer of the gods*, Waco: Baylor University Press, 2016, p.157.

sexual fidelity in marriage as stated in Genesis 2:24 applies to men just as much as to women. That is why men are told to 'abstain from unchastity' (1 Thessalonians 4:4), why St Paul forbids men having sex with prostitutes (1 Corinthians 6:12-20), and why a bishop has to be a 'one woman man' (1 Timothy 5:9) just as good wives were expected to be a 'one man woman.' To quote Hurtado again:

> …the decisive step taken in early Christian sexual teaching was to bring males under the same sort of behavioural requirements that in the larger cultural setting were expected of 'honorable' women. In the matter of marital fidelity and chastity, it seems that for early Christians what was good for the goose was also thought good for the gander![118]

Thirdly, a Christian marriage is to be marked by mutual equality between men and women with regard to sexual intercourse within marriage. This principle is taught by St Paul in 1 Corinthians 7:3-5:

> The husband should give to his wife her conjugal rights, and likewise the wife to her husband. For the wife does not rule over her own body, but the husband does; likewise the husband does not rule over his own body, but the wife does. Do not refuse one another except perhaps by agreement for a season, that you may devote yourselves to prayer; but then come together again, lest Satan tempt you through lack of self-control.

As Tom Wright observes, this is 'a striking statement of mutual equality between husband and wife.' In a culture in which male dominance in sexual relations was taken for granted Paul:

> …mentions first the husband's obligation to the wife, then the wife's to the husband. Then he stresses that, just as the wife doesn't have authority over her own body, because the husband does, even so the husband doesn't have authority over his own body, because his wife does.[119]

Furthermore, in a culture in which the sole purpose of marital sex was seen as the production of legitimate offspring for the husband, Paul tells the Corinthians that the mutual satisfaction of sexual desires was a key component of marriage. Timothy and Kathy Keller say that, in practical terms,

> Paul is telling married Christians that mutual, satisfying, sexual relations must be an important part of their life together. In fact, this passage indicates that

---

118 Ibid, pp.166-167.
119 Tom Wright, *Paul for Everyone - 1 Corinthians*, pp.78-79.

sex should be frequent and reciprocal. One spouse was not allowed to deny sex to the other.[120]

Submission, love and honour

The New Testament further tells us that in addition to being marked by equality in the way just described Christian marriage is also to be marked by submission, love and honour between husbands and wives. We can see this if we look at Titus 2:4-5, Colossians 3:18-19, Ephesians 5:21-33 and 1 Peter 3:1-7.

Titus 2:4-5

The Greek verb *hypotasso* and the cognate Greek noun *hypotage* which are translated in English as 'submit' and 'submission' contain the central idea 'that the one in submission does the will of the one to whom he or she submits, whether this will be good or bad, whether doing it will be welcome or unwelcome.'[121] Thus in Luke 2:51 the child Jesus is subject to his parents, in 1 Peter 5:5 St Peter teaches 'you that are younger be subject to the elders' and in Romans 13:1 St Paul teaches that everyone should be 'subject to the ruling authorities.'

In Titus 2:5 St Paul tells Titus that he should train Christian young women to submit in this way to their husbands. He should train them 'to be sensible, chaste, domestic, kind and submissive to their husbands, that the word of God may not be discredited.' In this verse the reason St Paul gives for young women to submit to their husbands is to enable them to bear witness to their faith to their husbands, or to their non-Christian neighbours in general, in a cultural setting in which such submission was seen as a key characteristic of a virtuous wife.

We can see this attitude, for example, in the *Advice to Bride and Groom* by the Greek biographer and moralist Plutarch in which he declares 'So it is with women also; if they subordinate themselves to their husbands, they are commended, but if they want to have control, they cut a sorrier figure than the subjects of their control.'[122] If a Christian wife was seen to be less virtuous than the good pagan wife in this regard then her witness to the gospel and the witness of the Church as a whole would be liable to be discredited.

Like any other verse in the Bible, Titus 2:5 should not be taken in isolation.

---

120 Tim and Kathy Keller, *The Meaning of Marriage*, London: Hodder & Stoughton, 2011, Kindle edition, Loc 3131

121 Christopher Ash, *Marriage—Sex in the service of God*, Leicester: IVP, 2003, p.312. See also G Delling, 'tasso etc' in the *Theological Dictionary of the New Testament*, Vol 8:27-48, Grand Rapids: Eerdmans, 1988.

122 Plutarch, *Advice to Bride and Groom*, conj, praec. 33 quoted in Gordon Fee, *1 and 2 Timothy, Titus*, Peabody: Hendrickson, 1988, p.192.

Titus 2:4 teaches that wives should not only be submissive to their husbands, but that they should 'love' them. This means that being submissive in verse 5 does not involve an unwilling subjection, but a willing subjection to a husband which is an expression of love. Furthermore, while Titus 2:5 on its own would indicate that submission in a Christian marriage only involves the submission of wives to husbands, Colossians 3:18-19, Ephesians 5:22-3 and 1 Peter 3:1-7 see submission as something that is required of husbands as well as wives.

Colossians 3:18-19

In Colossians 3:18-19 St Paul declares: 'Wives be subject to your husbands, as is fitting in the Lord. Husbands, love your wives, and do not be harsh to them.'

In these verses St Paul teaches that the obedience of a wife to her husband applies even in a marriage in which both the spouses are Christians and here the motive is not said to be to bear witness to those who are not yet Christians by conforming to expected cultural norms. As Dick Lucas notes in his commentary on Colossians, the entirety of Colossians 3 is a 'sustained exposition of the rule of Christ' and within this context when St Paul writes in verse 18 'Wives be subject to your husbands as is fitting in the Lord' what he is doing is explaining 'what it means to call Christ Lord.' To submit to the lordship of Christ means for wives also to submit to their husbands.[123]

In contrast to prevailing first century cultural norms, St Paul then goes on in verse 19 to tell husbands that submitting to the Lordship of Christ also has consequences for the way they conduct themselves within marriage. Husbands are told 'love your wives, and do not be harsh to them.' Whereas the prevailing cultural view was that the role of husbands was to rule over their wives (a view expressed for example in Aristotle's *Politics*),[124] what St Paul says is that they are to love them rather than acting harshly towards them and, by serving them in this way, to serve Christ.

Ephesians 5:21-33

Ephesians 5:21-33, develops further the call for wives to submit to their husbands and husbands to love their wives. This passage runs as follows:

> Be subject to one another out of reverence for Christ. Wives, be subject to your husbands, as to the Lord. For the husband is the head of the wife as Christ is the head of the church, his body, and is himself its Saviour. As

---

123 Dick Lucas, *The Message of Colossians and Philemon*, Leicester: IVP, 1980, pp.160-161.
124 See Ian Paul, 'Aristotle and the Household Codes,' *Psephizo*, 24 November 2013, https://www.psephizo.com/life-ministry/aristotle-and-the-household-codes/.

the church is subject to Christ, so let wives also be subject in everything to their husbands. Husbands, love your wives, as Christ loved the church and gave himself up for her, that he might sanctify her, having cleansed her by the washing of water with the word, that he might present the church to himself in splendour, without spot or wrinkle or any such thing, that she might be holy and without blemish. Even so husbands should love their wives as their own bodies. He who loves his wife loves himself. For no man ever hates his own flesh, but nourishes and cherishes it, as Christ does the church, because we are members of his body. "For this reason a man shall leave his father and mother and be joined to his wife, and the two shall become one flesh." This mystery is a profound one, and I am saying that it refers to Christ and the church; however, let each one of you love his wife as himself, and let the wife see that she respects her husband.

The first thing to note here, in verse 21, is the *mutual* submission of husband and wives ('Be subject to one another out of reverence for Christ').[125] As in Titus and Colossians, wives are called to submit to their husbands, but they do so within a context of the mutual submission of both wives and husbands. In his commentary on this verse Pope John Paul II helpfully expounds this mutual submission in terms of their love for one another:

The author speaks about the mutual submission of the spouses, husband and wife, and in this way shows how to understand the words he writes afterward about the submission of the wife to the husband. We read, 'Wives, be subject to your husbands, as you are to the Lord' (Eph 5:22). When he expresses himself in this way, the author does not intend to say that the husband is the 'master' of the wife and that the interpersonal covenant proper to marriage is a contract of domination by the husband over the wife. He expresses a different concept instead, namely that it is in her relationship with Christ—who is for both spouses the one and only Lord—that the wife can and should find the motivation for the relationship with her husband, which flows from the very essence of marriage and the family. This relationship is nevertheless not one-sided submission. According to the teaching of Ephesians, marriage ex-

---

125 As John Stott notes in his commentary on Ephesians, the verb in verse 21 translated 'Be subject to one another' in the RSV is a present participle and like the preceding participles in verses 19 and 20 depends on the command 'be filled with the Spirit' in verse 18. However, '…a Greek participle was sometimes used as an imperative, and undoubtedly the demand for mutual submissiveness leads on to the submission asked for from wives, children and slaves. Moreover, there is no verb at all in verse 22, because the call for submission in verse 21 is intended to be carried over into it.' John Stott, *The Message of Ephesians*, Leicester: Inter-Varsity Press, 1979, p.215.

cludes this element of the contract, which weighed on this institution and at times does not cease to weigh on it. Husband and wife are, fact, 'subject to one another,' mutually subordinated to one another. The source of this reciprocal submission lies in Christian *pietas* and its expression is love.[126]

The second thing to note is that the husband and wife have different roles within this relationship of mutual submission. These roles are summarised in verse 33: 'let each one of you love his wife as himself, and let the wife see that she respects her husband.' What we have here is a call to the giving and receiving of a gift. The husband is called to act as the 'head' of his wife by 'willing and affirming her existence together with his own, and her honour and welfare with and as his own, willing himself only as he wills her too.'[127] The wife is called to exercise 'submission' by accepting this gift rather than rejecting it. In both cases there is 'a readiness to subordinate one's own will and advantage for the benefit of the other.'[128]

The third thing to note is that these different roles are not based on any assumption that men are naturally superior to women or that husbands are naturally better suited to the exercise of a leadership role than wives (which was the prevailing first century view). Rather, these roles are based on the purpose of marriage.

Wives submit to their husbands (vv. 22-24), not the other way round, because Genesis 2:24 (quoted by Paul in vv. 31-32) is not, in the first instance, about marriage between human beings. Rather, it refers to what the *Book of Common Prayer* calls the 'mystical union that is betwixt Christ and his Church.'[129] Human marriage is a copy of the marital union between Christ. This is how Karl Barth explains it:

… the purely creaturely happening that a man leaves his father and mother and cleaves to his wife and they become one flesh—this is not a primary thing, the original, but a secondary, the copy. We have here to do with the great mystery and not just the small (v32). For the creation of man and for this climax, for this form of humanity, the normative pattern, the basic decree and the plan of all the plans of God is 'Christ and the community.'[130]

Just as in Ephesians 3:14 we read that God's fatherhood precedes human fatherhood, so also we learn in Ephesians 5:32 that the union between Christ and his community precedes human marriage. The purpose of human marriage is to be the living expression of its archetype, the union of Christ and his people. This ar-

126 John Paul II. op.cit.,p.473. Italics in the original.
127 Barth, *Church Dogmatics*, III.2, p. 316.
128 Mary Evans, *Women in the Bible*, Exeter: Paternoster, 1983, p.76.
129 *The Book of Common Prayer*, The Form of Solemnization of Matrimony.
130 Barth, *Church Dogmatics*, III.2, pp. 315-316.

chetype shapes its character. The husband is to love his wife to the point of death because of, and following the pattern of, Christ's love for the Church; the wife is to submit to her husband because of, and following the pattern of, the Church's submission to Christ.

When a husband and wife behave this way, they honour Christ. They testify to the world about their faith in who Christ is and what he has done for his people. They also learn humility: the husband learns that his role is not due to his own merit but to Christ's identity as head; and the wife learns to set aside any desires she has to use her abilities to rule over her husband, humbly obeying Christ. Christian faith (what John Paul II calls '*Christian pietas*') is about learning to put Christ first by serving other people. Christian marriage, as described in Ephesians 5, is a school in which we learn to do this.

1 Peter 3:1-7

St Peter gives further teaching about what constitutes right conduct for Christian wives and husbands in 1 Peter 3:1-7. He writes:

> Likewise you wives, be submissive to your husbands, so that some, though they do not obey the word, may be won without a word by the behavior of their wives, when they see your reverent and chaste behavior. Let not yours be the outward adorning with braiding of hair, decoration of gold, and wearing of fine clothing, but let it be the hidden person of the heart with the imperishable jewel of a gentle and quiet spirit, which in God's sight is very precious. So once the holy women who hoped in God used to adorn themselves and were submissive to their husbands, as Sarah obeyed Abraham, calling him lord. And you are now her children if you do right and let nothing terrify you. Likewise you husbands, live considerately with your wives, bestowing honor on the woman as the weaker sex, since you are joint heirs of the grace of life, in order that your prayers may not be hindered.

As Douglas Harink explains in his commentary on this passage, the submission which St Peter calls for from Christian wives is a proclamation of the gospel:

> In this case specifically—a believing wife married to an unbelieving husband—her subordination is an enacted sacrament of the revolutionary gospel to a husband who has not yet 'obeyed' the messianic 'word' or logic (logos; 3:1) of freedom. Indeed the husband, being unbelieving, is likely enslaved to other gods. But the wife's holy and reverent way of life....becomes the unspoken rhetoric that may yet persuade the husband to turn to Jesus Christ, be liberated

and himself take up the logic of revolutionary subordination (3:1-7 and Paul's word to Christian husbands in Eph. 5:25-33). She declares the truth of the gospel in her free 'action devoid of purpose.' The wife's aim is not to manipulate the husband into believing the word—he may finally refuse—rather, she takes up the gracious action of subordination because this is the way of Jesus Christ, and that itself is the end of her action. It is the gospel proclaimed.[131]

As she behaves in this way, he says, a wife manifests not an outward beauty resulting from her hairstyle, jewelry or clothing, but rather 'the hidden beauty of the crucified Christ' and as she does so:

> She enters into the illustrious company of the 'holy women' of old who confidently 'hoped in God' and became subordinate to their husbands. She becomes no less than a daughter of Sarah, who proclaimed the same gospel of subordination in her life with Abraham (1 Peter 3:5-6).[132]

Furthermore, the 'messianic domestic revolution' called for by St Peter is not confined to the behaviour of Christian wives, but also affects Christian husbands. They too are 'called to live in conformity with the gospel and be liberated by it.' In a way similar to St Paul in Ephesians 5, St Peter declares that:

> Husbands (and other males) in accordance with their own knowledge of the gospel...must show 'honor'... to their wives and (and other females in their households; 1 Peter 3:7). That females may be physically 'weaker' than males cannot be used as an excuse for husbands to dominate or abuse their wives. Rather, they owe them the same honor that they owe to 'everyone' and even to 'the emperor' (cf. 2:17). For women are 'coheirs'... of the grace of life (3:7). It is this common sharing in the gift graciously given, not the possession of a superior physical strength that established men in right relationship with women. For grace is how the gospel works. Males who do not acknowledge and live in the reality of that grace are still in bondage 'to the desires of the flesh that war against the soul' (2:11). The authoritarian husband or domineering male fails to understand God and the gospel—so much that his prayers, which depend

---

131 Douglas Harink, *1 & 2 Peter*, London: SCM, 2009, p.87 quoting Karl Barth *The Epistle to the Romans*. A classic example of such a proclamation of the gospel by a Christian wife to a non-Christian husband is recorded by St Augustine in Book 9 of his *Confessions* in which he records that his mother Monica: 'Being thus modestly and soberly trained and rather made subject by Thee to her parents, than by her parents to Thee, when she had arrived at a marriageable age, she was given to a husband whom she served as her lord. And she busied herself to gain him to Thee, preaching to him by her behaviour; by which Thou madest her fair, and reverently amiable, and admirable unto her husband' (*Confessions* IX.9 in *The Nicene and Post Nicene Fathers*, First Series Vol I, Edinburgh and Grand Rapids: T&T Clark/ Eerdmans, 1994, p.136.
132 Ibid, p.88.

from beginning to end on God's grace may also be 'hindered.' (3:7). For how can he call upon the grace of God when he refuses to acknowledge that he is a sharer in that grace with women?[133]

St Peter does not use the language of submission in 3:7. However, the setting of this verse within 1 Peter indicates that the honour that husbands are to show to their wives in conformity with the gospel is actually a form of submission. 1 Peter 3:7 is part of a section of 1 Peter beginning at 2:11 which lists how Christians should practice submission in a range of different contexts. Christians are to be subject to the governing authorities (2:13-17). Servants are to be submissive to their masters (2:18-25). As we have seen, wives are to 'likewise' be submissive to their husbands (3:1-6). Finally, 'likewise' husbands are to honour their wives.

The dual use of 'likewise' in 3:1 and 3:7 indicates that the instructions to both husbands and wives are part of the same general injunction to Christian submission that began back in 2:11. Furthermore, as Charles Cranfield notes, the parallel between being in subjection and showing honour in 2:13 and 17 shows that '*honour* has much the same force as *be in subjection to*. Husbands are also called to Christian subordination of self in relation to their wives.'[134]

Five objections to the view of marriage set out in this chapter

This chapter has set out a Christian view of marriage which says that marriage was created by God to be a reflection of the archetypal marriage between Christ and his Church. It further says that marriage is a lifelong and exclusive sexual relationship between a man and a woman who are not closely related to each other and is ordered towards the procreation of children. It is a relationship marked by equality, but it also a relationship in which husbands and wives have different callings in an overall context of submission to Christ and to each other. Wives are called to love their husbands and to be subject to them as the Church is subject to Christ. Husbands are called to not be harsh to their wives, but to love and care for them after the model of Christ's love for the Church and to show them the honour that is due to them as the co-heirs of the grace of God.

There are five objections that are now commonly made to this view of marriage.

The first objection is that it is unrealistic to expect people to remain together in an exclusive sexual relationship for the whole of their lives. There are two answers to this objection. First, the witness of a very large number of people down

---

133 Ibid, p.89.
134 Charles Cranfield, *I & II Peter and Jude*, London: SCM, 1960, p. 91. Emphasis in the original.

the centuries and still today shows that remaining together for a lifetime in a sexually exclusive relationship is entirely possible. They have done it. Secondly, God does not leave us without help in living in this way. He gives the supernatural power of the Holy Spirit to assist Christians to live in the way that he has laid down.

The second objection is that the New Testament teaching that wives should submit to their husbands represents a temporary accommodation of the gospel message to fit in with a patriarchal culture, an accommodation which we are now free to set aside since time and society have now moved on.

As Christopher Ash observes, this argument is 'appealing in an egalitarian culture' but it faces 'an enormous exegetical problem' in relation to the argument put forward by St Paul in Ephesians 5. As he notes:

> Paul develops the patriarchal theme in Ephesians with considerable warmth and passion along lines suggested to him by the long Old Testament theme of the marriage of the Lord to his people his bride (this development is in marked contrast to slavery, where the New Testament writers offer no such rationale). Best ignores this wider scriptural theme when he says, 'No logical reason dictates the drawing of a parallel between the relationship of Christ and the church and that of a husband and wife'… He claims that Christ could equally well have been portrayed as wife with the church as husband, and that the only reason the writer puts it this way is that he lived in a patriarchal culture (and the grammatical convention that ekklesia is feminine). On the contrary, there is a deeply scriptural and theological reason. This motif of the divine marriage is central to the grand story of the Bible, it is not an occasional or ad hoc argument produced to make a particular point at a specific situation. This theological motif strongly suggests that when Paul speaks of the submission of wives to husbands he does so, not with hesitation or regret, but because he understand that this theme ties the marriage relationship on earth to the great drama of salvation.[135]

In other words, as we noted when we looked at the teaching of Ephesians 5, the reason why wives are to submit to their husbands is because Christ is the head of his Church and the Church is called to submit to him. In the same way husbands are to love their wives because Christ loved the Church and gave himself up for her. This is as true in our egalitarian society as it was in the patriarchal society of the first century.

---

135 Ash, op.cit. p.321 quoting Ernst Best, *Ephesians*, Edinburgh: T&T Clark 1998, p.559.

The third objection is that the teaching that wives are to submit to their husbands gives license to husbands to abuse their wives.

There can be no doubt that this teaching has been, and still is, misused in this way and the seriousness of the abuse that has resulted should never be played down. However, the fact remains that such domestic abuse is a misuse of biblical teaching. This point is well made by Helen Thorne in her book *Walking with Domestic Abuse Sufferers*. She writes:

> One of the verses most twisted by the hands of an abuser is Ephesians 5:22: 'Wives, submit yourselves to your own husbands as you do to the Lord.'
>
> Out of context, this seems like carte blanche for husbands to make any demands they like of their wives. It gets twisted into a weapon that wounds deeply.
>
> That is certainly not what this verse is meant to induce!
>
> It's meant to be an encouragement to choose to submit in the way that Jesus chose to submit to the Father. It's meant to be a safe, trust-fuelled response to the call to husbands to love so very counter-culturally and sacrificially that they are willing to lay down everything (including, by inference, their desires) for the good of their wives. It's meant to be just part of the dynamic of love that includes both husband and wife exhibiting gentleness, kindness, patience and keeping no record of wrongs (1 Corinthians 13). Such godly submission can never be achieved by force.
>
> In abusive marriages those nuances get lost. As those who teach—formally or informally—it's our call to make sure that the context shines out in our words and in the ways we model family life to the wider church. It's our role to ensure that submission is seen as a gift from a loving God that teaches us much about how he humbled himself and first served us.[136]

The fourth objection is that even if it does not result in domestic abuse the idea that wives should submit to their husbands is inherently demeaning to women. Underlying this objection is the prevailing cultural assumption in the 'i world' that it is inherently demeaning for anyone to be subject to anyone else except through our own choice. Our culture teaches us that we need to shape our own lives, to be in control of our own destinies. For a wife to be asked to submit to her husband on the basis of biology appears to go directly against this.

---

136 Helen Thorne, *Walking with Domestic Abuse Sufferers*, London: Inter-Varsity Press, 2018, Kindle edition, Loc 476-486.

What this objection fails to take note of is the fact that what is being asked for is not that wives should give up control, but that they should voluntarily choose to exercise their control over their own lives by loving and submitting to their husbands. If they do this, their dignity as people able to make their own decisions remains intact. They simply choose to exercise their decision-making capacity in a particular way.

Furthermore, husbands are also asked to make a parallel choice. They are asked to exercise their control over their lives in acts of reciprocal submission by choosing to love, care for and honour their wives, putting their best interests before their own desires.

Neither of these callings is demeaning. As the Kellers note 'Both women and men get to 'play the Jesus role' in marriage—Jesus in his sacrificial authority, Jesus in his sacrificial submission.'[137] There can be no higher dignity for any human being than that.

The fifth and final objection, which is rarely expressed, but which is constantly in the background, is the feeling that even if what is being asked for of wives is not demeaning it is somehow unfair. Why cannot wives sometimes exercise sacrificial authority and husbands sacrificial submission? Would not this be fairer?

The question this objection raises is what we mean by 'fair.' What is fair means what is right or just in a particular context. Thus it is fair that the fastest skier gets the gold medal at the Winter Olympics and fair that the best candidate should be appointed to a particular job. In the case of marriage it is fair, in the sense of right, that the husband should be called to exercise sacrificial authority and the wife sacrificial submission because, as we have seen, it is part of the purpose of marriage to reflect the relationship between Christ the bridegroom and the Church his bride. The roles of husband and wife are not interchangeable because the roles of Christ and the Church are not interchangeable and marriage points to this truth.

It is important to be clear that living out a distinction of roles within marriage does not mean that husbands must carry out one specific set of domestic tasks while their wives carry out another. As the Kellers note: 'The Scripture does not give us a list of things men and women must and must not do. It gives no such specific directions at all.' This means, as they go on to say, that 'We must find ways to honor and express our gender roles, but the Bible allows for freedom in the particulars, while still upholding the obligatory nature of the principle.'[138] This

---

137 Keller, op.cit. Loc 2373.
138 Ibid, Loc 2478 and 2488.

means that it is up to each individual married couple to determine prayerfully before God how to live out the pattern of marital relations called for by the New Testament. In Appendix 1 at the end of this chapter some guidelines for the exercise of what is often described as 'male headship'[139] within marriage are noted as a starting point for reflecting on what applying New Testament principles should (and should not) mean in practice.

Marriage as spiritual warfare

We saw at the end of chapter two that, although the devil and his angels have been decisively defeated through Christ's death and resurrection, their assault on God's people continues. In the case of marriage they exploit the fact that it is a relationship between two people who are still influenced by their old fallen natures to stir up marital discord rather than the marital harmony that is God's intention.

This means that Christian marriage is a form of the spiritual warfare described in Ephesians 6:10-20. Nowadays we do not tend to think of marriage in this light, but our ancestors in the sixteenth century were wiser than we are in this respect. They knew that a marriage that seeks to follow the pattern God has laid down will inevitably attract the assaults of the devil. That is why the Church of England's homily 'Of the State of Matrimony' published in 1563 warns married Christians that

> …the devil will assay all things, to interrupt and hinder your hearts and godly purpose, if you will give him any entry. For he will either labour to break this godly knot, once begun betwixt you, or else at the least he will labour to encumber it with divers griefs and displeasures. And this is his principal craft: to work dissension of hearts of the one from the other; that whereas there is now a pleasant and sweet love between you, he will in the stead thereof, bring in most bitter and unpleasant discord.[140]

This being the case, how should spouses respond? The answer, according to the homily, is by a serious effort to maintain their unity, and constant prayer for the Spirit's assistance: 'married persons must apply their minds in most earnest wise, to concord, and must crave continually of God, the help of his Holy Spirit, so to

---

139 In the Church of England the word 'headship' has become toxic for many people because of its use in the debates about the ordination of women to the priesthood and the episcopate. Because 'the principle of headship' was appealed to by those opposed to women's ordination headship has become associated in many people's minds solely with men telling women that they should not do things. However, this negative association is not a valid reason for ceasing to use the term when discussing Christian marriage. We do have to think through what it means to apply St Paul's teaching that the husband is head of his wife (1 Corinthians 11:3, Ephesians 5:22) and 'headship' is as good a term as any for referring to this issue.

140 Ian Robinson (ed.), *The Homilies*, Bishopstone: Brynmill/Preservation Press, 2006, p. 364.

rule their hearts, and to knit their minds together, that they may not be dissevered, by any division of discord.'[141] Furthermore, they should:

….give thanks for this great benefit, in that you have taken upon you this state of wedlock; and pray you instantly, that Almighty God may luckily defend and maintain you therein, that neither ye be overcome with any temptation, nor with any adversity. But before all things, take good heed that ye give no occasion to the devil, to let and hinder your prayers, by discord and dissension. For there is no stronger defence and stay in all our life, than is prayer: in the which we may call for the help of God and obtain it; whereby we may win his blessing, his grace, his defence, and protection, so to continue therein to a better life to come.[142]

The Christian view of marriage and modern approaches to relationships

The Christian view of marriage that we have considered in this chapter provides a better alternative to two approaches to relationships that are central to our culture. The first of these approaches views relationships through the lens of the 'i worlds'' emphasis on individual authenticity. As Grant explains, this emphasis creates serious problems for people's ability to enter into and maintain intimate relationships.

Living in the age of authenticity has placed heavy burdens on intimate relationships and has left couples striving to build security and meaning on its hopelessly weak foundations. Because of our culture's move away from transcendence, or belief in God as the source of reality, we have come to place the full weight of our personal identity on ordinary life—our material, here-and-now existence. Rather than becoming free and expansive our relationships have become narrow and constrained, having no purpose beyond themselves. This exclusive focus has seismically destabilized them in two ways: (1) the burden they bear becomes overwhelming because of the expectation that all our psychological, emotional, material and sexual needs will met by one remarkable soul mate; and (2) the very bond we crave is undermined by the inwardly focused nature of the 'authentic' self. We do not so much give ourselves to a relationship as expect the relationship to give to us.[143]

Developing the last point, Grant goes on to say:

Our most intimate relationships are looked on by each partner as a primary source of happiness and self-actualization, measured in the narrow terms of

---

141 Ibid, p.364
142 Ibid, p.373.
143 Grant, op.cit, p. 37.

personal gratification. Am I getting what I need from this relationship? Does it make me happy? Do the benefits to me outweigh the costs? The assumption is that a relationship may last until death if it continues to fulfill each person, but to make a lifelong commitment at the beginning makes no sense. The cruel irony is that contemporary men and women view intimate relationships as essential to their personal identity, but they struggle to commit themselves fully to these same relationships. We can only find genuine personal meaning by making strong commitments beyond ourselves. Because relationships are no longer seen from a transcendent perspective, they are divorced from any other purpose than one's own personal happiness and intimacy[144]

In contrast to this approach to intimate relationships, the Christian faith says that marriage does have a purpose beyond itself. As we have seen, from a Christian perspective marriage exists to serve the purposes of God in three key ways. First, it points towards the marriage between Christ and his Church and the way this will be consummated in heaven and invites people to be a part of this marriage. Secondly, it provides a way in which men and women can provide each other with love and support as they obey their calling to serve as God's image bearers in the world. Thirdly, it provides a stable and supportive setting for the procreation and nurturing of children who in their turn can serve God and become married to him.

In addition, the Christian faith declares that marriage is about making a commitment beyond ourselves. From a Christian perspective, entering into marriage involves trusting God's care for us enough to commit ourselves to a permanent one flesh union with another person in which we do not seek to benefit ourselves, but seek instead to serve God by loving them and putting their needs above our own.

Furthermore, from a Christian perspective the very idea that we should look to have all our needs met by another human being is a mistake. God has not decreed that any human being should carry such a burden. Rather he has made us in such a way that our physical and emotional needs are to be met by God and by the whole community of God's people rather than by our spouse alone. As we shall see in the next chapter this is why it is also possible for someone to have a fulfilled and happy life even if they are not married at all.

The second modern approach to relationships, which is endlessly propagated by the media in all its forms and by commercial organizations seeking to make financial gain, is to see relationships as being primarily about romantic love. In this approach the thing that is most important in a relationship is the feeling of

---

144 Ibid, p.38.

romantic attraction that we have to the other person and keeping a relationship healthy involves keeping that feeling of romantic attraction alive.

As Grant notes, drawing on the work of the anthropologist Helen Fisher, neuroscience tells us that the feeling of romantic love is a form of infatuation that has its origin in the same areas of the brain that are associated:

> with basic drives such as wanting, motivation, craving, and focus. It works beneath the regions that deal with cognitive thinking and emotion. Romantic love, it turns out, is a powerful drug that connects with our basic drives.[145]

However, as he goes on to say:

> infatuation has a short natural life cycle. Like the boosters on the space shuttle, it burns bright for a while and then falls away. This explains why we feel so 'alive' in this early romantic stage and why people make such significant sacrifices—of careers, reputations, and existing relationships—in obedience to these feelings. The infatuation drug is so strong, Fisher explains, than anything associated with the object of our affection will seem to glow—his car in a crowded parking lot or her sweater hanging over a chair. It explains why the grass seems greener when we 'fall in love.'[146]

From a Christian perspective, the feeling of a romantic love has an important God-given purpose. Precisely because it is so powerful it can enable us to break free from our focus on ourselves and help us to begin to love someone else and by so doing can prepare us for that universal love to which God calls us. In the words of C S Lewis:

> In one high bound it has overleaped the massive wall of our selfhood; it has made appetite itself altruistic, tossed personal happiness aside as a triviality and planted the interests of another in the centre of our being. Spontaneously and without effort we have fulfilled the law (towards one person) by loving our neighbor as ourselves. It is an image, a foretaste, of what we must become to all if Love Himself rules in us without a rival. It is even (well used) a preparation for that.[147]

However, while recognizing the importance of romantic love, the Christian faith would add two words of caution. First, romantic love cannot justify breaking the law of God. To quote Lewis again, when people are 'in love' or, as he puts it, under the influence of Eros:

---

145 Grant, op.cit. p. 40 referring to Helen Fisher's TED talk 'Why We Love, Why We Cheat' at https://www.ted.com/talks/helen_fisher_tells_us_why_we_love_cheat.
146 Ibid, p.40.
147 C S Lewis, *The Four Loves*, London & Glasgow: Fontana, 1965, p. 1905.

It seems to sanction all sorts of actions they would not otherwise have dared. I do not mean solely, or chiefly, acts that violate chastity. They are just as likely to be acts of injustice or uncharity against the outer world. They will seem like proofs of piety and zeal towards Eros. The pair can say to one another in an almost sacrificial spirit, 'It is for love's sake that I have neglected my parents—left my children—cheated my partner—failed my friend at his greatest need.' These reasons in love's law have passed for good.[148]

However, the Christian faith teaches us that acts which breach the commands to love God and neighbour remain wrong even if they are performed under the influence of Eros, just as being violent and crashing cars remain wrong even when they are done under the influence of alcohol. Eros is not God and so what romantic love seems to require should not be given the same moral weight as the requirements of God's law.

Secondly, romantic love does not provide a sufficient basis to sustain marriage. As we have noted, romantic love can serve to bring a couple together by breaking down the walls of self and beginning to teach them what love involves, but it cannot sustain their relationship. As we have also noted, romantic love by its very nature passes quickly and when it has gone it is humility, charity and divine grace that are needed to maintain a marriage over the long term.

As Lewis warns, the people whose marriages will be in danger

…are those who idolized Eros. They thought he had the power and truthfulness of a god. They expected that mere feeling would do for them, and permanently, all that was necessary. When this expectation is disappointed they throw the blame on Eros, or more usually, on their partners. In reality, however, Eros, having made his gigantic promises and shown you in glimpses what his performance would be like has 'done his stuff.' He, like a godparent, makes the vows; it is we who must keep them. It is we who must labour to bring our daily life into even closer accordance with what the glimpses have revealed. We must do the work of Eros when Eros is not present. This all good lovers know, though those who are not reflective or articulate will be able to express it only in a few conventional phrases about 'taking the rough with the smooth,' not 'expecting too much,' 'having a little common sense,' and the like. And all good Christian lovers know that this programme, modest as it sounds, will not be carried out except by humility, charity and

148 Ibid, p. 104.

divine grace; that it is indeed the entire Christian life seen from one particular angle.[149]

The problem in our society is that the quest to discover and express the authentic self has become fused with the desire to perpetually experience romantic love. This means that many people pass on from relationship to relationship, and even from marriage to marriage, seeking each time to rediscover the joys of romantic love, while failing to realise that it was never designed by God to bring them the personal fulfilment for which they are vainly seeking.

In this chapter we have explored what putting love for God at the centre of our lives means in relation to marriage. In the next chapter we shall go on to consider what putting love for God at the centre of our lives means for those who are single. In addition, we shall look at the nature of friendship and why friendship is vital both for those who are married and for those who are single.

Appendix 1: Guidelines on male headship in marriage

The following helpful guidelines on the exercise of headship are set out by Timothy and Kathy Keller in their book *The Meaning of Marriage*. They provide a good starting point for anyone wanting to think about what obeying the pattern in Ephesians 5:21-33 might look like in practice.

> *The husband's authority (like the Son's over us) is never used to please himself but only to serve the interests of his wife.* Headship does not mean that the husband simply 'makes all the decisions', nor does it mean he gets his way in every disagreement. Why? Jesus never did anything to please himself (Romans 15:2-3). A servant-leader must sacrifice his wants and needs to please and build up his partner (Ephesians 5:21ff).

> *A wife is never to be merely compliant but is to use her resources to empower.* She is to be her husband's most trusted friend and counsellor, as he is hers (Proverbs 2:17). The 'completion' that embracing the other entails involves a lot of give and take. To complement each other means husband and wife need to hear each other out, make their arguments. Completion is hard work and involves loving contention (Proverbs 27:17), with affection (1 Peter 3:3-5) until you sharpen-enrich and enhance each other. She must bring every gift and resource that she has to the discussion, and he must,

---

149 Ibid, pp.105-106.

as any wise manager, know when to allow her expertise to trump his own, less well-informed, opinion.

A wife is not to give her husband unconditional obedience. No human being should give any other human being unconditional obedience. As Peter said, 'We must obey God rather than men' (Acts 5:29). In other words, a wife should not obey or aid a husband in doing things that God forbids, such as selling drugs or physically abusing her. If, for example, he beats her, the 'strong help' that a wife should exercise is to love and forgive him in her heart but have him arrested. It is never kind or loving to anyone to make it easy for them to do wrong.

Assuming the role of headship is only done for purposes of ministering to your wife and family. Some say, 'In the Biblical view, both husband and wife are to minister to each other unselfishly, so then what is the difference?' It is clear that the Son obeys his head, the Father, and that we obey our head, the Christ. But how does this authority work out in the context of mutually serving persons equal in dignity and being? The answer is that a head can only overrule his spouse if he is sure that her choice would be destructive to her and to the family. He does not use his headship selfishly to get his own way about the color of the car they buy, who gets to hold the remote control, and whether he has a 'night out with boys' or stays home to help with the kids when his wife asks him.[150]

Appendix 2: Sex and shame in the Christian tradition

The Christian tradition has a long history of seeing sexual activity as something shameful. This view is given classic expression by St Augustine in Book XIV of *The City of God* in which he argues that sexual desire is a result of the fall. For Augustine and the tradition following him marriage is a 'remedy for sin' in that the sinfulness of lust in the sexual act is remedied by the fact that the act is performed for the good end of having children: 'carnal or youthful incontinence, which is admittedly a defect, is applied to the honourable task of begetting children, and so intercourse within marriage engenders something good from the evil of lust.'[151]

If we ask how we know that sexual activity is shameful, the tradition gives two answers. First, Adam and Eve hide their nakedness after the fall (Genesis 3:7) and this is seen as emblematic of the shame about sex felt across human cultures in

---

150 Keller and Keller, op.cit. Loc 3228-3247. Italics in the original.
151 St Augustine, 'On the Good of Marriage 3,' in P.G. Walsh (ed), *Augustine: De bono coniugali, De sancta virginitate*, Oxford: OUP, 2001, p.7.

general. Secondly, under the Old Testament law discharges associated with sex (semen in men and menstrual blood in women) rendered people ritually unclean (Leviticus 15) and the people of Israel were required to abstain from sexual intercourse before entering the presence of God (Exodus 19:10-11, 14-15, 1 Samuel 21:4-7).

Neither of these arguments is convincing. First, in Genesis 3 Adam and Eve hiding their nakedness is an expression of the shame of sin in general rather than shame relating to sexual activity in particular. Secondly, the reason why the discharge of menstrual blood and semen rendered people unclean and why those entering the presence of God needed to refrain from sexual intercourse is:

(a) because the loss of blood and semen symbolically represent the way in which sin brings death to God's good creation and it this that is symbolically made right by purification;

(b) in order to clearly separate sexual activity from the act of worship in a cultural context in which non-Israelite religion regularly fused sex and worship together.[152]

Neither of these points renders sexual intercourse in itself shameful.

As we have seen, in the New Testament, as in Genesis 2:24, sexual activity is seen as an inherently good part of marriage. In recognition of this, the mainstream Christian tradition has in recent centuries moved away from the Augustinian view of sexual activity as something shameful. The *Catechism of the Catholic Church* thus speaks for the Christian tradition as a whole when it declares, 'The acts in marriage by which the intimate and chaste union of the spouses takes place are noble and honourable; the truly human performance of these acts fosters the self-giving they signify, and enrich the spouses in joy and gratitude.'[153]

Questions for discussion

1. What are the characteristics of marriage as created by God?

2. What does the New Testament teach about the relationship between husbands and wives?

3. How does the Christian view of marriage differ from modern approaches to relationships?

---

152 For these points see Davidson, op.cit. pp.327-32.
153 *Catechism of the Catholic Church*, Para. 2362, London: Geoffrey Chapman, 1994, p.506.

CHAPTER 6

Marriage, singleness, and friendship (II)

'I have called you friends'
(John 15:16)

Everyone is doing it

Everyone is having sex with everyone else, inside and outside of marriage, almost all of the time—or so it would appear from the media today. The notion of abstaining from sexual activity is not on our society's radar. Relationship education in schools assumes that all young people will be sexually active and that what they need is protection from any psychological or physical harm that may result. When celibacy is mentioned it is almost always viewed negatively. As Ed Shaw observes,

> The basic premise of Hollywood comedies like The 40-Year Old Virgin and 40 Days and 40 Nights demonstrates this—the first chronicles a man's increasingly desperate attempts to have sex for the first time; in the second another younger man struggles to last just forty days and nights without it. In the world around us, celibacy is a bad thing, to be avoided at all costs.[154]

What is more, the Church often colludes with the culture. Although many churches take a traditional Christian view of sexual ethics, and still teach that people should abstain from sex outside marriage, neither they, nor other more liberal churches, tend to teach that people might choose to abstain altogether and follow the path of singleness instead. As Shaw has found, 'When tackled, singleness is usually spoken of as a temporary problem happily solved by marriage. You're taught how to survive until your wedding day—not how to thrive as a single person until your dying day. Again, celibacy is a bad thing to be avoided at almost any cost.'[155]

Today's approach is similar to the cultural attitudes surrounding the Early

---

154 Ed Shaw, *The Plausibility Problem*, Nottingham: Inter-Varsity Press, 2015, p.107.
155 Ibid., p.107.

Church. Singleness and sexual abstinence was unusual and generally disapproved of. Within Jewish culture it was extremely rare.[156] The almost universal pattern was that when a Jewish man or woman reached marriageable age they would enter into a marriage arranged for them. They would then have sex, both because sexual intercourse was seen as a blessing from God and in order to have children to fulfil God's command in Genesis 1:28 to 'be fruitful and multiply' and God's promise to Abraham of descendants innumerable as the stars in heaven (Genesis 15:5).

Likewise within Greco-Roman culture, sex and marriage were the norm. Men who were free to do so proved their virility and pursued sexual pleasure by having sex with multiple partners outside marriage. They were also expected to marry and have sex with their bride in order to father legitimate heirs. Respectable women, by contrast, were expected to marry and to have sex, but only to provide their husbands with legitimate heirs.[157]

Intentional singleness

Things were different amongst Christians. As we have seen, the Early Church challenged the contemporary culture by insisting on the same standard of sexual ethics for both men and woman. Moreover, it held that intentional singleness (known then as 'virginity'), and the celibacy that went with it, was not only acceptable but, in fact, a more excellent form of Christian discipleship than being married. The contrast could hardly be more striking.

St Cyprian of Carthage warned every Christian to glorify God in their bodies by observing a strict sexual discipline in his treatise *On the dress of Virgins* (c.248 AD). His reason, citing St Paul, was that the body is God's temple (1 Corinthians 6:19):

> Let us glorify and bear God in a pure and chaste body, and with a more complete obedience; and since we have been redeemed by the blood of Christ, let us obey and give furtherance to the empire of our Redeemer by all the obedience of service, that nothing impure or profane may be brought into the temple of God, lest He should be offended and forsake the temple which He inhabits.[158]

He then praises intentionally single virgins:

> This is the flower of the ecclesiastical seed, the grace and ornament of spiritual endowment, a joyous disposition, the wholesome and uncorrupted work of

---

156 Josephus, *Jewish War* 2:120-121 mentions celibacy among the Essenes, but this is the exception that proves the rule.
157 The only recognised exceptions to the norm of sex and marriage were the Vestal Virgins and the eunuch priests of the cult of Cybele.
158 St. Cyprian of Carthage, *On the Dress of Virgins*, in *The Ante-Nicene Fathers*, Vol.5, Edinburgh and Grand Rapids: T&T Clark/Eerdmans, 1995, p.430.

praise and honour, God's image answering to the holiness of the Lord, the more illustrious portion of Christ's flock. The glorious fruitfulness of Mother Church rejoices by their means, and in them abundantly flourishes; and in proportion as a copious virginity is added to her number, so much the more it increases the joy of the Mother.[159]

Timothy Keller says that this positive estimation of virginity in the Early Church

....de-idolized marriage. There was no more radical act in that day and time than to live a life that did not produce heirs. Having children was the main way to achieve significance for an adult, since children would remember you. They also gave you security, since they would care for you in your old age. Christians who remained single, then were making the statement that our future is not guaranteed by the family, but by God.

Single adult Christians were bearing testimony that God, not family, was their hope. God would guarantee their future, first by giving them their truest family—the church so that they never lacked for brothers and sisters, fathers and mothers, in Christ. But ultimately, Christians' inheritance is nothing less than the fullness of the kingdom of God in the new heavens and the new earth.[160]

Jesus' intentional singleness

Where did this countercultural de-idolisation of marriage come from? The answer, as Cyprian made clear, is from Jesus himself.

St John succinctly expressed the basic Christian belief that, in Jesus, God assumed human nature in order to bring about our salvation. In the prologue to his Gospel he tells us that 'the Word became flesh and dwelt among us, full of grace and truth' (John 1:14). To grasp the full significance of this we need to note that the word 'flesh' (*sarx*) is used in the verse immediately preceding, where it means human sexual desire. Andy Angel, in his book *Intimate Jesus*, comments that

....these two verses are the only places in the prologue which use the term sarx, which makes it rather difficult not to read the usage in v.14 in the light of that in v.13. So, when John describes the physical humanity of Jesus, he does so by using a word which he also uses in the immediate context to refer to sexual desire. Through his choice of words, John suggests that sexual desire was part of God's human experience.[161]

He goes on to say that John 'introduces Jesus' sexuality in terms that suggest that

---

159 Ibid, p.431.
160 Keller and Keller, op.cit. loc. 2617.
161 Andy Angel, *Intimate Jesus—The Sexuality of God Incarnate*, London: SPCK, 2017, p.25.

Jesus experienced sexual desire in all the frailty and weakness of normal people. He had to face his sexuality as any other human being, with all the difficulties that entails.'[162] Thus, we are told in Hebrews 4:15, 'we have not a high priest who is unable to sympathize with our weaknesses, but one who *in every respect* has been tempted as we are, but without sin.'

John, like the other three Gospel writers, describes Jesus as a bridegroom who has come to seek his bride (See Matthew 9:14-17, Mark 2:19-20, Luke 5:34-35). Where he goes further is in his use of explicitly sexual language. In 3:29 he quotes St John the Baptist declaring that he the friend of the bridegroom who 'rejoices greatly at the bridegroom's voice.' Angel argues that the most plausible explanation of 'the bridegroom's voice' is the cry of the bridegroom consummating his marriage: 'By picturing the Word as making love to his bride, John pictures God consummating his marriage to his covenant people.'[163]

But how did Jesus, as God incarnate, consummate his marriage to his covenant people? All four Gospels agree that he did so precisely by not getting married and not having sex. As we have noted, Jesus was a human male with human sexual desires, yet he chose not to fulfil them in marriage or sexual intercourse. They were precluded if he was going to carry out his mission of service to the kingdom of God in obedience to his heavenly Father.

To return to Angel's reading of John, he points out that the story of Jesus meeting the Samaritan woman at the well (John 4:7-42) adopts the standard form of a Jewish betrothal story—boy meets girl at a well. What we would normally expect, after various adventures on the way, is a romantic conclusion in which they get married and live happily ever after. What John gives us instead is 'a story of chastity and sexual healing. But surely that is the point. The sexuality of a truly loving person is no less real for abstaining for the benefit of another.'[164] Jesus abstains from sex and marriage with the Samaritan woman, and anyone else, for the benefit of the whole human race and for the sake of the coming kingdom.

In addition, Jesus reconstructed the normal meaning of family. He established an alternative family to the one he belonged to by birth:

---

162 Ibid. p.26.
163 Ibid. p.35. See also William Loader, *Sexuality in the New Testament: Understanding the Key Texts*, London: SPCK, 2010, p.37. It should be noted that even if this specific interpretation of John 3:29 is rejected, the text clearly does refer to Christ as the bridegroom marrying his bride.
164 Angel, op.cit. p. 60.

While he was still speaking to the people, behold, his mother and his brothers stood outside, asking to speak to him. But he replied to the man who told him, "Who is my mother, and who are my brothers?" And stretching out his hand toward his disciples, he said, "Here are my mother and my brothers! For whoever does the will of my Father in heaven is my brother, and sister, and mother." (Matthew 12:46-50)

Jesus is not repudiating his earthly family (as we know from the New Testament as a whole), but he is showing 'that there is a tie that is even closer than that of family.'[165] Jesus first commitment is not to his earthly family but to his spiritual family, which consists of everyone who has God as his or her Father through him (Matthew 11:27). It would eventually include his earthly family as well.

What Jesus asks of himself he also asks of his followers, calling them to put their relationship with him before their membership of a human family. In Luke 14:26, for example, we read, 'If any one comes to me and does not hate his own father and mother and wife and children and brothers and sisters, yes, and even his own life, he cannot be my disciple.' As George Caird explains, the word 'hate' is a semitic way of saying 'prefer less' (e.g., Genesis 29:30-31, Deuteronomy 21:15-17). Consequently, 'for the followers of Jesus to hate their families meant giving the family second place in their affections. Ties of kinship must not be allowed to interfere with their absolute commitment to the kingdom.'[166] Just as Jesus put the service of his Father's kingdom before his relationship with his earthly family, so his disciples must be prepared to do the same.

Jesus also called his followers to consider the possibility of living a celibate life like his own. In Matthew 19:12 he says:

For there are eunuchs who have been so from birth, and there are eunuchs who have been made eunuchs by men, and there are eunuchs who have made themselves eunuchs for the sake of the kingdom of heaven. He who is able to receive this, let him receive it.

Making oneself a 'eunuch' does not mean literal castration. What it does mean is that there are some people for whom marriage is not on the table because they have accepted God's call to live a celibate life for the sake of the kingdom of God. In a radical way they put God before the possibility of marriage and family life.

However, it is important to note that this radical choice not to be married but to remain single does not mean a depreciation of the value of marriage.

---

165 R T France, *Matthew*, Leicester: Inter-Varsity Press, 1985, p.215.
166 G B Caird, *Saint Luke*, Harmondsworth: Penguin, 1971, p. 179.

As Pope John Paul II puts it, 'this renunciation is at the same time a particular form of affirmation of the value from which the unmarried person consistently abstains by following the evangelical counsel.'[167] The point that he is making is that marriage involves someone making a 'sincere gift' of themselves to someone else.[168] Those who embrace a call to live a single life affirm the value of making such a sincere gift of oneself to another by giving themselves wholly to God.

From this perspective embracing a single life is primarily a positive step. Obviously it involves renouncing marriage and therefore sex, but, like the renunciation of family ties that we looked at earlier, this is done for the sake of positively obeying Christ's call to 'follow me.'

It is also important to note that Jesus implies that not everyone will be able to accept the call to renounce marriage. It is those who are able to receive this call who are called to receive it: '…whether one is married or not is not a matter of 'better' or 'worse,' but of God's gift which is not the same for all disciples.'[169]

In 1 Corinthians 7:32-35 St Paul, who was himself unmarried, emphasises the advantages of remaining single for the sake of the service of God:

> I want you to be free from anxieties. The unmarried man is anxious about the affairs of the Lord, how to please the Lord; but the married man is anxious about worldly affairs, how to please his wife, and his interests are divided. And the unmarried woman or girl is anxious about the affairs of the Lord, how to be holy in body and spirit; but the married woman is anxious about worldly affairs, how to please her husband. I say this for your own benefit, not to lay any restraint upon you, but to promote good order and to secure your undivided devotion to the Lord.

Paul's concern here, writes Geoffrey Bromiley, is that:

> ….unmarried men and women are free from the cares and attachments of the married and can thus give themselves with greater devotion to the Lord and the things of the Lord…Other people, relationships and things can, of course, divert Christians from full commitment to Christ. But marriage might be described as the most intimate and demanding of all human com-

---

167 John Paul II, op.cit. p. 441.
168 Ibid, p.442.
169 France, op.cit. p. 283.

mitments. Hence the possibility of a clash or division of interests is especially high at this point.[170]

In view of these conflicting commitments, Paul concludes that 'he who marries his betrothed does well; and he who refrains from marriage will do better' (1 Corinthians 7:38). Like Jesus in Matthew 19:12, Paul recognises that the call to singleness is a gift given to some people but not to everyone: 'I wish that all were as I myself am. But each has his own gift from God, one of one kind and one of another' (1 Corinthians 7:7).

Singleness misunderstood

The Early Church followed Jesus and St Paul in de-idolising marriage. Marriage was not the only godly way of life; an alternative call to singleness enabled people to give themselves to the service of God in a radically wholehearted way, free of the inevitable responsibilities of marriage and family life.

Furthermore, such singleness also pointed forward to God's coming kingdom in which those who have been resurrected 'neither marry nor are given in marriage, but are like the angels in heaven' (Matthew 22:30). In the words of O'Donovan

> To this eschatological hope the New Testament church bore witness by fostering the social conditions which could support a vocation to the single life. It conceived of marriage and singleness as alternative vocations, each a worthy form of life, the two together comprising the whole Christian witness to the nature of affectionate community. The one declared that God had vindicated the order of creation, the other pointed beyond it to its eschatological transformation.[171]

As O'Donovan goes on to say, the co-existence of marriage and singleness in the Early Church did not means that the character of either vocation lost its integrity

> Each had to function as what it was, according to its own proper structure. The married must live in the ways of marriage, the single in the ways of singleness. Neither would accommodate itself or evoke in the other an evolutionary mutation. Marriage that was not marriage could not bear witness

---

170 Bromiley, op.cit, p., 59. It is sometimes suggested that there is a tension between what is said about marriage in 1 Corinthians 7 and Ephesians 5, with the latter being St Paul's more mature reflections which we should now follow. However, it can be more plausibly argued that it was precisely because the Apostle held that marriage was the demanding vocation set out in Ephesians 5 that he believed that there could be a conflict between marriage and unhindered attention to the service of God.

171 O'Donovan, op.cit. p. 70.

to the goodness of the created order, singleness that was not singleness could tell us nothing of the fulfilment for which that order was destined.[172]

We can see this distinction between marriage and singleness in 1 Corinthians 6-7 where there is a clear expectation that marriage will involve sexual intercourse whereas singleness will involve sexual abstinence. St Paul denies that those who are married should practice permanent sexual abstinence or that the unmarried may enter into sexual unions.[173]

Although the Church maintained the New Testament pattern of affirming both marriage and singleness, it began to characterise the choice between them as a moral one. For Jesus and Paul the call to singleness is a gift, that is to say a state of life to which someone is called by God,[174] and while the recipient ought to live in light of that gift, doing so does not make them morally superior to someone who had been called to marriage. From the Patristic period onwards, however, singleness came to be seen as a morally superior state. An individual might choose singleness as a higher degree of spiritual attainment.[175]

During the Middle Ages this misapprehension contributed to the requirement of clerical celibacy and to the belief that those who embraced a (celibate) monastic way of life won greater merit before God. Becoming a monk or a nun even came to be seen as a 'second baptism' wiping away the sins committed after one's original baptism. The Protestant Reformers rightly rejected these ideas as incompatible with biblical teaching,[176] but what they arguably failed to do was to give any positive account of the value of singleness. They taught Christians to aspire to marriage and family life but treated single people as nothing more than 'the un-married'.[177] This significant oversight has persisted to the present day in churches shaped by the Reformation, including the Church of England.

---

172 Ibid, p.70.

173 It is for this reason that we should reject the proposal by Robert Song in his book *Covenant and Calling* (London: SCM 2014) for the recognition by the Church of non-procreative, but sexual, unions for those with same sex attraction. This proposal blurs the line between marriage and singleness.

174 It is important to distinguish between the objective fact that someone has been called to live in a certain way by God and a subjective desire to live in that way. Through the circumstances of their lives arranged by the providence of God someone may have an objective call to live as a single person even if this is not what they subjectively desire.

175 This idea of singleness as a higher form of spirituality can be seen, for instance in St Augustine's treatise *Of Holy Virginity* (*The Nicene and Post Nicene Fathers*, First Series, Vol. III, Edinburgh and Grand Rapids, T&T Clark/Eerdmans, 1998, pp. 417-38.

176 See , for instance, Article XXXII of the *Thirty Nine Articles* and Articles XXIII and XXVII of the *Augsburg Confession*.

177 It is noteworthy for, example, that while the *Second Book of Homilies* has a homily on marriage it does not have a corresponding homily on singleness. The single are given no guidance on how they should live godly lives in the single state.

A monastic tradition was re-launched in the Church of England in the nineteenth century. It had the positive effect of allowing those with a vocation to singleness to pursue that vocation in the context of structured religious communities. However, it is has unhelpfully associated the call to the single life solely with monasticism and the Anglo-Catholic tradition. There is still little recognition that the call to singleness is something that *all* traditions within the Church need to consider. Embracing a permanent monastic vocation is only one way of responding to God's call to singleness.

Singleness and marriage as dual vocations

What would it look like in practice to recognise singleness and marriage as the two possible calls from God?

First, it would mean that those who are unmarried and who feel a positive sense of calling to serve God in the single state permanently should prayerfully pursue that vocation. They should explore whether it should mean simply living as a single person within the normal life of the Church, or joining some form of monastic community.

Secondly, it would mean that those who are unmarried and who do not feel a particular sense of calling to the single state, but who have not yet met someone who they feel they could marry, should not anxiously seek to be married, but should be content to accept 'and to take full advantage of' their present state as God's current call to them unless or until this situation changes.

Thirdly, it would mean that those who are unmarried should be willing to accept God's call to marry if they meet someone of the opposite sex in whom they delight (Genesis 2:23), feel that with God's help they are able to make a lifelong commitment (encapsulated in Genesis 2:24 and set forth in the promises in the marriage service), and after prayerful reflection do not feel marriage would conflict with some other form of service that God is asking of them.

Fourthly, it would mean those who are married recognizing that they too may find themselves single again in the future and that therefore they too need to understand and be prepared to embrace a potential call to a single life.

Everyone is called to friendship

God calls human beings either to singleness or to marriage, and both these ways of life are undergirded by his call to friendship. The key passage setting out this call is John 15:12-17 where Jesus' speaks to his disciples on the eve of his crucifixion:

This is my commandment, that you love one another as I have loved you. Greater love has no man than this, that a man lay down his life for his friends. You are my friends if you do what I command you. No longer do I call you servants, for the servant does not know what his master is doing; but I have called you friends, for all that I have heard from my Father I have made known to you. You did not choose me, but I chose you and appointed you that you should go and bear fruit and that your fruit should abide; so that whatever you ask the Father in my name, he may give it to you. This I command you, to love one another.

These words are addressed, in the first instance, to Jesus' first disciples, but they also apply to everyone he calls to follow him and, thus, potentially, to all human beings. They tell us that Jesus is our friend and that he has shown his friendship by laying down his life for us (v.13) and by teaching us all that he has heard from the Father (i.e., making know to us the saving plan of God and our part in it) (v.15). In turn, we are Jesus' friends if we do what he commands (v.14), which is to love one another as he has loved us (vv.12 and 17).

Jesus' love for his disciples was clearly not the sexual love between a husband and wife, nor does he expect his disciples to express their love for each other in that way (unless they are in fact husband and wife). The kind of love in view here is friendship.

In our society we tend to contrast love and friendship. Thus someone might say, 'I don't love him. We're just good friends.' In reality, however, friendship is arguably the overarching form of love, of which the love between husband and wife is one subset. In the twelfth century Aelred of Rievaulx, famously paraphrased 1 John 4:16, 'God is love', by saying 'God is friendship'.[178] In light of John 15 he was right to do so; in Christ, God loves us as our friend and in response we are called to love one another as friends.

What does it mean, then, to love one another as friends? The Kellers identify three characteristics that mark out friendship: constancy, transparency, and common passion. Friends are always there for each other, they are open and honest, and they share a common enthusiasm for something or somethings (in the words of C S Lewis 'even if it were only an enthusiasm for dominoes or white mice').[179] In the Bible we find that all three of these characteristics apply to the relationships of love that should exist within the life of God's people.

---

178 Aelred of Rielvaux, *Spiritual Friendship*, Cistercian Publications, 1977, pp.65-66.
179 Keller and Keller, op. cit, Loc. 1441-1462 quoting C S Lewis *The Four Loves*.

First, Christians, by virtue of being Christians, share a common vision and passion, a joint enthusiasm:

> For believers in Christ, despite enormous differences in class, temperament, culture, race, sensibility, and personal history, there in an underlying commonality that is more powerful than them all. This is not so much a 'thread' as an indestructible steel cable. Christians have all experienced the grace of God in the gospel of Jesus. We have all had our identity changed at the root, so now God's calling and love are more foundational to who we are than any other thing. And we also long for the same future, journey to the same horizon, what the Bible calls the 'new creation.'[180]

This commonality means that 'any two Christians with nothing else but a common faith in Christ, can have a robust friendship, helping each other on their journey toward the new creation, as well as doing ministry together in the world.'[181]

Secondly, Christians are called to show spiritual constancy to each other:

> Christian friends bear each other's burdens (Galatians 6:2). They should be there for one another through thick and thin (1 Thessalonians 5:11, 14-15), sharing their goods and their very lives with each other if there is need (Hebrews 13:16; Philippians 4:14; 2 Corinthians 9:13). Friends must encourage one another through honour affirmation (Romans 12:3-6, 10; Proverbs 27:2). They are to identify and call out another's gifts, strengths, and abilities. They are to build up each other's faith through study and common worship (Colossians 3:16; Ephesians 5:19).[182]

Thirdly, they are called to practice spiritual transparency:

> Christian friends are not only to confess their own sins to one another (James 5:16), but they are to lovingly point out their friend's sins if he or she is blind to them (Romans 15:14). You should give your Christian friends 'hunting licenses' to confront you if you are failing to live in line with your commitments (Galatians 6:1). Christian friends are to stir one another up, even provoking one another to get them off dead centre (Hebrews 10:24). This isn't to happen infrequently but should happen at a very concrete level every day (Hebrews 3:13). Christians friends admit wrongs, offer or ask forgiveness (Ephesians

---

180 Ibid, 1462-1473.
181 Ibid, p.1473.
182 Ibid, Loc.1483.

4:32) and take steps to reconcile when one disappoints another (Matthew 5:23ff; Matthew 18:15ff).[183]

What all this means, say the Kellers, is that friendship between Christians is 'not simply about going to concerts together, or enjoying the same sporting event. It is the deep oneness that develops as two people journey together toward the same destination, helping one another through the dangers and challenges along the way.'[184] A classic literary example of this is found in J. R. R. Tolkien's *The Lord of the Rings* where the Fellowship of the Ring, and then just Frodo and Sam alone, journey together to deliver the Ring to destruction in the fires of Mount Doom. Christian discipleship is that kind of serious joint endeavour.

Friendship is something that every Christian needs. Friendship is at the heart of Christian marriage. It is the concrete form of the 'mutual society, help, and comfort' referred to in the *Book of Common Prayer* marriage service. Yet, for all Christians, including single Christians, 'it is not good that the man should be alone' (Genesis 2:18). Jesus, as a single man, needed and cultivated a circle of friends; single Christians today have the same need. Kate Wharton, reflecting on her experience as a single Christian, writes,

> I need other people in my life. I need them to offload to after a bad day; I need them to work alongside me in ministry; I need them to share a bottle of wine with me as we put the world to rights; I need them to point out to me the parts of my character than need working on; I need them to celebrate with me when good things happen; I need them to spend my days off and holidays with. I need them to give me a hug and tell me everything's going to be OK.[185]

The Church is called to friendship

So where does all our discussion of marriage and singleness lead us? Jesus refers to the Church as his alternative family (e.g., Mark 12:30). The Church is called to be the community that offers loving, intimate friendship to its members, married and single. Monastic communities help to achieve this goal by providing a framework within which friendship can flourish, but friendship cannot be left to monastic communities alone. All Christians have a responsibility to offer friendship to other members of the body of Christ. Mere casual acquaintance is not enough. It needs to be the kind of deep friendship that we have just described. Obviously there is a limit to the number of people any one individual

---

183 Ibid. Loc. 1473-1483.
184 Ibid, Loc. 1483-1493.
185 Kate Wharton, *Single Minded: Being Single, Whole and Living Life to the Full*, Oxford: Monarch, 2013, 173.

can befriend intimately, but the net of friendship should be cast as wide as possible, even as we give particular care and attention to particularly committed friendship relationships.

While the Church rightly stresses the importance of family life and seeks to foster and support it, it must also avoid the danger of seeing friendship as a 'consolation for those who fail to cross the finishing line of the nuclear family'.[186] The Church's identity in John 15 is as the community of Jesus' friends, so friendship needs to be at the heart of its life. This means that the Church ought to be intentional about a range of friendships, encouraging not only friendships between married couples and amongst single people, but also between single people and married people. Jesus, after all, was friends with people who were married.

In light of Wharton's reference to the value of hugs and St Paul's injunction to 'greet one another with a holy kiss (Romans 16:16) Christian friendships need to include opportunities for physical intimacy. Human beings, as embodied souls created by God, need to be able to give and receive love using physical contact. Our culture is cautious about physical contact because we associate it with sexual intercourse. That is why we wrongly suspect a sexual relationship in the physical intimacy between David and Jonathan (1 Samuel 20:41) or when we read St Anselm's letter to another monk recalling 'our not-forgotten love when we were together eye to eye, exchanging kiss for kiss, embrace for embrace'.[187] It is also why we are now increasingly wary about physical contact between adults and children. We need to overcome our prejudices and inhibitions and learn to develop appropriate ways of using physical intimacy to convey love, affirmation, support and comfort between friends without it carrying sexual meaning or leading to sexual intercourse.

A final point to note is that the Christian vision of 'singleness embedded within corporate relationships'[188] which we have explored in this chapter is an affirmation rather than a rejection of sexuality. We live in a society that tends to equate sexuality with sexual intercourse, but to quote Grant:

….the greater part of sexuality is 'affective' or 'social sexuality.' Affective sexuality describes our fundamental need for relational rather than strictly sexual, intimacy across a broad range of nurturing friendships. The challenge for Christian identity and daily living is to express our sexual energy in line with

---

186 Robert Wainwright, 'Male Friendship and Homosexuality,' Unpublished paper, 2016, p.83.
187 St. Anselm, Epistle 130, quoted in R W Southern, *Saint Anselm: Portrait in a Landscape*, Cambridge: CUP, 1990, p.146.
188 Grant, op.cit. p. 158.

this divine purpose, thereby resisting our culture's misdirection of sexual desire into desire for sex or consumer goods. We need this range of deep and diverse relationships—with parents, friends and elders—to properly affirm our personhood and sexuality. These networks of connections are important for single and married people alike.[189]

In this chapter we have explored the challenge to the Church to affirm singleness and friendship. In the next four chapters we will look at a range of other challenges the Church is currently facing, beginning with the issues of intersex and transgender.

Questions for discussion

1. How and why did the Early Church de-idolize marriage?

2. How has singleness been misunderstood in the history of the Church?

3. Why is friendship fundamental to the life of the Church?

---

189 Ibid, p.158.

PART II

Challenges facing a Christian approach

CHAPTER 7

Intersex and Transgender

'So God created man in his own image, in the image of God he created him; male and female he created them' (Genesis 1:27).

Recognizing reality

For most of us our sex is not a problem. We accept that we are either male or female because that is how we are born, and we are happy to live as either male or female according to the sex into which we were born. However, those of us for whom this is the case need to recognize the reality that there are a minority of people for whom their sex can be a huge problem. This can be because the way their body has developed means that they have elements of both male and female in their physical make up, or it can be because they feel that their biological sex does not accord with who they feel they truly are.

In this chapter we shall recognize this reality by looking by at both of these reasons why people find their sex problematic. We shall assess the issues involved theologically and also consider what it means to support pastorally the people involved.

INTERSEX

Might there be more than two sexes?

As we have seen, both our physical human nature and the Bible testify to the existence of two sexes, male and female. The Christian faith further tells us that this characteristic of human existence is not accidental, but is willed by the infinitely wise and good creator God who has created us in his image and likeness. Although this is a conviction that Christians have always held, it is now being challenged by a small, but growing, number of people within the Church.

A good example of this challenge can be seen in the statement *Christians Unit-*

ed in Support of LGBT+ Inclusion in the Church (2017). Article 5 declares: 'We affirm that while the male and female gender identity reflects a majority of the human family, God has created individuals whose gender identity does not fall on such a binary spectrum.'[190]

In this affirmation we see an example of the confusion between 'sex' and 'gender' that we noted in chapter three. The affirmation is not talking about 'gender' in the proper sense (i.e., the way people experience or live out their sexual identity). Rather, it is referring to 'sex' (i.e., the reality of human sexual differentiation which is experienced and expressed in terms of gender). Nevertheless, the radical claim it is making is clear. God has created people who are neither male nor female.

The reason why this claim is being made is because of the existence of people who are described as intersex. Thus Susannah Cornwall writes in her paper *Intersex Conditions (DSDs)[191]: A Guide for Christians*: 'Most Christians, like most other people in our society, assume that there are only two human sexes, male and female. However, intersex people's bodies don't fit into either box.'[192] Since the bodies of intersex people do not fit into the two categories of male and female, and since their bodies are created by God, it follows—so the argument goes—that God has created some human beings who fall outside the binary male/female divide

What causes physical sexual differentiation?
In order to grasp more fully the point being made by Cornwall about intersex conditions, we need to understand that physical sexual differentiation between human beings is a matter of differences in what are known as the 'genotype' and the 'phenotype.'

The genotype is the genetic constitution of human beings. The phenotype is the observable physical characteristics of a human being, including their appearance, development and behaviour. The phenotype results from the interaction of a person's genetic makeup and their environment. At the level of the genotype every human being has 46 chromosomes (thread like structures in human cells which transmit inherited genetic information) arranged in 23 pairs.

What determines a person's sex are the X and Y chromosomes, which are pres-

---

190 Christians United in Support of LGBT+ Inclusion in the Church, Article 5, text at http://www. christiansunitedstatement.org/.
191 'DSDs' stands for 'disorders of sexual development' which is a technical medical term for what are also known as 'intersex' conditions.
192 Susannah Cornwall, *Intersex Conditions (DSDs): a Guide for Christians*, Manchester: Lincoln Theological Institute, N.D. p.4.

ent in the foetus from the moment of conception.[193] Most women are 46XX and most men are 46XY. The existence of this chromosomal difference leads to the observable physical differences between men and women that exist at the level of the phenotype (differences in genitalia, body shape, the sound of the voice, etc.) and it is what is ultimately responsible for the ability of human beings to have children by means of sexual reproduction.[194]

Everyone agrees that intersex people have bodies that differ from what is typical for male or female human bodies at the level of either their genotype or their phenotype or both. There is disagreement, however, over how many people can rightly be regarded as intersex.

How many people are intersex?

Advocates on behalf of intersex people frequently claim that between 1% and 2% of the population can be classed as intersex, which in the United Kingdom would mean approximately 650,000 people. Human Rights Watch asserts, in an article entitled 'I want to be like nature made me', that sex is a spectrum:

> Intersex people are not rare, but they are widely misunderstood. Biology class-es often oversimplify a fundamental reality. We are taught that sex is dimor-phic: simply male or female. But sex, in reality, is a spectrum—with the ma-jority of humans appearing to exist at one end or the other. In fact, as many as 1.7 percent of babies are different from what is typically called a boy or a girl.[195]

The belief that 1.7% of babies can be classed as intersex ultimately comes from

---

193 What this means is that two terms that are now commonly used in discussions of human sex-ual identity are unhelpful. The term 'birth sex' wrongly suggests that someone's sex is deter-mined at birth, or that it could be changed subsequently. In reality sex determination takes place before birth from conception onwards (which is why an ultrasound scan can reveal that the developing baby is a boy or a girl) and someone's sex cannot be changed after birth. The term 'sex assigned at birth' wrongly suggests that someone's sex is arbitrarily given to them at birth. This again is not true. What happens at birth is that the existing sex of a new baby is acknowledged. The sex of a person has been assigned by God working through nature long before birth takes place.

194 The suggestion has been made that the normally accepted division between men and wom-en on the basis of their genotype and phenotype is simply a cultural construct which we do not have to accept. It is true that this division is a cultural construct, but the key question is whether it is a helpful construct in the sense of being one that helps us to understand reality better. The answer to this question is 'yes.' The genotype/phenotype approach helps us to understand clearly what the difference between males and females are and why they exist. No one has yet come up with a better way of doing this. In terms of the theology of the Book of Genesis the distinction enables us to use our God-given reason to name reality properly (Genesis 2:19-20). For a helpful introduction to how human sex develops through the influ-ence of the genotype see Ryan Anderson, *When Harry Became Sally*, New York: Encounter Books 2018, Ch.4.

195 Human Rights Watch, 'I want to be like nature made me,' 25 July 2017, text at https://www.hrw.org/report/2017/07/25/i-want-be-nature-made-me-medically-unnecessary-surgeries-intersex-children-us.

a book called *Sexing the body: Gender politics and the construction of sexuality* published in 2000 by the developmental biologist Anne Fausto-Sterling.[196] In her book she argues that human sex should not be seen as a male-female dichotomy but as a continuum, with 1.7% of the population (17 out of every 1000 live births) sitting somewhere between male and female and therefore to be regarded as intersex. The book received enthusiastic reviews that highlighted the 1.7% claim and argued that it challenged the consensus that humanity can be divided simply into male and female. The book review in the journal *American Scientist*, for example, noted the figure:

> Most people believe that there are only two sex categories. Yet 17 out of every 1,000 people fail to meet our assumption that everyone is either male or female. This is the approximate incidence of intersexuals: individuals with XY chromosomes and female anatomy, XX chromosomes and male anatomy, or anatomy that is half male and half female.[197]

Similarly, the review in *The New England Journal of Medicine* said the book showed 'that intersexual newborns are not rare (they may account for 1.7% of births), so a review of our attitudes about these children is overdue.'[198]

On the basis of Fausto-Sterling's book and its reviews the 1.7% figure gained general currency, forming the basis for the more general 1-2% figure. However, as Leonard Sax pointed out when he reviewed Fausto-Sterling's work in 2002, the 1.7% figure is actually highly problematic. It is based on too broad a definition of what constitutes intersex.

Fausto-Sterling defined intersex as any individual 'who deviates from the Platonic ideal of physical dimorphism at the chromosomal, genital, gonadal, or hormonal levels.'[199] Within this definition she includes five conditions that, in Sax's view, cannot be considered intersex in any 'meaningful clinical sense': late-onset congenital adrenal hyperplasia, Klinefelter syndrome, Turner syndrome, other chromosomal variants such as XXX and XYY, and vaginal agenesis. [200]

Sax's objection is that, although these conditions do involve disorders of sexual development, they do not involve any confusion as to whether the individual

---

196 Anne Fausto Sterling, *Sexing the body, Gender politics and the construction of sexuality*, New York: Basic Books, 2000.
197 C. Moore, 'Sorting by Sex,' *American Scientist*, 88, 2000, p. 545.
198 M. Breedlove, Sexing the body. *New England Journal of Medicine*, 343, 2000, p.668.
199 M. Blackless, A. Charuvastra, A.Derryck, A. Fausto-Sterling, K. Lauzanne, & E. Lee, 'How sexually dimorphic are we? Review and synthesis,' *American Journal of Human Biology*, 12, p 161.
200 Leonard Sax, How common is intersex?', *Journal of Sex Research*, 1 August, 2002, text at http://www.leonardsax.com/how-common-is-intersex-a-response-to-anne-fausto-sterling/.

concerned is male or female. If we subtract these five conditions we are left with truly intersex conditions in which the person concerned has a mixed genotype and phenotype, an inconsistency between their genotype and their phenotype, or a phenotype that cannot be classified as either male or female. For example, in the case of Complete Androgen Insensitivity Syndrome:

> These individuals are genetically male (XY), but owing to a defect in the androgen receptor, their cells do not respond to testosterone or other androgens... As a result, these individuals do not form male genitalia. Genetically male (XY) babies with this condition typically are born with a vaginal opening and clitoris indistinguishable from those seen in normal female (XX) babies. In almost all cases, the diagnosis is not suspected until puberty, when these 'girls' are brought to medical attention because they have never menstruated. Investigation at that point will invariably reveal that these 'girls' are in fact genetically male, that they have undescended testicles, and that neither the uterus nor the ovaries are present. These individuals are genotypically male, but phenotypically female.[201]

Far from representing 1.7% of live births, these true intersex conditions amount to around 0.018%, almost 100 times lower than Fausto-Sterling's estimate.

To put it the other way around, this means that more than 99.98% of human beings are clearly either male or female. By any reasonable definition of what counts as 'normal', being either male or female is overwhelmingly normal for human beings. It follows that any argument against the traditional Christian division of humanity into male and female that depends on the claim that intersex conditions are relatively common is untenable. True intersex conditions are very rare indeed.

Are people with the intersex a third type of human being?

In spite of how rare true intersex conditions are, it might still be argued that the existence of such people is a positive part of the diversity that God wills for his human creation, and therefore something Christians should affirm. The argument would go that God in his wisdom and goodness has chosen to create a very small number of special human beings who are neither male nor female, but some third type of human being.

This argument is put forward, for example, by the American writer Megan De-

---

201 Ibid.

Franza in her book *Sex Difference in Christian Theology* in which she writes that 'Male, female and intersex are all created in the image of God and all called to be conformed to the image of Jesus.'[202]

De Franza builds on the truth that people with intersex conditions are indeed created in God's image and likeness to make the argument that we must acknowledge the existence of more than two sexes. However, there are two problems with this line of argument.

First, De Franza's argument builds on the teaching of the creation narratives in Genesis 1 and 2. However, as we have seen, these narratives view God's creation of human beings in exclusively dimorphic terms. God creates humanity as male and female, declares that his creation is very good, and then ceases to create because he has created everything that it is good for him to create. The biblical account says nothing about God also creating a third, intersex, form of humanity as an additional part of his good creation.

Secondly, the idea of a third type of human being misunderstands the nature of the intersex phenomenon. As Alastair Roberts observes in a response to De-Franza, 'few of us would consider denying that humanity is a bipedal species on account of children born without a leg and persons who have legs amputated later in life.'[203] The existence of one-legged people or people without legs does not lead us to believe that God has created a special type of one-legged or no-legged human beings. Instead we would conclude that something has gone wrong, either in the course of that person's development in the womb or at some point later in their life. The reason behind our conclusion is that there is no good end served by human beings lacking one or both legs, whereas having two working legs enables them to move around.

Roberts goes on to argue, in a similar fashion, that the existence of intersex conditions serves no good purpose, whereas the normal development of human sexual differentiation can be seen to serve a good purpose in creating sexually dimorphic human beings who are fitted to engage in sexual reproduction. Intersex is thus a form of disorder that goes against the good order that God originally put into his creation. As Roberts explains:

Medical science has acquainted us with processes of sex differentiation in the womb and, from its vantage point, most intersex conditions would seem to be

---

202 Megan K DeFranza, *Sex Difference in Christian Theology*, Grand Rapids: Eerdmans, 2015, p.288.

203 Alastair Roberts, Podcast, Intersex, *Mere Fidelity*, 25 August, 2015, text at https://alastairad-versaria.com/2015/08/25/podcast-intersex/

appropriately classified as 'disorders of sex development'. The natural purposes of the sex organs and the human reproductive system—of which male and female both possess a half—are not just dark and unknown mysteries to us and it would seem strange not to be able to speak of natural processes going awry in certain cases.

It seems clear to me, as it generally seems to be to medical science, that human bodies are structured to be sexually reproductive—to be male and female—and humanity is a sexually dimorphic species. There is clearly considerable natural variation consistent with humanity's dimorphic form, but there is an obvious difference in principle between variation and defect, even if not always clear in the most marginal cases in practice, where, for instance, function may be retained in an abnormal or impaired form (abnormal forms are not necessarily defective forms, although they frequently are). Sexual organs with intersex conditions are typically characterized by defect—usually manifested in infertility, for instance—and can't adequately perform certain functions that sexual organs are supposed to perform.

This being the case, he says:

Intersex bodies and bodies with intersex conditions are not evidence of further sexes in addition to male and female, even though particular types of intersex conditions may possess distinct and identifiable characteristics. The sexual organs of intersex persons are not ordered to some different sexual end of their own, but are abnormally and/or defectively lacking in the typical functional male or female form, imperfectly related to the ends of male and female sexual organs. Their abnormality is usually connected with evidence that the ordinary processes of sexual differentiation have gone awry in some recognizable manner. That they are generally considered defective doesn't arise from the rarity of such conditions, but from the fact that they can't effectively do what sexual organs are supposed to be able to do. They are disordered male or female bodies, or bodies that are neither male nor female. At the very least, to claim that they are a further sex would seem to require some far-reaching re-evaluation of how we determine bodily organs to be functional or not.

There may be some sort of an empirical spectrum between male and female, albeit one overwhelmingly populated at the poles. However, the existence of such an empirical spectrum is not proof against sexual dimorphism, because there remain only two functional forms of sex around which specific human beings are clustered. All intermediate forms are departures from these, without an integral purpose of their own.[204]

How can people with intersex conditions live rightly before God?

What we find in the bodies of people with intersex conditions is, therefore, in the words of Oliver O'Donovan, 'an ambiguity which has arisen by a malfunction in a dimorphic human sexual pattern.'[205] Once we have acknowledged the existence of that malfunction, acknowledging that there is indeed a defect of some kind, Roberts encourages us to think about the specific 'possibilities of vocation' for people who live with this defect.[206] How can they live rightly before God as the people they are?

Firstly, it must be emphasised once again that people with intersex conditions are first and foremost human beings made in God's image and likeness. The *Christians United* statement is right to declare, 'We affirm that those who are born as intersex are full and equal bearers of the image and likeness of God and are worthy of full dignity and respect.'[207] Even though the development of their male or female identity has become disordered, people with intersex conditions bear witness to their creation as human beings in God's image and likeness through the male and female elements that exist in their genotype and phenotype.

Secondly, they, like all other human beings, are summoned to live as people created by God and redeemed by God through Jesus Christ, having faith in the Gospel, loving God and neighbour, and living lives marked by the offering and receiving of friendship.

Thirdly, they, like all other human beings, are summoned to live in a way that reflects God's creation of humanity as male and female.

In cases where there is distinct male or female genotype but where problems have occurred in the development of the corresponding phenotype, the proper way forward would seem to be for them to live according to the sex of their genotype, receiving spiritual and psychological support and (where necessary) medical intervention in the form of reconstructive surgery to help them live more comfortably in their given sex and, when possible, to allow

---

204 Ibid.
205 O'Donovan, *Transsexualism: Issues and Argument*, Cambridge: Grove Books, 2007, p. 8.
206 Roberts op.cit..
207 *Christians United*, Article 4.

them to have children.[208] Like other people they may either be called to marry a member of the opposite sex, or called to serve God through a life of singleness.

In the very rare cases where the genotype has both XY and XX chromosomes and the phenotype has both male and female sexual characteristics (for example both a penis and a vagina) the question of whether it would be proper to live as male or female becomes much less clear cut. A possible way forward that would bear witness to the truth of who they are would be to live as either male or female (thus responding to God's general call to humans to live as a man or a woman) while acknowledging the presence of elements of the other sex in their bodily make up. If this way forward were adopted then any marriage would need to be with a member of the opposite sex to that in which they have chosen to live.

What would arguably not be appropriate would be for them to live as a non-binary (i.e., neither male nor female) person. This is because the truth about who they are is not that they are *neither* male nor female, but that the way their biology has developed means that they are both male *and* female.

TRANSGENDER

What does transgender mean?

Intersex and transgender are often confused nowadays, but there is a crucial distinction between them. When people have intersex conditions there is a degree of ambiguity about their sex at the level of their genotype or their phenotype. In the case of most transgender people, however, there is no ambiguity. They are, for the most part, people whose bodies are unambiguously either male or female, but who have difficulty accepting, or living according to, the sex of their body. As Mark Yarhouse puts it, 'Transgender is an umbrella term for the many ways in which people might experience and/or present and express (or live out) their gender identities differently from people whose sense of gender identity is congruent with their biological sex.'[209]

The main forms of transgender can be classified as follows:

* There are those who accept that they are male or female according to their bodily sex, but who have a desire to dress in the clothes of the opposite sex

---

208 Such medical intervention is not (as is sometimes suggested) an attempt to impose some ideal model of what it means to be human. It is simply an acknowledgement that something has gone wrong in the course of a person's development and an attempt to correct it as far as possible, which is what doctors regularly do in other cases such as when babies have a cleft palette or a hole in the heart.

209 Mark Yarhouse, *Understanding Gender Dysphoria*, Downers Grove: IVP Academic, 2015, Kindle edition, Loc.252.

either because they find this sexually arousing or because they find it desirable to do so for other reasons. This is what used to be called transvestitism.

- There are those who accept that they are male or female according to their bodily sex, but who experience gender dysphoria (a sense of distress caused by a mismatch between one's psychological and emotional sense of identity and one's biological sex) and who seek to relieve this sense of distress through cross-dressing.

- There are those whose gender dysphoria leads them to feel that the sex of their body is at variance with the fact that are really a member of the opposite sex (thus someone with a male body feels that they are female or vice versa) and who choose to identify as a member of the opposite sex while retaining their current body.

- There are those whose gender dysphoria leads them to feel that the sex of their body is at variance with the fact that are really a member of the opposite sex and who not only choose to identify as a member of the opposite sex, but who also undergo hormone treatment and plastic surgery in order to try to make their bodily appearance approximate as closely as possible to a body of that sex.

- There are those who feel their sense of personal identity is not expressed by describing themselves as either male or female. For example, the online Non-binary Gender Wiki explains that:

  - Those with non-binary genders can feel that they:
  - Have an androgynous (both masculine and feminine) gender identity, such as androgyne.
  - Have an identity between male and female, such as intergender.
  - Have a neutral or unrecognized gender identity, such as agender, neutrois, or most xenogenders.
  - Have multiple gender identities, such as bigender or pangender.
  - Have a gender identity which varies over time, known as genderfluid.
  - Have a weak or partial connection to a gender identity, known as demigender.
  - Are intersex and identify as intersex, known as amalgagender
  - Have a culturally specific gender identity which exists only within their or their ancestor's culture.[210]

---

210 http://gender.wikia.com/wiki/Non-binary.

Those who identify as non-binary may also prefer to use alternative pronouns such as 'ze', 'hir', 'hirs', 'zir', 'xe', 'xem' or 'xyr' in order to express the fact that they are neither male nor female and are therefore not 'him' or 'her.'

Why is the transgender phenomenon problematic?

There can be no doubt that gender dysphoria really exists and that it is extremely distressing for the people who experience it. Any Christian approach to gender dysphoria has to first of all acknowledge the reality of this distress for the people concerned and the fact that Christians have an obligation to do all they can to help and support them.

This having been acknowledged, there remains an issue about the form this help and support should take.

There is today a growing body of material arguing that compassion for people with gender dysphoria means that Christians should accept that it is right for people to live according to their preferred gender identity rather than their biological sex.[211] This argument draws on testimonies such as the following which declare that experience makes clear that it is God's will that people should live according to their preferred (or as they would say, God given) gender identity:

> My experience has shown me that to seek to change the mind orientation of the Transsexual is not only useless, but also wrong and against the will of God. Let me explain. For over 30 years I agonised before God in prayer over my condition. My cultural religious conditioning had taught me that such thoughts, and the desires which followed were evil, and I sought God for healing in earnest desperation. Although after severe self-abasement before the Lord I seemed to have a short period of release this never lasted long, and certainly I was not granted healing by God in this way. I turned to the only way I believe healing is possible which is by seeking the way of changing my bodily form to the gender I knew to be my real gender. I have found healing now through full gender reassignment.[212]

However, in spite of such testimony and the argument built upon it, the belief that it is right for people to assume an identity that is contrary to the sex of their body is deeply problematic from a Christian perspective for four reasons.

---

211 See, for example Christina Beardsley, *The Transsexual person is my neighbour*, 2007, at http://changingattitude.org.uk/resources/publications/the-transsexual-person-is-my-neighbour, Christina Beardsley and Michelle O'Brien (eds.), *This is my body—Hearing the theology of transgender Christians*, London: Darton, Longman and Todd, 2016, Marcella Althaus-Reid and Lisa Isherwood (eds.), *Trans/Formations*, London: SCM, 2009 and Justin Tanis, *Trans-Gendered, Theology, Ministry and Communities of Faith*, Cleveland: The Pilgrim Press, 2003.
212 Anonymous testimony in *Some Issues in Human Sexuality*, London: CHP, 2003, p. 221.

First, it is problematic because it goes against reason to claim that someone can be of the opposite sex to their body, or that that they can be of no sex at all, or that they can have some form of sexual identity other than male or female.

A person's sex is their bodily sex because that is what the term 'sex' means. As we have already seen, sex is a biological reality. This means that someone's sex is their existence as male or female by virtue of the biology of their body. Because it is an immaterial entity, the soul does not have a sex of its own but its sex is the sex of the body with which it is united.

To put it simply, this means that my body is me. If someone strikes my body it makes sense for me to say 'they hit me', or for someone to say 'you hit me' if my body strikes them. Except in the very rare cases of truly intersex people, my body is either male or female. Therefore I am either male or female according to the body that I have. Two consequences follow:

1. For someone to say they have no sex at all, or that they are neither male nor female, is simply not true. No one can escape the existence of their biology in this way. They can deny the truth of who their body makes them, but they cannot abolish it. As we have seen, even those who are intersex have a biology which they cannot escape and which is determined by the dimorphic pattern of human sexual development (even if in their case this has gone awry).

2. It makes no sense to say that I am a man trapped in a woman's body or vice versa because my body is me. There can be no self of the opposite sex trapped in my body. I am not an entity separate from my body that can obeserve my body and say 'that is not me.' This is because even the very act of looking at, or thinking about my body (like any other action I take) involves my body and thus proves the identity I have with my body. As before, I can deny the truth of who I am, but I cannot abolish it.

The biology of my body can never be fundamentally changed. It is possible by means of hormones and plastic surgery to change someone's phenotype to a certain extent, but the underlying biological reality of who they are remains un-changed and will re-assert itself unless heavy doses of hormones continue to be taken. Medical procedures can produce what Paul McHugh calls 'feminized men or masculinised women,' but as he goes on to say, these are only 'counterfeits or impersonators of the sex with which they 'identify'.[213] What medicine cannot do, because it is impossible to do, is to change a man into a woman or vice versa.

---

213 Paul McHugh, 'Transgenderism: A Pathogenic Meme,' *Public Discourse*, 10 June 2015, text at http://www.thepublicdiscourse.com/2015/06/15145/.

Secondly, transgender is problematic because it involves a denial of the basic truth that we have noted throughout this study that our sexed bodies are a good gift to us from God that we are to receive with gratitude and in the light of which we are called to live. O'Donovan makes this point well when he writes:

> The sex into which we have been born (assuming it is physiologically un-ambiguous) is given to us to be welcomed as the gift of God. The task of psychological maturity—for it is a moral task, and not merely an event which may or may not transpire—involves accepting this gift and learning to love it, even though we may have to acknowledge that it does not come to us without problems. Our task is to discern the possibilities for personal rela-tionship which are given to us with this biological sex, and to seek to develop them in accordance with our individual vocations. Those for whom this task has been comparatively unproblematic (though I suppose that no human being alive has been without some sexual problems) are in no position to pronounce any judgement on those for whom accepting their sex has been so difficult that they have fled from it into denial. Nevertheless, we cannot and must not conceive of physical sexuality as a mere raw material with which we can construct a form of psychosexual self-expression which is determined only by the free impulse of our spirits. Responsibility in sexual development implies a responsibility to nature—to the ordered good of the bodily form which we have been given.[214]

As he goes on to say:

> When God made mankind male and female, to exist alongside each other and for each other, he gave a form that human sexuality should take and a good to which it should aspire. None of us can, or should, regard our difficulties with that form, or with achieving that good, as the norm of what our sexuality is to be. None of us should see our sexuality as mere self-expression, and forget that we can express ourselves sexually only because we participate in this generic form and aspire to this generic good. We do not have to make a sexual form, or posit a sexual good. We have to exist as well as we can within that sexual form, and in relation to that sexual good, which has been given to us because it has been given to humankind.[215]

This means that it is not legitimate to deny the God-given form by rejecting the 'gender binary', or to deny the particular version of that form that God has given

---

214 Oliver O'Donovan, *Begotten or Made?*, Oxford: OUP, 1984, pp.28-29.
215 Ibid, pp.29-30.

to us by making us either male or female. However difficult this form may be for us to accept, to deny it would be a form of sin because it would involve refusing to say to God 'thy will be done.'

Thirdly, transgender involves violating the biblical teaching that we should live as the members of the sex that God has given to us. This teaching can be found in Deuteronomy 22:5 which prohibits cross-dressing on the grounds that 'to dress after the manner of the opposite sex was to infringe the normal order of creation which divided humanity into male and female.'[216] It can also be found in 1 Corinthians 11:2-16 where St Paul tells the Corinthians that men should follow the dress and hair codes which proclaim them to be male and women the codes which proclaim them to be female because 'God's creation needs humans to be fully, gloriously and truly human, which means fully and truly male and female.'[217] This does not mean that Christians should uncritically embrace the gender stereotypes of any given society. What it does mean is that they should live in a way that proclaims to that society the truth of God's creation of human beings as male and female.

Fourthly, it is often claimed that embracing a transgender identity is an effective way of relieving the mental anguish caused by gender dysphoria. However, there is a growing body of evidence that calls this claim into question.

The available evidence shows that being transgender is linked to serious issues of both mental and physical health. For example, the biggest ever survey of transgender people in the United States indicates that there is a far higher prevalence of mental and physical health issues among transgender people than among the population as whole. The survey, undertaken by the National Center for Transgender Equality, surveyed 27,715 self-described transgender people in 2015. The key findings were that

- 39% of transgender people had suffered serious recent psychological stress (as compared to 5% among Americans generally);

- 40% of transgender people had attempted suicide (as compared to 4.6% among Americans in general);

- 7% of transgender people had attempted suicide in the last year (as compared to 0.6 among Americans in general);

- 1.4% of transgender people were infected with HIV (as compared to 0.3%

---

216 P.J. Harland 'Menswear and Womenswear: A Study of Deuteronomy 22:5,' *Expository Times*, 110, No.3, 1988, p.76.
217 Wright, *1 Corinthians*, p.143.

among Americans in general. In particular, 3.4% of male to female transsexuals and 19% of black male to female transsexuals had HIV.[218]

Furthermore, the evidence suggests that that gender transition will not necessarily be effective in resolving the mental health issues experienced by those with gender dysphoria. Thus Dr Chris Hyde of the University of Birmingham notes that a study of the issue by the university's Aggressive Research Intelligence Facility in 2004 showed that 'there's still a large number of people who have the surgery but remain traumatized—often to the point of committing suicide.'[219] Likewise a major Swedish study from 2011 looking at the long term outcomes for people who had undergone sex-reassignment surgery found 'substantially higher rates of overall mortality, death from cardiovascular disease and suicide, suicide attempts, and psychiatric hospitalisations in sex-reassigned transsexual individuals compared to a healthy control population.'[220]

In 2014 the highly respected American medical research company Hayes Inc. undertook a review of the evidence for the long-term benefits of gender transition. It gave the studies supporting transition its lowest rating for quality and concluded that 'Statistically significant improvements have not been consistently demonstrated by multiple studies for most outcomes.'[221] In 2016, on the basis of their survey of the evidence, Lawrence Meyer and Paul McHugh likewise found that it 'suggests we take a skeptical view toward the claim that sex-reassignment procedures provide the hoped for benefits or resolve the underlying issues that contribute to elevated mental health risks among the transgender population.'[222]

A growing body of testimony from people who have 'de-transitioned' (that is, reverted to living in their original sex) also points in the same direction. For example, the American writer Walt Heyer, who underwent male to female transition, reports in his article 'I was a trangender woman':

> I knew I wasn't a real woman, no matter what my identification documents said. I had taken extreme steps to resolve my gender conflict, but changing genders hadn't worked. It was obviously a masquerade. I felt I had been lied to.

---

218 James, S. E., Herman, J. L., Rankin, S., Keisling, M., Mottet, L., & Anafi, M, *The Report of the 2015 U.S. Transgender Survey*. Washington, DC: National Center for Transgender Equality, 2016.

219 David Batty, 'Mistaken identity,' *The Guardian*, July 30, 2004, http://www.theguardian.com/society/2004/jul/31/health.socialcare.

220 Cecilia Djehne et al, ' Long-Term Follow-Up of Transsexual Persons Undergoing Sex Reassignment Surgery: Cohort Study in Sweden,' *PLoS One*, 6 (No.2), 2011.

221 Hayes, Inc 'Hormone therapy for the treatment of gender dysphoria' and 'Sex reassignment surgery for the Treatment of gender dysphoria,' in *Hayes Medical Technology Directory*, Lansdale Pa: Winifred Hayes, 2014.

222 Lawrence Meyer and Paul McHugh, 'Gender Identity,' in *New Atlantis*, Fall 2016, p.113.

How in the world had I reached this point? How did I become a fake woman? I went to another gender psychologist, and she assured me that I would be fine; I just needed to give my new identity as Laura more time. I had a past, a battered and broken life that living as Laura did nothing to dismiss or resolve. Feeling lost and depressed, I drank heavily and considered suicide.[223]

For another example, Cari Stella, another American, who underwent female to male transition declares:

I will say, from my own experience and from my conversations with other de-transitioned and re-identified women: transition is not the only way, or even necessarily the best way, to treat gender dysphoria. I felt a strong desire, what I would have called a 'need' at the time, to transition….And it wasn't weeks, or months, that I stayed on hormones, before I realized that I needed to stop. I was on them for over three years, cumulatively. I know women who were on testosterone, three, four, five, even ten years before they were able to recognize that it was f**king them over. It can be dam hard to figure out that the treatment you're being told is to help you is actually making your mental health worse. Testosterone made me even more dissociated than I already was.[224]

What all this suggests is that from a mental health perspective we need to find a better approach to helping transgender people.[225]

How should Christians respond to transgender?

With these problems in mind, how should Christians respond to the transgender phenomenon? The answer offered by Andrew Walker in his book *God and the Transgender Debate* is by being a people of both truth and love:

If Christians have anything to offer in this contentious age it is truth, and we should not shy away from the truth. But equally, if we use truth as blunt force trauma against those who are coming to grips with what discipleship means,

---

223 Walt Heyer, 'I was a Transgender Woman,' *Public Discourse*, 1 April, 2015, article at http://www.thepublicdiscourse.com/2015/04/14688/.

224 Cari Stella, 'Response to Julia Serano: Detransition, Desistance and Disinformation' posted on You Tube 9 August, 2016 at https://www.youtube.com/watch?v=9L2jyEDwpEw. For further testimonies pointing in the same direction see Anderson, op.cit. ch. 3.

225 A particular area of concern is the way in which children and young people who exhibit confusion or distress about their sexual identity are now being encouraged to identify themselves as members of the opposite sex and are given powerful drugs to prevent the onset of puberty. Since we do not know what the long term psychological and physiological consequences will be, this amounts to dangerous experimentation on the nation's children and is something the Church needs to challenge. For an introduction to the issues involved see Anderson, op.cit. ch.6.

woe to us. Woe to us if we demand conformity from those who are struggling more than we are willing to walk alongside them while they are struggling.

It is only loving to hold to biblical truth if that truth comes wrapped in love. We are only firmly anchored, able to grow and to share the gospel without being tossed about by every idea and argument from both the conservative and progressive ends of the spectrum, if we are 'speaking the truth in love' (Ephesians 4 v 15). Neither love nor truth is an optional bolt on to our Christianity.[226]

As people of truth we are called to teach in our churches, and to declare in public debate, the key truths we have been looking at in this chapter:

- Sex and gender are not the same thing;

- Reason and Scripture tell us that people's sex is defined by their biology;

- Reason and Scripture tell us that there are two sexes, male and female;

- Reason and Scripture tell us that while a person's sexual identity can be denied, it cannot be changed or eradicated;

- Reason and Scripture tell us that the path of wisdom and godliness lies in accepting the truth of our sexual identity and living accordingly.

- A growing body of evidence challenges the claim that changing one's sexual identity will be effective in providing lasting relief from the distress caused by gender dysphoria. Reason therefore suggests that encouragement should instead be given to alternative forms of treatment that address the underlying mental health issues that lead to gender dysphoria.

As people of love, who value the God given dignity of transgender people as those whom God has created and for whom Christ died, we should be proactive in ensuring that transgender people are not subject to harassment or violence, or discriminated against in the provision of goods, services, or opportunity for appropriate employment.

As people of love, who recognize and value as a work of God the sex into which transgender people were born, we should encourage transgender people not to engage in cross-dressing or go down the path of gender transition. If they have gone down either of these paths, love means helping them to accept and live out their original, God given, sexual identity, whilst acknowledging the acute

---

226 Andrew T Walker, *God and The Transgender Debate*, Epsom: The Good Book Company, 2017, p.128.

challenges doing this will raise, particularly for those who have undergone gender re-assignment surgery or formed families in their assumed identity.

Finally, as people of love we should give transgender people an unconditional welcome into our churches and provide them with appropriate pastoral care. As a Lutheran Church – Missouri Synod report helpfully explains, the starting point for such pastoral care is the truth that:

> ...the deepest need of such a man or woman—as it is for every person—is to know that he or she is beloved by God. Christ's love and forgiveness are in this case as always one's greatest needs. Sorrow, confusion, frustration, shame, and despair are likely present in any individual dealing with gender dysphoria or struggling with questions about his or her identity as male or female. If such an individual has not already sought psychotherapeutic care, the pastor should seek to encourage and, to whatever degree possible, facilitate the individual in securing competent therapy that is not hostile to the Christian faith.[227]

Such pastoral care also needs to be based on:

> ....the development of genuine Christian friendship modelled after the One whose friendship knows no boundaries (Luke 7:34). Loving pastoral care for the individual seeks to provide a spiritually nurturing, encouraging, and accepting 'safe place' to someone who may well have suffered from actual or perceived ostracism, mockery, and animosity. He or she may view the church with suspicion or share the common assumption that Christianity is more concerned with moral judgments, cultural battles, or political victories than about broken and suffering people. In accepting the struggling individual, a relationship of interpersonal trust develops. Within that relationship there will be natural opportunities to make Christ known, to call the person to trust in his promises and love, and to show that the purposes and commands of God for our lives are for our good.[228]

Since 'the pathway of growth, sanctification and change can be expected to be slow and painful' and 'struggle and relapse can be anticipated'[229] our pastoral care needs to involve patience and a long term commitment to praying for, loving, listening to, and assisting the person concerned in any way necessary. It will also mean continuing to love and support them even if progress is slow or relapses occur, trusting that God is in the process and has the capacity to bring about

---

227 The Lutheran Church -Missouri Synod, 'Gender Identity Disorder or Gender Dysphoria in Christian Perspective,' 2014.
228 Ibid.
229 The Evangelical Alliance, *Transsexuality*, Carlisle: Paternoster Press, 2000. p.82.

the result that he desires, even if this takes years. As Walt Heyer reminds us in *A Transgender's Faith*: 'we must never give up on people, no matter how many times they fail or how long recovery takes. We must never underestimate the healing power of prayer and love in the hands of the Lord. We must never give up hope.'[230]

The reason we must never give up hope is because God can and does change people's hearts. We noted earlier that there are a growing number of testimonies from people who have de-transitioned following gender reassignment. Among these are Christians who testify how God has enabled them to accept their biological sex as a gift from him and live accordingly. A good example is the following testimony from Robert John bearing witness to what God has done for him:

> I had irreversible gender reassignment surgery in 1997 absolutely convinced I was a woman in a man's body. I anticipated living happily ever after, however I had persistent difficulties and fell into deep depression. I began reading the Bible, unsatisfied with superficial proclamations of diversity, inclusiveness, and tolerance. I happened upon King David's famous repentance Psalm 51 and discovered, like David, I could be forgiven for all my sins. I also learned God chastens those whom He loves and I was being guided to seek repentance, and faith in the finished work of Jesus Christ. I knew identifying as a woman was not living in truth, and returned to my given names and birth gender without further surgery. My victory has come by allowing the Lord in my heart, becoming God-focused instead of self-centered, and am thankful for my birth sex and many blessings. Despite the consequences and challenges. God has led me to witness His truth and love, and I can testify: indeed, God's grace, mercy and truth do set one free.[231]

It could be argued that the pro-transgender testimony cited at the beginning of our consideration of the transgender issue cancels out this testimony since they point in opposite directions. However the difference between them is that the second testimony has the support of Scripture and reason while the first does not for the reasons which we have explored.

---

230 Heyer, op.cit. p.141.
231 Text from the website Sex Change Regret http://www.sexchangeregret.com/examples. For other such testimonies see Heyer, A Transgenders Faith and the documentary film Tranzformed which contains the witness of fifteen 'ex-transgender' Christians, https://tranzformed.org/.

Appendix: The ordination of transgender people and services to mark gender transition

The general requirement that ordained people should model Christian truth in the way they live their lives make it inappropriate for the Church to ordain someone who is going through, or who has gone through gender transition, or who identifies as gender non-binary. There would be no issue, however, with ordaining someone who struggled with gender identity or who had de-transitioned, providing they meet the normal requirements for ordination.

In July 2017 the General Synod passed a motion brought to it by the Diocese of Blackburn stating

> that this Synod, recognising the need for transgender people to be welcomed and affirmed in their parish church, call on the House of Bishops to consider whether some nationally commended liturgical materials might be prepared to mark a person's gender transition.

In response to this motion the House of Bishops then produced GS Misc 1178 *An update on 'Welcoming Transgender People.'*[232] This paper suggests that rather than new liturgical material being produced those who want to do so should use the existing rites of Baptism, Confirmation and the Affirmation of Baptismal Faith to mark someone's gender transition.

The bishops promise more detailed guidance later in the year. However, on the basis of existing unofficial services created to mark gender transition it seems likely that what would be involved would be people who had undergone gender transition being baptized, or confirmed, or re-affirming their baptism, in their assumed identity, using a name and pronouns consistent with that identity. Thus if Mark became Carol in a male to female transition then Carol would be the name that would be used and so would female pronouns and terms such as 'daughter' rather than 'son.'

Such rites would be understood both by the person concerned and by the Church as an acceptance of the reality of their new identity and as an affirmation that God accepts this new identity as well. They necessarily involve the claim that it is possible for someone to have a sexual identity that is at variance with their biology. As we have seen, this claim is untrue. A biological male cannot be female and vice versa. Since liturgy should not proclaim falsehood, and since Mark can

---

232 The full text can be found at https://goo.gl/c84iys

not in fact become Carol, it follows that such services should not take place. What the bishops propose therefore needs to be rejected.[233]

Questions for discussion

1. Is it correct to say that people with intersex conditions constitute a third sex?

2. Why is the transgender phenomenon problematic from a Christian perspective?

3. How should Christians respond to transgender people with both truth and love?

---

233 On the issue of services to mark gender transition see Martin Davie, *Transgender Liturgies*, London: Latimer Trust, 2017.

CHAPTER 8

Sex outside marriage

'For this is the will of God, your sanctification: that you abstain from un-chastity' (1 Thessalonians 4:3).

Christianity's challenge to pagan sexual standards

One of the distinctive features of early Christianity was its challenge to the double standard in sexual practice that operated in the Greco-Roman world when the New Testament was written (see chapter five). This double standard meant that, while honourable women were expected to be sexually abstinent before marriage and sexually faithful to their husbands within it, men were free to have sex with a wide range of sexual partners both before and during marriage. The caveat was that they should not have sex with the wives of other men or with freeborn virgins. Having sex outside marriage with courtesans, prostitutes, and even children was seen as a good thing if it meant that men abstained from sex with other men's wives or with freeborn virgins.

Christianity challenged this double standard not by suggesting that women should henceforth have the same sexual freedom as men, but by requiring that men should adhere to the same standard of sexual conduct as honourable women. Men should be sexual abstinent before marriage and faithful to their wives within it. As St Paul made clear, the two choices open to Christian believers were either to be married or to be single (1 Corinthians 7). Marriage involved sexual activity, but only within the marital relationship, and singleness meant sexual abstinence (in the terms of Matthew 19:12, making oneself a eunuch for the sake of the kingdom of God).

What is wrong with sex outside marriage?

In line with this single standard for sexual conduct, the New Testament tells us time and again that sexual activity outside marriage is a sin that Christians are to avoid. Four examples will serve to illustrate this.

First, Jesus lists *porneia* (RSV 'fornication') as one of the things that comes out of the human heart and renders people unclean in the sight of God (Matthew 15:19 and Mark 7:21). *Porneia* was a comprehensive term which was used to refer to all sexual acts outside of marriage.[234] As Michael Brown notes, by using this term Jesus taught that:

> …all sexual acts outside marriage make us unclean. Yes, heterosexual fornication, homosexual acts, bestiality, incestuous acts, all of these are included by Jesus under the category of 'sexual immoralities' and all of them defile us and make us unclean.[235]

Secondly, St Paul tells the Christians in Galatia:

> Now the works of the flesh are plain: fornication, impurity, licentiousness, idolatry, sorcery, enmity, strife, jealousy, anger, selfishness, dissension, party spirit, envy, drunkenness, carousing, and the like. I warn you, as I warned you before, that those who do such things shall not inherit the kingdom of God. (Galatians 5:19-21)

The words translated 'fornication', 'impurity' and 'licentiousness' (*porneia, akatharsia* and *aselgeia*) are all general terms for sexual immorality, which in the New Testament context means sexual activity outside marriage. Paul makes clear that engaging in it will mean losing one's place in God's coming kingdom. In later Christian terminology, he is saying that sexual immorality leads to eternal damnation.

Thirdly, the writer to the Hebrews declares, 'Let marriage be held in honour among all, and let the marriage bed be undefiled; for God will judge the immoral and adulterous.' (Hebrews 13:4) F. F. Bruce takes this as an 'injunction to honour the marriage union and abstain from sexual sin.'[236] 'The immoral' whom God will judge are *pornous*, which means those who commit *porneia*. If we want to honour marriage as the context ordained by God for sexual activity, we must not only refrain from adultery, but from all forms of sexual activity outside marriage. The writer warns that those who do engage in sexual immorality will be judged by God, implying that their behaviour will be condemned as part of God's general condemnation of all human sin.

---

234 See James Moulton and George Milligan, *The Vocabulary of the Greek New Testament Illustrated from the Papyri and Other Non-Literary Sources*, Grand Rapids: Eerdmans, 1980), s.v. 'porneia', H. Reisser, "Porneuō," in Colin Brown (ed.), *The New International Dictionary of the New Testament Theology*, Grand Rapids: Zondervan, 1975, 1:499 and John Nolland, 'Sexual Ethics and the Jesus of the Gospels,' *Anvil*, Vol 26:1, 2009, pp. 21-30.

235 Michael L Brown, *Can you be Gay and Christian?*, Lake Mary: Front Line, 2014, p.132.

236 F. F. Bruce, *The Epistle to the Hebrews*, London: Marshall, Morgan and Scott, 1967, p.392.

Fourthly, St Peter writes, 'Let the time that is past suffice for what the Gentiles like to do, living in licentiousness, passions, drunkenness, revels, carousing, and lawless idolatry.' (1 Peter 4:3) Converted Christians should no longer live as they did when they were Gentile pagans. They must give up sinful forms of behaviour, including 'licentiousness' (*aselgeia*) which, as in Galatians 5:19, is a general term for sexual activity outside marriage.

Why does it matter what we do with our bodies?

The bodies of Christian people matter. St Paul says that this basic theological truth stands behind the Christian rejection of sexuality immorality. In 1 Corinthians 6:12-20 he insists that what Christians do in and with their bodies must reflect the reality that they belong to God and are destined for eternal glory:

'All things are lawful for me,' but not all things are helpful. 'All things are lawful for me,' but I will not be enslaved by anything. 'Food is meant for the stomach and the stomach for food'—and God will destroy both one and the other. The body is not meant for immorality, but for the Lord, and the Lord for the body. And God raised the Lord and will also raise us up by his power. Do you not know that your bodies are members of Christ? Shall I therefore take the members of Christ and make them members of a prostitute? Never! Do you not know that he who joins himself to a prostitute becomes one body with her? For, as it is written, 'The two shall become one flesh.' But he who is united to the Lord becomes one spirit with him. Shun immorality. Every other sin which a man commits is outside the body; but the immoral man sins against his own body. Do you not know that your body is a temple of the Holy Spirit within you, which you have from God? You are not your own; you were bought with a price. So glorify God in your body.

In these verses Paul's emphasis, explains Hurtado:

…is very much on believers' bodies as the crucial venue, so to speak, in which they are to live out their faith commitment. 'Your bodies are members of Christ,' he declares, and so believers must not have illicit sex—with a prostitute for example (6:15). Indeed, in an astonishing move, citing a statement from the Genesis creation account—'the two shall be one flesh,' which was typically seen as referring to the physical/bodily union effected in marriage—Paul applies this biblical statement to having sex with a prostitute! Even such casual sex, he says, is a bodily union, which is precisely what makes it all the more seriously wrong. He proceeds then to emphasize further the bodily nature of the sin of *porneia* (6:18) for believers, declaring that their bodies are individually 'a temple of the Holy Spirit within you, which you have from God.' Paul then ends this passage by urging. 'You were brought with a price [alluding to Jesus' sacrificial death for them]; therefore glorify God *in your body*' (6:19-20).[237]

Porneia was not the term that men of Paul's day typically used to describe their extra-marital sexual activities:

> Instead they used the term specifically to refer to what prostitutes did, 'prostitution.' Paul's usage of the term, however, reflects ancient Jewish, and then Christian usage, in which the term designated a wider variety of male sexual activities that appear to have been tolerated in the wider society, including men having sex with prostitutes, courtesans, and slaves. By referring to these activities collectively as porneia, Paul labels them as sinful and completely off-limits for believers.[238]

Paul not only forbids such practices but also provides 'a distinctive new basis for doing so and for framing appropriate sexual behaviour for believers.'[239] This is because in 1 Corinthians 6 he:

> ....cites the bodily resurrection of Jesus as an emphatic affirmation of embodiment and so underlines the importance of what believers do with/in their bodies. As Paul makes clear a bit later in 1 Corinthians 15, Jesus' resurrection is the pattern and basis for the future resurrection of believers, which is their ultimate hope. So, in keeping with his understanding of Jesus' resurrection, Paul held that the future resurrection of believers will mean the transformation of their mortal body into a new and glorious one, to be sure, but nevertheless an embodiment, not some other kind of bare 'spirit' existence.

> In Paul's thought this means that, even now, what believers do with their mortal body has significance, and so he insists that, precisely because it is unquestionably a bodily activity, sexual behaviour is a crucial matter. The bottom line in the passage is that the diverse sexual activities covered in Paul's use of porneia, even though they may have been approved in the wider culture and even among Christian believers, are to be completely off-limits for them.[240]

What does Jesus say about rejecting sexual immorality?

In the Sermon on the Mount Jesus goes even further than Paul in 1 Corinthians

---

237 Hurtado, op.cit. p.162, italics in the original.
238 Ibid, pp.162-163.
239 Ibid, p.163.
240 Ibid, p.163.

6:12-20. Not only must Christians shun all forms of sexual intercourse outside marriage, they must also avoid the desire for sexual intercourse outside marriage. Jesus declares:

> You have heard that it was said, 'You shall not commit adultery.' But I say to you that everyone who looks at a woman lustfully has already committed adultery with her in his heart. If your right eye causes you to sin, pluck it out and throw it away; it is better that you lose one of your members than that your whole body be thrown into hell. And if your right hand causes you to sin, cut it off and throw it away; it is better that you lose one of your members than that your whole body go into hell. (Matthew 5:27-30)

Jesus draws out here the full meaning of the Old Testament command 'You shall not commit adultery' (Exodus 20:14, Deuteronomy 5:18). As John Stott puts it:

> …he affirmed that the true meaning of God's command was much wider than a mere prohibition of acts of sexual immorality. As the prohibition of murder included the angry thought and insulting word, so the prohibition of adultery included the lustful look and imagination. We can commit murder with our words; we can commit adultery in our hearts and minds.[241]

Stott emphasises that Jesus rules out all forms of sexual immorality:

> To argue that the reference is only to a man lusting after a woman and not vice versa, or only to a married man and not an unmarried, since the offender is said to commit 'adultery' and not 'fornication,' is to be guilty of the very casuistry which Jesus was condemning in the Pharisees. His emphasis is that any and every sexual practice which is immoral in deed is immoral also in look and in thought.[242]

Since sexually immoral looks and thoughts are as sinful as sexually immoral physical acts, they must be addressed with the same degree of ruthless self-denial that Jesus refers to when he talks about plucking out our right eye and cutting off our right hand in verses 29 and 30. This does not mean literal self-mutilation but the strict rejection of everything that causes us to entertain illicit sexual desire. To quote Stott once more:

> If your eye causes you to sin because temptation comes to you through your eyes (objects you see), then pluck out your eyes. That is, don't look. Behave as

---

241 John Stott, *The Message of the Sermon on the Mount*, Leicester: Inter-Varsity Press, 1978, p. 87.
242 Ibid, pp.87-88.

if you had actually plucked out your eyes and flung them away and so *could* not see the objects which previously caused you to sin. Again, if your hand or foot causes you to sin, because temptation comes to you through your hands (things you do) or your feet (places you visit), then cut them off. That is: don't do it! Don't go! Behave as if you had actually cut off your hands and feet, and had flung them away, and were now crippled and so *could* not do the things or visit the places which previously caused you to sin.[243]

What does it mean to exercise chastity?

Archbishop William Wake explains Jesus' teaching as meaning that 'we are to abstain not only from adultery, but from all manner of carnal pollutions whatsoever; from all the most distant approaches to it, and incitements towards it.'[244] In other words, Christians are called to exercise the virtue of chastity by practising strict sexual self-denial in thought and deed outside marriage and strict sexual fidelity in thought and deed within marriage in both.

This raises the question of what counts as sexual activity? Sexual activity involves the penetration of the vagina by the penis and all other forms of bodily activity that are intended to accompany or lead to such penetration, or to stimulate the physical pleasure produced by such penetration by some other means such as anal or oral sex. Performing such actions outside marriage is illicit sexual activity. Illicit sexual desire consists in entertaining the thought of engaging in such activity when it would be wrong to engage in it, or engaging in inappropriate sexual activity in our imagination.

Simply looking at a man or a woman and finding them attractive is not in itself illicit sexual desire. Showing physical affection to another person by hugging or kissing them, for instance, is not in itself sexual activity. Looks and physical contact are only problematic if they lead to illicit sexual desire or activity, or if they cause problems for other people by making them think that we are engaging in inappropriate behaviour, or if they encourage other people to behave in a way which in their case would lead to sexual sin.

Exercising the virtue of chastity requires knowing where the line is between licit and illicit thought and behaviour and exercising appropriate self-discipline so as not to cross it.

---

243 Ibid, p.89. Italics in the original.
244 William Wake, *The Principles of the Christian Religion Explained*, Forgotten Books, p.257.

Why is chastity so difficult?

Exercising the virtue of chastity has always been difficult, and will always be difficult, because we are fallen creatures who live in a fallen world. To be chaste goes
against the grain of our fallen natures, but as C S Lewis notes in *Mere Christianity,*
there are three reasons why chastity is particularly difficult for us today. Firstly, he
says chastity goes against what we feel is 'natural':

> ...our warped natures, the devils who tempt us, and all the contemporary
> propaganda for lust combine to make us feel that the desires we are resisting
> are so 'natural,' so 'healthy,' and so reasonable, that it is almost perverse and
> abnormal to resist them. Poster after poster, film after film, novel after nov-
> el, associate the idea of sexual indulgence with the ideas of health, normality,
> youth, frankness and good humour.[245]

These positive associations reflect the truth that sex is indeed something healthy
and normal, but they also contains the lie 'that any sexual act to which you are
tempted at the moment is also healthy and normal.'[246] This suggestion, writes
Lewis, is nonsense:

> Surrender to all our desires obviously leads to impotence, disease, jealousies,
> lies, concealment, and everything that is the reverse of health, good humour,
> and frankness. For any happiness, even in this world, quite a lot of restraint is
> going to be necessary; so the claim made by every desire, when it is strong, to
> be healthy and reasonable, counts for nothing.[247]

We need to realize that the propaganda for sexual indulgence is precisely that:
propaganda. We are being sold a big lie and we need to recognise this fact.

Secondly, Lewis says that 'many people are deterred from seriously attempting Christian chastity because they think (before trying) that it is impossible.'[248]
Therefore, he offers some advice:

> ...when a thing has to be attempted, one must never think about possibility or
> impossibility. Faced with an optional question in an examination paper, one
> considers whether one can do it or not: faced with a compulsory question,
> one must do the best one can. You may get some marks for a very imperfect

---

245 Lewis, *Mere Christianity*, pp.89-90.
246 Ibid, p. 90.
247 ibid, p.90.
248 Ibid, p.90.

answer: you will certainly get none for leaving the question alone.[249]

The very attempt to be chaste has value, even if we are not immediately successful. Even when we have asked for God's help to be chaste:

> …it may seem to you for a long time that no help, or less help than you need, is being given. Never mind. After each failure, ask forgiveness, pick yourself up, and try again. Very often what God first helps towards is not the virtue itself but just this power of always trying again. For however important chastity (or courage, or truthfulness, or any other virtue) may be, this process trains us in habits of the soul which are more important still. It cures our illusions about ourselves and teaches us to depend on God. We learn, on the one hand, that we cannot trust ourselves even in our best moments, and, on the other, that we need not despair even in our worst, for our failures are forgiven. The only fatal thing is to sit down content with anything less than perfection.[250]

Thirdly, Lewis writes, people are deterred from attempting chastity because they misunderstand the psychology of sexual repression. Psychology does indeed teach that ''repressed' sex is dangerous,'[251] but:

> ….'repressed' is here a technical term: it does not mean 'suppressed' in the sense of 'denied' or 'resisted.' A repressed desire or thought is one which has been thrust into the subconscious (usually at a very early age) and can now come before the mind only in a disguised and unrecognisable form.[252]

This means that attempting to be chaste does not involve repression:

> … when an adolescent or adult is engaged in resisting a conscious desire, he is not dealing with a repression nor is he in the least danger of creating a repression. On the contrary, those who are seriously attempting chastity are more conscious and soon know a great deal more about their own sexuality than anyone else. They come to know their desires as Wellington knew Napoleon, or as Sherlock Holmes knew Moriarty; as a rat-catcher knows about rats, or a plumber knows about leaky pipes. Virtue—even attempted virtue—brings light; indulgence brings fog.[253]

So far in this chapter we have seen that Christians are called to a life of strict chastity. We are called to reject extra-marital sex not only in deed but also in thought. Fur-

---

249 Ibid, pp.90-91.
250 Ibid, p.91.
251 Ibid, p.91.
252 Ibid, p.91.
253 Ibid, pp.91-92.

thermore, we have seen that Christians should not be deterred from following the path of chastity as if it were unhealthy, too difficult, or psychologically damaging.

In chapter two we noted that through the death and resurrection of Christ and the work of the Spirit we are set free to become the men and women we were created to be by saying 'no' to our old disobedient way of life and 'yes' to the life of holiness that Christ has made possible for us . Saying 'no' to *porneia* and 'yes' to chastity is a key part of what it means to live this kind of life.

Certain patterns of behavior such as adultery are still widely and rightly viewed as sins against chastity in both society and the church. There are, however, a range of other forms of sexual behaviour which are prevalent today and which are increasingly defended as morally acceptable. These form of behavior are prostitution, the production and use of pornography, masturbation, the use of sex surrogates, cohabitation, and same-sex relationships.

In the remainder of this chapter we will look at these six forms of behavior and explore why, despite the important differences between them, they all constitute departures from the New Testament's path of chastity

Prostitution

Prostitution is always wrong from a Christian perspective because it involves sex outside marriage, and is therefore a departure from chastity by both the prostitute and his or her client. As we have seen, sexual intercourse is meant to be an act of interpersonal communion which take place within a marital relationship open to the gift of children. In prostitution, sexual intercourse takes place outside of marriage in a commercial relationship in which the begetting and raising of children is not in view. For this reason, as the *Catechism of the Catholic Church* says, 'it is always gravely sinful to engage in prostitution.'[254]

This means that as Christians we should never be involved in purchasing sex for money ourselves (see 1 Corinthians 6:15-20) and that we need to make clear to others that such activity is wrong and that they should repent of it, seeking God's forgiveness and committing themselves, with God's help, to never purchase sex in future.

However, our approach as Christians to those involved in providing sex for money needs to involve more than simply telling people they should stop. This is because although some people say that they are involved in the sin of prostitution as a matter of choice, the evidence suggests that most prostitutes are victims who have been forced

---

254 *Catechism of the Catholic Church*, p.504.

into it, whether as a result of financial desperation, or because they have become trapped in some form of sexual slavery. The stories of 'Sharon' and 'Carol' taken from the CARE material on prostitution illustrate this point in graphic fashion.

Sharon's story

Both Sharon's parents were heroin users; her mother was also a manic depressive. Sharon grew up in and out of the care home system. Aged 17, a boyfriend introduced her to drugs and encouraged her into prostitution to fund both of their addictions. Working on the street selling sex, Sharon, now 25, has experienced severe violence, been raped many times and made to perform degrading acts with 'clients'. Her drug habit and chaotic lifestyle have left her homeless many times and forced to have sex in order to have a roof over her head. Her desperation for drug money means she often has unprotected sex and has contracted several sexually transmitted infections. She has given birth to two children, both adopted as babies.

Claire's Story

Claire grew up in a loving family, but in her late teens found herself in the big city a long way from home, having been greatly misled about the circumstances she was coming to. Soon her money ran out and the pressure to get involved in prostitution began. Claire went from being a happy trusting girl to finding herself standing in a penthouse being looked over by a madam. Claire was involved in the supposed 'high end' of prostitution in London but experienced degrading and violent behaviour from 'clients' and at one point she was trafficked from the UK to a prostitution ring in another country. Just before she managed to escape from prostitution Claire was so traumatised by her experiences that she had frequent panic attacks and lost the ability to speak, communicating only through written notes.[255]

From a Christian perspective prostitutes are never just prostitutes. They are individual people who were created by God in his image and likeness and for whom Christ died. This means they have an intrinsic value and dignity which should always be respected. As a result we need as Christians to support political action to prevent the exploitation of people like 'Sharon' and 'Claire.' The question is what form this action should take.

It is now often suggested that the legalisation of prostitution would help to prevent the exploitation of people engaged in it and increase their safety, since prostitution could take then place on a properly regulated basis. However, the

---

255 CARE, Commercial Sexual Exploitation, text at https://goo.gl/VNKEzs

evidence from places such as the Netherlands, Germany and New Zealand where prostitution has been legalised tells a different story.

As one academic study of the issue notes: 'not only can none of the legalisation or decriminalisation regimes examined here provide strong evidence that the law and policy has delivered the promised rights and material benefits to women who sell sex, several admit failure in this respect.'[256]

A German psychologist has gone further, noting that in Germany:

> Since the law [legalising prostitution] destroyed any questioning of the harm in men buying women for sex, the acts are becoming increasingly dangerous, violent and degrading. Buyers pick from a long list of sexual acts, most of which could easily be defined as torture [...] These acts cause extremely deep, enduring and traumatizing harm to the women.[257]

Rather than supporting calls for the legalisation of prostitution, we should instead support more effective action against those who traffic people for the purposes of prostitution. They should also support the introduction into England, Wales and Scotland of the so called 'Nordic' approach which was pioneered in Sweden and Norway from 1999, and has subsequently been adopted in other jurisdictions, including Northern Ireland.

The Nordic approach involves reducing demand for prostitution by making it a criminal offence to purchase sexual services, while at the same time decriminalising those who offer such services. Reports from Sweden and Norway suggest that this approach has had three beneficial results. (a) It has reduced the amount of on-street prostitution and resulted in lower than expected prostitution levels overall. (b) It has reduced the number of men saying they have purchased sexual services. (c) The police have reported deterrent effects on trafficking and organised crime involvement in prostitution.[258]

However, as Christians we are not only called to take political action to try to prevent the exploitation of people like 'Sharon' and 'Claire,' but also to minister directly to them. We need to follow Jesus' example by welcoming them (Mark 2:15-17, Luke 7:36-50), assuring them that they are loved and forgiven by God, telling them about the new life that God offers, and supporting them in embracing it.

---

256 L. Kelly, M Coy and, R Davenport. *Shifting Sands: A comparison of Prostitution Regimes Across Nine Countries*, London: The Home Office 2008.

257 'Germany wins the Title of 'Bordello of Europe': Why doesn't Angela Merkel Care?' *Huffington Post*, 27 May 2015.

258 See CARE, Commercial Sexual Exploitation—Supporter Briefing, May 2017, p.3 at https://goo.gl/CnaQx6.

We also need to help them to escape from their involvement in prostitution. As CARE notes:

> There is evidence that many of those in prostitution would like to stop, but they face significant barriers in doing so. In particular, they need tailored drug treatment, safe and supported housing, mental health support, financial counselling and access to education and training programmes.[259]

We need to be willing to be involved in providing these sorts of support services and we also need to support bodies such as CARE in lobbying the government to provide better funding and access for such services.

Pornography

Pornography is the depiction of sexual activity through art, the written word, dramatic performance or other means in order to stimulate sexual excitement and desire among those viewing or reading the material concerned. Pornographic material has always existed, but as Grant explains, due to the growth of the internet and the proliferation of internet connected devices it is now, in the shape of cyber porn, 'significantly more available, more neurologically powerful, and more extreme than it used to be.'[260]

Those involved in the production of pornography are guilty of a sin against chastity. They are deliberately stimulating sexual desire outside the context of a marital relationship. As in the case of prostitution, however, the degree of culpability is much less when people take part in pornography though financial need, or because they are trapped in sexual slavery. What they are doing is still sinful, but they are the victims as well as the perpetrators of sin.

Those who view or read pornographic material are also guilty of a sin against chastity by putting themselves in a position to be stimulated. What is more, pornography, particularly cyber pornography, is highly addictive. It creates a need for more and stronger pornographic material and this has a negative effect on peoples' marriages, jobs and mental health.[261] In addition, as Dennis Hollinger explains:

> ... pornography creates an inability to actually experience the fullness of pleas-

---

259 Ibid, p.4. For information about work to help people exit prostitution see the website of the charity Beyond the Streets at http://beyondthestreets.org.uk/.

260 Grant, op.cit. p.16.

261 For details see Pamela Paul, *Pornified: How Pornography is Transforming Our Lives, Our Relationships and Our Families*, New York: Henry Holt, 2005 and Gary Wilson, *Your Brain on Porn: Internet Pornography and the Emerging Science of Addiction*, Margate: Commonwealth Publishing, 2015.

ure in God's good gift of sex. Naomi Wolf in an article in New York Magazine says that pornography is not making men into raving beasts. On the contrary: 'The onslaught of porn is responsible for deadening male libido in relation to real women, and leading men to see fewer and fewer women as 'porn-worthy'. Far from having to fend off porn-crazed young men, young women are worrying that as mere flesh and blood, they can scarcely get, let alone hold, their attention.' She goes on to say, based on her interactions with university students, that pornography is dulling the appetite and creating a situation in which it takes more and more to provide sexual stimulation. 'For the first time in human history, the images' power and allure have supplanted that of real naked women. Today real naked women are just bad porn.'[262]

As Grant comments, the issue is that pornography:

> … changes the individual's sexual character, that is, his or her fundamental capacity to enter into and sustain genuine intimacy and love. The most powerful deception of cyber porn is its promise to fulfill desire while ultimately killing it. The most ironic fallout of the pursuit of sexual gratification online is that it can render the chronic user incapable of the very sexual satisfaction he or she is seeking.[263]

In the words of Vaughan Roberts, whereas we tend to think that the problem with pornography is that it shows too much, the reality is that it shows too little.

> Because it focuses on the physical and the visible it completely misses out on the far greater and more wonderful thing that God has given to us. Porn does not show us the joy of human love and commitment; the deep nurturing satisfaction of two people made one flesh; the fulfilment and fruitfulness of two lives lived together to the glory of God; and the nurture of a family. Porn is the equivalent of burning a priceless Stradivarius violin for a few moments of warmth and missing out on a lifetime of beautiful glorious music.[264]

To put it another way, pornography is like cheap fast food. It fills you up with unhealthy things and leaves you with no appetite for things which are healthy and truly life enhancing.

---

262 Dennis P Hollinger, *The Meaning of Sex*, Grand Rapids: Baker Academic, 2009, pp.142-143, quoting Naomi Wolf, 'The Porn Myth,' New York Magazine, 20 October 2003. The phenomenon to which Hollinger and Wolf refer also means that an increasing number of young women feel forced to provide ever more explicit and provocative images of themselves to try to hold on to their boyfriend's interest, what is known as 'sexting.'
263 Grant, op.cit. p.110.
264 Vaughan Roberts, *The Porn Problem*, Epsom: The Good Book Company, 2018, pp.37-38.

For all these reasons as Christians we must completely avoid using pornography ourselves. As Roberts notes, avoiding using pornography will involve the exercise sex-discipline, 'we will need to do all we can to protect ourselves where we are most vulnerable.' [265] In specific terms, we will need to identify and avoid the occasions when we are likely to be tempted to access pornography, we will need to make use of technological aids such as computer filters, and (as with other forms of addiction) we will need to have people to whom we are accountable for our behaviour.

However, as Roberts also notes, these forms of discipline will be not enough. We will need to do two other things as well. First of all we will need to focus not primarily on saying 'no' to pornography, but on saying 'yes' to Jesus Christ. Roberts quotes the words of Heath Lambert:

> You need to be the kind of person who fights for a close relationship with Jesus more than you fight against pornography… When you find yourself working to look to Christ more than you find yourself working to avoid porn, you'll know you've turned the corner….A living breathing relationship with Jesus will drive porn out of your life quicker than anything else. When you turn your eyes to Jesus, there isn't room for anything else in your heart because he fills it up.[266]

Secondly, we will need to trust the promises of God. God has promised 'I will never fail you nor forsake you' (Deuteronomy 31:6, Hebrews 13:5) and he has promised forgiveness when we fall back into sin as we inevitably will in one way or another (1 John 1:8-9). There will be times when the fight against pornography may seem unwinnable and we are tempted to give up, but if we keep trusting in God and his promises and acting on the basis of them we shall begin to experience the victory over sin that Christ died and rose to give us, partially in this life and then fully in the life to come.

However, not only must we reject pornography ourselves, but out of love for our neighbour we must also do all that we can through prayer, witness and practical support to assist others who are tempted by, or addicted to, pornography. In addition, we must do all that we can through prayer, witness and practical support to help those involved in the production of pornography to break free from their involvement with it. They too are victims of pornography, particularly if, as is often the case, they are vulnerable people who are been subject to people trafficking or exploited in other ways.

---

265 Ibid, p.68.
266 Ibid, p.64 quoting

Masturbation

Masturbation is the sexual stimulation of a person by himself or herself. It used to be argued that the story of Onan in Genesis 38:1-11 was a biblical condemnation of masturbation (hence the old term 'onanism') but Old Testament scholars would now agree that the story is not about masturbation but about an unwillingness to produce an heir for his dead brother.[267] If we set Onan aside we find that the real issue with masturbation is that it involves the detachment of sexual pleasure from the context of sexual union with another person in marriage (this is similar to the case of pornography, with which masturbation is often connected). That is to say, it detaches sexual activity from being the means of entering into a one flesh union with another person and potentially producing children.

As C S Lewis argues, whereas the God given pattern of sexual activity within marriage leads us out of ourselves into relationship with others (our spouse and then any offspring we have) masturbation encourages us to remain locked up in a prison of self-love:

> For me the real evil of masturbation would be that it takes an appetite which in lawful [i.e. proper] use, leads the individual out of himself to complete (and correct) his own personality in that of another (and finally in children and grandchildren) and turns it back: sends the man back into the prison of himself, there to keep a harem of imaginary brides. And this harem, once admitted, works against his ever getting out and really uniting with a real woman. For the harem is always accessible, always subservient, calls for no sacrifices or adjustments, and can be endowed with erotic and psychological attractions which no real woman can ever rival. Among these shadowy brides he is always adored, always the perfect lover: no demand is made on his unselfishness, no mortification is ever imposed on his vanity. In the end, they become merely the medium through which he increasingly adores himself...After all, almost the main work of life is to come out of ourselves, out of that little, dark prison we are all born in.[268]

There is an old saying that goes 'Don't knock masturbation. It is sex with the person you truly love.' What Lewis is reminding us is that this is precisely why masturbation is a problem.

It is sometimes argued that masturbation can be beneficial as a means of ob-

---

267 See, for example, Davidson, op.cit. pp.464-465.
268 Letter from C S Lewis to Keith Masson. 3 June 1956, Marion E Wade Center, Wheaton College, quoted in Grant, op.cit. p.111.

taining a purely physical release of sexual tension and of controlling illicit sexual desire. However, as Sean Doherty comments:

> Perhaps masturbation without lust is possible purely as a physical release of sexual tension. But lust and masturbation are usually very closely connected. Rather than relieving lustful desire, it can also stimulate it. So, whilst I am reluctant to say outright that masturbation is a sin, it could be playing with fire, and hinder the pursuit of a healthy, integrated sexuality.[269]

If masturbation encourages us to remain trapped in self-love and involves 'playing with fire' as Doherty argues, it follow that it is something which as Christians we should warn others against and avoid engaging in ourselves. We should instead learn to deal with sexual tension by the traditional means of prayer, fasting, exercise, and hard work.

Sexual surrogacy

Sexual surrogacy, highlighted in the film *The Sessions* (2012),[270] is about someone making himself or herself available to provide sexual experience to people who would not otherwise be able to experience it, whether due to physical or mental disability or to illness, like the polio experienced by the hero in *The Sessions*.

The issue with sexual surrogacy is that it implies that ill or disabled people are a separate class of human beings who should be able to experience sex without marriage. The Christian counter-argument would be that, precisely because ill or disabled people are people, God calls them to either marriage or singleness like he calls all other human beings.

If ill or disabled people have the mental and physical capacity to enter into marriage then, as we saw in chapter five, there is no reason why they should not do so. Marriage is the path they should explore. If, however, like people who are not ill or disabled, they are not able to find anyone to marry, then they should accept that God has called them to a life of singleness and that, as we saw in chapter four and six, he is able to fulfil their desire for love and physical intimacy both through relationships of friendship in this world and, even more abundantly, through the life they will enjoy in the world to come.

What ill or disabled people are not entitled to do (because no one is entitled to do it) is to claim the right to enter into a relationship that is neither marriage nor singleness, as in the case of a relationship with a sex surrogate. They, like everyone

---

269 Sean Doherty, *The Only Way is Ethics—Part 1: Sex and Marriage*, Milton Keynes: Authentic Media, 2015, p.84.
270 *The Sessions*, Fox Searchlight Pictures, Such Much Films and Rhino Films, 2012.

else, need to embrace and find their true joy in the pattern for human relationships that God in his wisdom and goodness established at creation.

The current development of sex robots designed to simulate the sexual activity of real human beings[271] can best be seen as an attempt to provide a non-human form of sex-surrogacy. The problem with this development is that once again it detaches sex from a marital relationship with another human being.

In her book *Alone Together* MIT Professor Sherry Tuckle records an encounter with a young student at a conference on the development of anthropomorphic robots:

> During a session break, the graduate student, Anne, a lovely, raven-haired woman in her mid-twenties, wanted specifics. She confided that she would trade in her boyfriend 'for a sophisticated Japanese robot' if the robot would produce what she called 'caring behavior.' She told me that she relied on a 'feeling of civility in the house.' She did not want to be alone. She said 'if the robot could provide that environment, I would be happy to help produce the illusion that there is somebody really with me.' She was looking for a 'no-risk relationship' that would stave off loneliness. A responsive robot, even one just exhibiting scripted behavior, seemed to her better than a demanding boyfriend. I asked her, gently, if she was joking. She told me she was not.[272]

What Anne wants is the upside of a relationship with another human being in terms of companionship without the downside of having to relate to someone who will make demands of her. In Lewis's terms she is still trapped in the prison of self. What she wants is a benefit to herself without having to pay the cost of giving of herself to someone else.

It is possible to imagine a relationship with a sex robot working on exactly the same terms. Someone in such a relationship would choose to have the upside of a sexual relationship with another human being in terms of sexual stimulation without the downside of having to engage with the sexual or emotional needs of another person. The prison of self would remain intact.

Such an unwillingness to relate to another human being would involve a rejection of the call to love their neighbour and there would also be a failure to love

271 See, for example, Jenny Kleeman, Tom Silverstone and Michael Tait, Rise of the Sex Robots—Video, The Guardian, 27 April 2017, https://www.theguardian.com/technology/video/2017/apr/27/rise-of-the-sex-robots-Video and David Levy, *Love and Sex with Robots: The Evolution of Human-Robot Relationships*, New York: Harper Collins, 2008.
272 Sherry Tuckle, *Alone Together: Why We Expect More from Technology and Less from Each Other*, New York: Basic books, 2012, p.8 cited in Grant, op.cit. p.85.

God. It would be a rejection of his decision recorded in Genesis and 1 and 2 that the proper sexual companion for another human being is another human being and the that the proper context for sex is a marital relationship open to the gift of children. To love God involves loving what God in his wisdom and goodness has laid down and this is what the person concerned would be unwilling to do.

It is also possible, however, to imagine a relationship with a sex robot being entered into by someone who would really like to be married and have sex with a spouse, but despairs of this ever being a possibility. They would choose a relationship with a sex robot as second best, but as something better than a life of loneliness and sexual abstinence.

In this latter case there would not be a rejection of the call to love their neighbour, but there would be a failure to love God's decision that sex should take place in the context of a marital relationship with another human being open to the gift of children and a failure to trust that if God wants them to be married then he will arrange this and that he can provide an answer to loneliness through relationships of friendship among God's people.

God has designed sex to be about a relationship with another human being. We cannot love God and second guess this decision. Therefore the idea of sex with robots is one that we need to reject.

Cohabitation

An increasing number of people are now cohabiting in the United Kingdom and across the Western world as a whole. The latest available figures from the Office for National Statistics in 2016 give a figure of 5,917,724 people cohabiting in England and Wales. This was 9.8% of the population, a rise of 3% since 2002. In addition, the 2015 statistics listed cohabiting couples as the fastest growing family type in the UK, with 3.2 million cohabiting-couple families (now 17% of all families although the percentage of people who have cohabited is much higher).[273]

Cohabiting couples include both opposite-sex couples and same-sex couples. Opposite-sex cohabiting couples have relationships which can seem similar to traditional marriage: they consist of a man and a woman living together, in a sexual relationship, and often having children together.

There are, however, two crucial differences between cohabitation and marriage. First and most importantly, those who cohabit make a conscious choice not

---

273 Office for National Statistics, 'Population estimates by marital status and living arrangements, England and Wales: 2002 to 2016.' https://www.ons.gov.uk/

to marry. They choose to live in a way that is explicitly not the pattern of relationship between a man and a woman established by God at creation and taught by the Church. Secondly, there is no requirement that cohabitation involves any of the basic elements of marriage. It need not be a permanent or sexually-exclusive relationship, it need not involve a commitment to the pattern of mutual love set out in Ephesians 5, and it need not be open to the possibility of having children. All that is required for a couple to cohabit is that they live together at the same address.

Although a particular instance of cohabitation might exhibit many of the positive forms of behavior associated with marriage (sexual faithfulness, mutual caring, the procreation and nurturing of children etc.) from a Christian perspective it is definitely not a marriage.

It might be argued that a sexually exclusive relationship between one man and one woman that they intend to be permanent should count as actually being a form of marriage. This is the view taken, for instance, by the Church of England report *Something to Celebrate* which declares 'in terms of the theology of marriage, cohabitation which involves a mutual, life-long, exclusive commitment may be a legitimate form of marriage, what might be called 'pre-ceremonial' or 'without ceremonial marriage.'[274] However, by deliberately choosing not to make their relationship a marital one, as they could have chosen to do, the couple involved are themselves rejecting the idea that they should be married and are thus rejecting God's gift of marriage. They have chosen not to be married and as such are not married. As we have seen, God's will is that his human creatures should be either married or single, but those who are cohabiting are neither married nor single. This means that the old description of cohabitation as 'living in sin' is accurate, however unhelpful it may be to single out one sinful pattern of life in this way. To live in sin is to live in a way that is contrary to God's will for his human creatures. By choosing not to be single yet also choosing not to marry, those who cohabit are living in contradiction of God's will.

The common notion that cohabitation is a good way to prepare for marriage because it enables you to 'try before you buy,' is not supported by the available evidence. On the contrary, David Olson and Amy Olson-Sigg report that:

> …the social science evidence suggests that living together is not a good way to prepare for marriage or avoid divorce. In fact, virtually all the major studies

---

274 Church of England Board for Social Responsibility, *Something to Celebrate*, London: Church House Publishing 1995, p. 116.

have shown a higher divorce rate among couples that cohabited before marriage than those that did not. No positive contribution of cohabitation to a successful marriage has been found to date.[275]

In a similar fashion, the report on cohabitation from the American College of Pediatricians in 2015 states:

> In summary, although it may appear to be a practical, positive stepping stone to a healthy marriage, research indicates living together before marriage (cohabitation) can bring significant harm to the relationship and the individuals involved. Cohabitation makes it more likely that couples will break up, and more likely that they will divorce if they do marry. Partners who cohabitate are also more likely to be unfaithful than are married spouses, and are more likely to be violent toward the other partner.[276]

As Hollinger observes, these findings should not surprise us:

> Sexual involvement with a lack of commitment, combined with strong personal autonomy to test compatibility, are sure ways to end up not preparing for marriage, which by its very nature calls for mutuality, covenant commitment, and a one-flesh union that symbolizes and embodies the oneness of our total selves.[277]

The higher rates of relationship breakdown linked to cohabitation also means that cohabitation is extremely bad news for children, the major casualties when adult relationships fall apart. As Glynn Harrison notes, 'divorce isn't the biggest threat to kids today; it's the seemingly unstoppable rise of cohabitation.'[278]

What all this means is that the sympathetic view of cohabitation taken in *Something to Celebrate* was a serious mistake. For all the reasons just noted, the growth of cohabitation is definitely not something that should be celebrated.

Something to Celebrate was right to warn against being 'disapproving and hostile towards people who cohabit.'[279] As the report says this 'only leads to alienation and breakdown in communication.'[280] However, a distinction needs to be made between disapproval and hostility towards people who cohabit and disapproval of cohabitation as a way of life.

---

275 David Olson and Amy Olson-Sigg, 'Overview of Cohabitation Research, ' Prepare/Enrich, March 2007, text at https://www.prepare-enrich.com/pe/pdf/research/overviewcohab.pdf
276 The American College of Pediatricians, 'Cohabitation: Effects of Cohabitation on the Men and Women Involved—Part 1 of 2', March 2015, text at https://www.acpeds.org/the-college-speaks/position-statements/societal-issues/cohabitation-part-1-of-2.
277 Hollinger, op.cit. p.131.
278 Glynn Harrison, op.cit. Loc 1486.
279 Ibid, p.118.
280 Ibiid, p.118.

Christians need to be welcoming and supportive to those who are cohabiting in the same way as they would be towards anyone else. We need to listen sympathetically to their stories and come to understand the fears and social pressures that have caused them to cohabit rather than marry. However, just as in the case of anyone else, we also need to encourage them to become disciples of Jesus Christ and to accept that discipleship involves turning away from a way of life that is contrary to God's will.

Pastoral care will then involve coming to understand more deeply the particular situations of the people concerned and helping them to discern whether they should return to living an overtly single life, or whether, particularly in cases where children are involved, they should convert their relationship into marriage. If the latter is the right way forward then Christians need to give maximum support to the new marriage to help make the transition from cohabitation as successful as possible.

Furthermore, as Christians we should be proactive in the public square, not only in warning that cohabitation is contrary to God's will and not conducive to human flourishing, but also in explaining unashamedly why marriage is a better alternative. They might make common cause with pro-marriage groups such as the Marriage Foundation in order to do this.[281]

Same-sex sexual relationships

The most high profile challenge for the Church of England at present is how to respond faithfully, lovingly, and sensitively to people who are same-sex attracted. It is under pressure from both inside and outside its own ranks not only to accept same-sex relationships in general, but same-sex marriage in particular, as the right response. The motion passed by the Hereford Diocesan Synod in October 2017 was intended to move the Church of England firmly in this direction by calling for clergy to be allowed to hold services of prayer and dedication after people have entered into same-sex civil marriages and a Private Members Motion on similar lines in the name of Christina Baron of the Diocese of Bath and Wells is also currently gathering signatures among the members of General Synod.[282]

It is important to affirm that much of the pressure to recognise same-sex marriage is well motivated and to acknowledge the fact that it seems self-evident to many people today: it seeks to recognise that people attracted to members of

---

281 http://marriagefoundation.org.uk
282 'Liturgies for same sex couples' at https://www.churchofengland.org/more/policy-and-thinking/work-general-synod/private-members-motions#na

the same-sex can exhibit the same positive qualities of faithful commitment and genuine intimacy as those involved in heterosexual relationships. Consequently, same-sex marriage is seen as a symbol of the equal dignity and value of men and women who are sexually attracted to members of their own sex. Since they are equal in dignity and value to people who are attracted to members of the opposite sex, they should not be victims of hatred, violence, or unjust discrimination, and their affections need to be taken seriously.

Christians should support this motivation as being consistent with basic Christian beliefs, and the question does not permit easy answers, but it does not follow that they should support same-sex marriage as the right way to affirm the equality and dignity of same-sex attracted people. In order to respond faithfully, lovingly and sensitively to same-sex attraction, we must first be clear about the reality of what same-sex sexual relationships are.

Although it may be difficult for our society to comprehend, from an orthodox Christian perspective same-sex 'marriage' is not marriage at all, even if, in Jeffrey John's words, the relationship concerned is 'permanent, faithful and stable.'[283] Marriage is what God created it to be: a one-flesh union between a man and a woman which is in principle open to the procreation of children. As something created by God, marriage is not subject to change until his eternal kingdom comes. This means that, in spite of prevailing contemporary feeling, a relationship between two people of the same sex, intrinsically closed to procreation, cannot be a marriage any more than a triangle can have a fourth corner, a truth can be a lie, or an elephant can be a penguin. Although the British Parliament and others have declared that there is such a thing as same-sex marriage, this is an example of human beings trying to do something they have no power to do. No parliament has power to change the nature of reality as God has established it. A parliament might legislate against the existence of gravity, but this would not stop apples falling from trees or people hurting themselves when jumping from tall buildings.

So what are same-sex sexual relationships if they are not marriages? Since they are a form of sexual activity taking place outside marriage, the Bible regards them as one form of *porneia*, as we have already seen above. Any form of sexual activity outside of marriage is morally wrong and so, when the New Testament declares that Christians should flee sexual immorality (1 Corinthians 6:18), this includes same-sex sexual relationships.

---

283 Jeffrey John, *Permanent, Faithful, Stable—Christian Same-Sex Marriage*, rev.ed. London: Darton, Longman and Todd, 2012.

The New Testament builds on the condemnation of male homosexual activity in the Old Testament law (Leviticus 18:22, 20:13) by declaring that both male and female same-sex relationships are symptoms of the way human beings have turned away from God (Romans 1:26-27). They are one of the sinful ways of life from which God has rescued Christians (1 Corinthians 6:9-11). They are examples of conduct which is contrary to 'sound doctrine' and the 'glorious gospel' (1 Timothy 1:10-11). In addition, Jude 7 sees the destruction of Sodom in Genesis 19 as resulting from God's judgement on homosexual lust.

For millennia Christians of all traditions have agreed 'that homosexual practice is incompatible with Christian discipleship'[284] and the renewed study of the biblical text over the past few decades has only served to underline the correctness of this position.[285] Although revisionist scholars have recently attempted to argue that these texts refer to exploitative same-sex activity, or to same-sex activity linked to idolatry, the arguments they advance in support of this re-reading are unconvincing.

Since a same-sex relationship cannot be a marriage it would be inappropriate to hold services of prayer and dedication to mark them as if they were, as the Hereford motion proposes. Furthermore, since they are examples of *porneia* and the Church is not permitted to invoke God's blessing on sin, it would be wrong for the Church of England to authorize services to bless them. The requirement that authorised ministers should be 'wholesome examples and patterns to the flock of Christ'[286] means that it would also be wrong for the Church of England to permit people who are in same-sex sexual relationships to be ordained or to serve as Readers.

This leaves us with the question of how the experiences of same-sex attracted people are to be taken seriously when their capacity for relationship may exhibit so many praiseworthy characteristics.

Responding rightly to those of us who are same-sex attracted

The clarity of Christian teaching on marriage can leave those of us who are sexually attracted to members of their own sex feeling marginalized to greater or lesser degrees by the Church. Christians need to be sensitive to the variety of these experiences and prepared to learn from them. Same-sex attracted people should be

---

284 S. Donald Fortson III and Rollin G Grams, *Unchanging Witness—The Consistent Christian teaching on homosexuality in Scripture and Tradition*, Nashville: B&H Academic, 2016, p.141.

285 For helpful introductions to the debate about the interpretation of the biblical text on this issue see Robert Gagnon, *The Bible and Homosexual Practice*, Ian Paul *Same-Sex Unions* and Martin Davie, *Studies on the Bible and same-sex relationships since 2003*, Malton: Gilead Books, 2015.

286 *Book of Common Prayer*, The Ordering of Priests.

viewed as human beings in exactly the same way as everyone else. They are made in God's image and likeness and Christ died for them, so they have exactly the same worth and dignity as all other people. This means that they should never be attacked or insulted because of their same-sex attraction, or be subject to unjust discrimination. It also means that they should be offered the same loving friendship as everyone else along the lines discussed in chapter six. Having same-sex attraction should never lead to people being excluded or lonely, and we should seek to understand the particular dimensions that same-sex attraction may involve in friendship. Jesus loves and welcomes everyone and so must his people.

An initial step concerns identity: those of us with same-sex attraction should not be identified according to our sexual attraction, which is a mark of a disordered world, but according to God's good creation renewed in Christ. Like all other human beings our sexual identity is defined by our bodies which mark them out as either male or female. 'God did not create straight women, straight men, gay women and gay men,' says Doherty. 'God created two sexes, with the capacity to relate to one another sexually.'[287]

Like everyone else, those of us who are-sex attracted should be encouraged to live as men and women. This means being open either to entering into (heterosexual) marriage or living lives of sexual abstinence as single people. As with people with opposite-sex attraction, either of these vocations may represent God's calling to a particular individual. Neither is better than the other. We saw in chapters five and six that they are equally good ways to 'glorify God in your body' by celebrating God's good creation and pointing towards God's coming kingdom.[288]

It might well be asked whether it is it realistic to suppose that those with same-sex attraction can successfully marry someone of the opposite sex? In fact there are plenty of examples to show that it is realistic: the Anglican statistician and blogger Peter Ould is one,[289] the American writer Rosaria Butterfield is a second [290] and Doherty is a third. Doherty records how being reminded that God created two sexes liberated him to be able to marry:

---

287 Doherty, op.cit. p. 10.

288 The point made in this paragraph is the correct response to the suggestion that is often made that it is unjust of God to create a special class of gay people who can never marry and therefore, according to traditional Christian teaching can never have sex. The reality is that God has not created a special class of gay people. He has created men and women who, like all other men and women, may be called to marriage, or may be called to singleness and therefore sexual abstinence.

289 Living Out, Stories, Peter, at http://www.livingout.org/stories/peter.

290 Rosaria Butterfield, *The Secret Thoughts of an Unlikely Convert*, 2ed, Pittsburgh: Crown and Covenant, 2014.

I realized my sexual desire was not discerned in my sexual desires but in the plain, tangible fact that I am a man. Thus as a man, God's original intention for me in creation was to be able to relate sexually to a woman (not that all women and men will be called to relate sexually to someone of the opposite sex). This was still true, even though currently my feelings did not match it. That opened up for me the possibility of marriage… What this meant for me was that without denying or ignoring my sexual feelings I stopped regarding them as being who I was, and started regarding my body as defining my sexual identity. I felt God calling me to stop identifying myself as gay—even though at this stage I had not experienced any change in my sexual orientation. When I stopped identifying myself as gay, I did experience some change—enough that subsequently I fell in love with and eventually married Gaby, who had been a good friend for many years.

The overall pattern of my sexual desires has not changed. I am still predominantly same-sex attracted. In a sense it has ceased to matter to me whether I am attracted to women or men in general. But it matters a great deal that I am attracted to my wife! Of course, nearly all married people are attracted to other people at times. But marriage is about being attracted and being called to be faithful to one person in particular, and our marriage is certainly a happy and fulfilling one. We face our share of challenges but they are usually things such a tidying the house, juggling work with family commitments, and how grumpy I feel in the mornings, and hardly ever about sex![291]

Nevertheless, it is important not to try to push people into marriage if that is not God's call on them. There are numerous anecdotes about people trying to do this, but it is both unkind to the people involved and potentially disastrous if it means that someone enters into a relationship to which they are not called insofar as they are not suited to it. To repeat: marriage is not better than singleness and so people should not be pushed into it.

Is it realistic to suppose that people with same-sex attraction can lead fulfilled Christian lives as single people? Again, there are numerous examples to show that it is. For example, Sam Allberry, who is a single same-sex attracted Christian, writes from his own experience that:

Singleness is not just the absence of marriage, but is a good and blessed thing in and of itself. Each state (married and single) has its own ups and downs, opportunities and challenges, griefs and joys.

He goes on to say:

---

291 Doherty, op,cit.pp.10.

Single people often have a greater capacity for friendship, greater flexibility of lifestyle, and are free to serve in a greater range of ministries than might be the case with their married friends. As a single man, I am grateful that I have been able to drop everything to spend time with friends in great need. It has meant the world to me to be able to do that, and it would not have been so easy if I were married. I'm thankful, too, for the wide range of good friendships I have been able to cultivate. It is a privilege to be involved in the lives of many other people in this way.

Those of us who are single must make the most of the opportunities singleness provides for deepening and expressing our devotion to God. Far from being a shackle, singleness can be a wonderful blessing, both to us and to others....

The history of the church is filled with lifelong singles who have been an enormous blessing to God's people and the wider world. Some through missionary activity, others through church ministry, and others through faithful friendship and support for others. What an honour to be used in such a way.[292]

In another example, 'Donald' gives the following testimony about his own experience as a single sex-attracted Christian in his article 'Radical Inclusion (Donald's Story)' on the True Freedom Trust website:

After I came out as gay in my all-boys boarding school when I was 15, no one would sit near me or associate with me for weeks. I was already uncomfortable about my gay feelings, and this added to a deep sense of shame. It didn't help when I was sent to see the house master, then the headmaster, and then the chaplain. They each asked sick-makingly embarrassing questions and told me "It was probably just a phase". Nobody told me I would be okay if it wasn't. Around that time, I was invited to the school Scripture Union group. I went because they offered cake. The leaders there welcomed me without asking any questions and their acceptance gave me a safe place to learn about Christ. I wrote to a local minister and his gracious letters told me the shame was not from God, and that although I had not chosen my sexuality, I had a choice about how to live my life. It took time to sink in but when, a year later, God led me to 1 Corinthians 6.9-11, I realised it meant that people like me could be included in the church. I felt the shame fall away, replaced by a profound sense

---

292 Sam Allberry, *Is God Anti-Gay?* Epsom: The Good Book Company, 2013, Kindle Edition. Loc. 538 & 549-558.

of Christ's love and acceptance. I became a Christian there and then, knowing that the cost would be singleness, but that God had given me a new hope.

When I went to university, I became afraid again of being exposed as gay and rejected by my Christian friends. When I was offered a place on the Christian Union leadership team, I felt I had to 'confess' my sexuality before I accepted. I was sure that "If they really knew who I was", they would realise they had made a terrible mistake thinking I was suitable. After several desperately awkward conversations, it turned out my fears were unfounded. Not only was I not rejected, but my friends celebrated the choices I had made about my sexuality. That small group of leaders was the first time I felt part of a Christian family, and 25 years later we are still in touch.

Over time, I learned that my identity is in Christ, and not to be defined by my sexuality. Slowly, it didn't feel threatening to be open with Christian friends, and their responses were consistently supportive and encouraging. At a new church in London, this time my pastor already knew about my sexuality when he asked me to serve on the leadership team. In seeing not my weaknesses, but Christ's grace at work in me, he 'put skin on' the acceptance I had found in Christ. His persistent determination to include unmarried people in all areas of church life is an example well worth following.

Around this time, most of my friends were pairing up and getting married, and I encountered a new fear, of being 'left behind' on my own. At times, it seemed the whole church was made up of happy couples producing children with alarming proficiency, and to be honest I felt left out. My pastor said it would help to join a fellowship group, but I was sceptical that that could replace a "real" family, and I signed up grudgingly. To my surprise, the leaders were the only couple there. Many others, like me, were single not exactly by choice but through circumstances. I realised I was not alone at all and we made for a warm and motley family. Psalm 68.6 says 'God sets the solitary in families', and indeed he does.

Later, I moved to Leeds for a new job and again I've settled into a small group of similarly non-standard-issue Christians who have become my family. Most of us live near an estate with its fair share of challenges. Our hope is to work with the community there, to be an example for Christ, and to grow God's family. I am not very good at this, but I am learning from those who do it better. We go to several different churches and work with some secular community organisations, so it can get a bit messy. We don't compromise on what the Bible teaches, but I think this willingness to tolerate a little untidiness, and to reach out to the least and the lost, is at the heart of what it is to be radically inclusive.[293]

It is true that the call to singleness can bring with it a great emotional burden of longing for sexual intimacy and family life for people with same-sex attraction, but this is equally true of single people attracted to members of the opposite sex. In either case Christians are not authorised to take this burden of singleness and sexual abstinence away by saying God does not require them to carry it.

What we can and should do, however, is to try to reduce the weight of the burden by providing loving friendship and emotional support.[294] Indeed, the Church should seek to learn from same-sex attracted people about the potential depths of Christian friendship independent of the assumption that intimacy is to be found primarily in an opposite sex relationship. There is plenty of scope to explore patterns of chaste intimacy within friendship as an alternative to the pursuit of same-sex marriage, taking into account the challenges and insights which constitutes experience of same-sex attraction.

As well as treating same-sex attracted people as human beings like everybody else, we should also be careful to avoid the false identification of godliness with heterosexuality. This point is immediately obvious when you stop to think about it. There are plenty of people who are same-sex attracted who lead godly lives and plenty of people who are attracted to the opposite sex who lead very ungodly lives. Indeed, as Shaw notes, there are same-sex attracted people who would say that learning to live with their same-sex attraction has helped them to become more godly people.[295] Godliness does not depend on the nature of your sexual attraction, but on the way you live your life in obedience to God in the face of that attraction. We should not assess a person's godliness by whether they are 'gay' or 'straight,' but by whether or not they are living lives that glorify God as married or single people.

Two points that flow from this are, first, that there is no reason why someone's same-sex attraction should be a bar to Christian ministry. This is because someone can be a 'wholesome pattern and example to the flock' as they live their life in the presence of same-sex attraction just as much as if they lived their life in the presence of opposite sex attraction.

---

293 'Radical Inclusion (Donald's Story)' at http://truefreedomtrust.co.uk/radical-inclusion-don-alds-story. See also the stories section at Living Out (http://www.livingout.org/stories) and Shaw, *The Plausibility Problem*.
294 Wainwright, op.cit. has useful material on this.
295 Ibid, pp.101-102.

Secondly, we should not see 'progress in Christ-likeness', as Shaw puts it, purely in terms of steps forward or backward in reshaping one's sexual orientation: 'To stake everything on one area of thought and behaviour is not a biblical approach to godliness.'[296] Although someone may legitimately choose to try to reduce their same-sex attraction if it is making it hard for them to live a godly life, and while there is plenty of evidence that changes in sexual attraction occur,[297] there is no promise in Scripture that God will take away the effects of the Fall this side of the kingdom. He often says, as he said to St Paul, 'My grace is sufficient for you, for my power is made perfect in weakness' (2 Corinthians 12:9). What ultimately counts is not a reduction of same-sex attraction but the grace of God always being available to help people live godly lives whatever their sexual attraction may be.

Living a life of love

One of the major arguments against opposition to same-sex marriages (and also to opposition to cohabitation) is that it involves a rejection of love. Christians, the argument goes, should be affirming rather than rejecting loving relationships.[298] However, as we have noted earlier in this study, love involves recognizing and valuing another person as they truly are and acting towards them accordingly.

In the case of same-sex relationships, as in the case of cohabitation, there is dual failure of love. This is because they involve either a failure to recognize that the other person is someone created by God and called by him to a live of chastity involving marriage with a member of the opposite sex or singleness, or a refusal to act upon this knowledge. They also involve a failure to love God since loving God means relating to him as God by living out the way of life he created you for and which he died and rose in Christ to make possible.

It might be argued in response that on the traditional Christian view of the matter God himself is being unloving in denying people the opportunity to experience love. However, as we saw in chapter six, even if people are called to a life of singleness this does not mean that they are prevented from experiencing love in the form of loving friendship. It is true that they are unable to experience sexual intercourse, but as St Paul put it in 2 Corinthians 4:17 'this slight momentary affliction is preparing for us a weight of glory beyond all comparison.' As we saw in

296 Ibid, p.103.
297 The most authoritative study is Stanton Jones and Mark A. Yarhouse, *Ex-Gays? A Longitudinal Study of Religiously Mediated Change in Sexual Orientation* (Downers Grove, IL: IVP Academic, 2007). See also the material available on the Core Issues Trust website at https://www.core-issues.org/.
298 For this argument see, for instance, Andrew Davison (ed), *Amazing Love*, London: Darton, Longman and Todd, 2016.

chapter four, sex in this world is just a pale shadow of the reality of intimacy and communion which God has prepared for us in the marriage that awaits us in the life to come and those who live rightly before God in this world (by, among other things, living lives of chastity) will experience this reality for ever.

Questions for discussion

1. How and why did the Early Church challenge the sexual double standard of Greco-Roman culture?

2. What is chastity and why is it so difficult?

3. How should Christians view the various forms of extra-marital sexual activity surveyed in this chapter and how should they seek to help those involved in them?

CHAPTER 9

Divorce and re-marriage

''For this reason a man shall leave his father and mother and be joined to his wife, and the two shall become one flesh'...So they are no longer two but one flesh. What therefore God has joined together, let not man put asunder'
(Matthew 19: 5-6).

The prevalence of divorce

As we have seen in the course of this study, God created marriage to be a permanent relationship. However, in this country a very large number of marriages are not permanent. According to the most recent figures on the issue from the Office of National Statistics, 42% of marriages in the United Kingdom now end in divorce.[299] Although this means that the rate of divorce has fallen to levels last seen in 1975, it still means that that thousands of marriages in this country end in divorce each year, which in turn means that almost everyone will have some personal experience of the painful effects of divorce, either because it has happened to them personally, or because it has happened to people in their family or in their circle of friends.

Is the Church of England inconsistent on marriage?

In the face of the growth of divorce since the end of the Second World War the Church of England has changed its position from saying that marriage is indissoluble and re-marriage in church after divorce is therefore impossible, to saying that marriages can die and that when they do re-marriage in church is permissible.

This change of position raises the charge that the Church of England is inconsistent in its approach to marriage. It does not permit the marriage of same-sex couples in church because it believes that marriage is between two people of the opposite sex. However, even though it believes that marriage is meant to be for

---

299 *Marriage Foundation, 'Divorce Rates back at 1975 levels,'* http://marriagefoundation.org.uk/wp-content/uploads/2016/09/NEW-MF-briefing-note-Divorce-stats-for-2014.pdf

life, it nevertheless allows the re-marriage of people who are divorced and who have a former spouse still living.

Even if it were true that the Church of England ought not to permit the re-marriage of people who are divorced and whose former spouse is still living, that would be a very weak argument for allowing same-sex marriage. The fact that it should not allow re-marriage after divorce would not mean that it should allow marriage between two people of the same sex. Nevertheless, it does highlight a genuine issue: why does the Church of England allow re-marriage of divorcees when God has ordained marriage to be a life-long union? Is it right for the Church of England, or indeed any Christian Church, to hold that marriage can end, and that the re-marriage of divorcees in church of people should be permitted? If so, under what circumstances?

How has the Church of England's position changed?

Reflecting a tradition in the Western Church going back to the early Middle Ages the Roman Catholic Church holds that a sacramental marriage, that is, a marriage validly entered into by two baptised Christians, is indissoluble. It is a union that can only be ended by the death of one or both spouses.[300]

> This is set out in the *Catechism of the Catholic Church*. Paragraph 1614 declares:

> In his preaching Jesus unequivocally taught the original meaning of the union of man and woman as the Creator willed it from the beginning: permission given by Moses to divorce one's wife was a concession to the hardness of hearts. The matrimonial union of man and woman is indissoluble: God himself has determined it 'what therefore God has joined together, let no man put asunder.'[301]

> Paragraph 1640 goes on to say:

> ...*the marriage bond* has been established by God himself in such a way that a marriage concluded and consummated between baptized persons can never be dissolved. This bond, which results from the free human act of the spouses and their consummation of the marriage, is a reality, henceforth irrevocable, and gives rise to a covenant guaranteed by God's fidelity. The Church does not have the power to contravene this disposition of divine wisdom.[302]

---

300 Marriages involving people who are not baptised, so called 'natural marriages' are, however, viewed as dissoluble, but only in the very specific circumstance when to do so would support the maintenance of the Christian faith by a Christian spouse in line with 1 Corinthians 7:15.
301 *Catechism of the Catholic Church*, pp. 361-362.
302 Ibid, p. 367. Italics in the original.

Up until the Reformation the Church of England shared the Western view that marriage was indissoluble and it therefore made no provision for divorce.

The English Reformers moved away from the indissolubilist position, however. They embraced instead the view that had always been held in the Eastern Church that divorce, and re-marriage after divorce, should be permitted in some circumstances. This shift was reflected in the *Reformatio Legum Ecclesiasticarum*, the proposed code of Canon Law drawn up during the reign of Edward VI. It would have allowed divorce and the re-marriage of the innocent party in cases of adultery, desertion, 'deadly hostility' and prolonged ill-treatment of a wife by a husband.[303] This code was never adopted, however, and the Church of England's Canons of 1597 and 1604 provided only for the annulment of 'pretended marriages' and for divorce *mensa et thoro* (of table and hearth) on the grounds of adultery and desertion. This latter provision was a legal separation of a married couple that could only take place if they gave a definite pledge not to marry again, which meant that English Church law had no need to offer a basis for the remarriage of those who had been divorced.

From the end of the seventeenth century divorces became possible through private Acts of Parliament. These had the effect of granting a dispensation from the law and when this took place re-marriage in church normally followed. However, this was very rare. Only 317 of these private Acts were passed between 1670 and 1857, an average of less than two a year.

In 1857 the *Matrimonial Causes Act* transferred jurisdiction in matrimonial matters from the Church to the secular courts. Rather than requiring private Acts of Parliament for divorce, divorce and re-marriage were permitted on the grounds of adultery. The clergy were not compelled to marry those who had been divorced, but they did have to make their churches available for such marriages to take place. This changed under the *Matrimonial Causes Acts* of 1937 and 1965, both of which exempted Church of England clergy both from having to perform a marriage in a case where a former spouse was still living and also from having to make their churches available for this purpose. Section 8.2 of the latter, which remains the current law on the subject states:

No clergyman of the Church of England or a clerk in orders, shall be compelled (a) to solemnise the marriage of any person whose former marriage has been dissolved and whose former spouse is still living or (b) to permit the

---

303 *The Reformatio Legum Ecclesiasticarum*, 10, in Gerald Bray (ed), *Tudor Church Reform*, Woodbridge: The Boydell Press/Church of England Record Society. 2005, pp. 265-279.

marriage of such a person to be solemnised in a church or chapel of which he is the minister.[304]

Although re-marriage in church had become legal, the Church of England and the Anglican Communion stood strongly against the practice from the end of the nineteenth century. In fact they returned to the position held prior to the Reformation that that marriage was indissoluble. Even if a marriage were ended legally by the state, the relationship established by God remained in place, and therefore remarriage during the lifetime of a former spouse could not be permitted.[305]

The Lambeth Conferences of 1908, 1930 and 1948 all passed resolutions against allowing remarriage.[306] In 1938 the Convocations of Canterbury and York (the meetings of the bishops and elected clergy of the Provinces of Canterbury and York) also passed resolutions against the practice, which were re-affirmed as an Act of Convocation by the Convocation of Canterbury in 1957. The 1957 Act of Convocation declared that 're-marriage after divorce during the lifetime of a former partner always involves a departure from the true principle of marriage as declared by Our Lord' and laid down that:

> in order to maintain the principle of lifelong marriage which is inherent in every legally contracted marriage and is expressed in the plainest terms in the Marriage Service, the Church should not allow the use of that service in the case of anyone who has a former partner still living.[307]

Although the decisions of the Convocations had very strong moral weight because they represented the mind of the Church, they were not legally binding. Some clergy continued to marry divorced people in church using the marriage service on the grounds of their freedom to do so under the *Matrimonial Causes Acts* which left the decision whether or not to re-marry people up to individual members of the clergy. [308]

From the 1960s opinion in the Church of England began to move away from the

---

304 *Matrimonial Causes Act 1965*, 8.2. Text at http://www.legislation.gov.uk/ukpga/1965/72.

305 For details see A R Winnet, *Divorce and Remarriage in Anglicanism*, London: Macmillan 1958.

306 Resolution 94 of 1948, for instance, declares 'that the marriage of one whose former partner is still living may not be celebrated according to the rites of the Church, unless it has been established that there was no marriage bond recognised by the Church.' (Roger Coleman (ed), *Resolutions of the Lambeth Conference 1867-1988*, Toronto: Anglican Book Centre, 1992, p.115).

307 Act of the Convocation of Canterbury 1957, Regulations Concerning Marriage and divorce 1.2 and 3 cited in *Marriage in Church after Divorce*, London: CHP, 2000, p.62.

308 In 1996, for example 10% of all marriages in Anglican churches in England and Wales were remarriages (*Marriage in Church after Divorce*, pp.21-22).

indissolubilist view towards permitting the remarriage in church of those whose former spouses were still living. In 1981 the General Synod passed a motion that declared that while 'marriage should be undertaken as a lifelong commitment' it considered nonetheless that 'there are circumstances in which a divorced person may be married in church during the lifetime of a former partner.' After extensive further debate the matter was finally resolved by a resolution of General Synod in July 2002. It rescinded the Convocation resolutions and the Act of Convocation, declaring

That this Synod

a) Affirm in accordance with the doctrine of the Church of England as set out in Canon B30, that marriage should always be undertaken as a solemn, public and life-long covenant between a man and a woman";

b) Recognize –

   i) That some marriages regrettably do fail and that the Church's care for couples in that situation should be of paramount importance; and

   ii) That there are exceptional circumstances in which a divorced person may be married in church during the lifetime of a former spouse;

c) Recognize that the decision as to whether or not to solemnize such a marriage in church after divorce rests with the minister (or officiating cleric if the minister is prepared to allow his/her church or chapel to be used for the marriage) and;

d) Invite the House of Bishops to issue the advice contained in Annex 1 of GS 1449.

The material contained in the General Synod document 1449, which was subsequently issued by the House of Bishops, was described as 'advice' because it was held that the personal discretion given to the clergy under the Matrimonial Causes Act of 1965 was absolute and they therefore could not be directed to re-marry or not re-marry anyone. Under this advice the clergy are invited to bear in mind the following questions when deciding whether to permit re-marriage in church:

(a) Do the applicants have a clear understanding of the meaning and purpose of marriage?

(b) Do the applicants have a mature view of the circumstances of the breakdown of the previous marriage and are they ready to enter wholeheartedly and responsibly into a new relationship?

c) Has there been sufficient healing of the personal and social wounds of marriage breakdown?

d) Would the effects of the proposed marriage on individuals, the wider community and the Church be such as to undermine the credibility of the Church's witness to marriage?

e) Would permitting the new marriage be tantamount to consecrating an old infidelity?

f) Has either of the parties been divorced more than once? In the case of multiple divorces, the sheer complexity of relationships that may have developed will inevitably make any assessment by you more difficult. However, the Church witnesses to lifelong marriage, and should not find itself being a party to 'serial monogamy', hence neither of the parties should normally have been married and divorced more than once.

g) Do the applicants display a readiness to explore the significance of the Christian faith for their lives so that their further marriage is not an isolated contact with the Church?'

The clergy are also advised to consult with the parish, their local Anglican clergy and with ecumenical partners in cases where a Local Ecumenical Partnership is in operation.

In cases where is not felt appropriate to permit re-marriage in church or in other circumstances where a previous civil marriage has taken place, the clergy can make use of 'An Order for Prayer and Dedication after a Civil Marriage' which is a service 'in which the couple-already married—wish to dedicate to God their life together.[309]

A significant feature of the Church of England's thinking since the 1960s has been the replacement of a distinction between guilty and innocent parties in divorce with an emphasis simply on the fact that a marriage can be seen to have failed. There are two reasons for this change. The first is the perception that 'it is unwise and may also be uncharitable, for those outside the marriage to attempt to say precisely where the fault lies in any case.'[310] The second is the perception that what really brings a marriage to an end is not simply the performance of certain specific acts (such as acts of adultery) but the fact that the couple involved are no longer able, for whatever reason, to fulfil their marriage vows by providing each other

---

309 For this service see *Common Worship Pastoral Services*, London: CHP 2000, pp.173-183.
310 *Marriage*, p.16.

with a relationship of 'mutual society, help and comfort.' At the heart of marriage is a relationship of love and when this dies then the marriage dies with it, even if it still exists formally.[311]

This is the Church of England's current position with regard to divorce and re-marriage. Like the Roman Catholic Church, it holds that 'marriage is in its nature a union permanent and life-long, for better or worse, till death them do part,' as Canon B30 puts it. However, unlike the Roman Catholic Church, it also holds that 'some marriages do fail', that divorce is then possible and there are circumstances in which it may be judged right to allow a divorced person to marry in church even while their former spouse is still alive.

What are we to make of the contrasting positions taken by the Roman Catholic Church and the Church of England? To answer this question we shall look in turn at what the Old and New Testaments have to say about divorce.

What does the Old Testament say?

Genesis 2:24

The relationship ordained by God in Genesis 2:24 is a permanent union. As we saw in chapter three, the word used to describe this union is the same word used to describe the permanent bond between God and Israel. Just as God is in a permanent and unbreakable covenant with his people, so also he has ordained that marriage should be a permanent and unbreakable union between one man and one woman.

Malachi 2:13-16

In Malachi 2:13-16 we read that God is opposed to divorce:

> And this again you do. You cover the Lord's altar with tears, with weeping and groaning because he no longer regards the offering or accepts it with favour at your hand. You ask, 'Why does he not?' Because the Lord was witness to the covenant between you and the wife of your youth, to whom you have been faithless, though she is your companion and your wife by covenant. Has not the one God made and sustained for us the spirit of life? And what does he desire? Godly offspring. So take heed to yourselves, and let none be faithless to the wife of his youth. 'For I hate divorce, says the Lord the God of Israel, and covering one's garment with violence, says the Lord of hosts. So take heed to yourselves and do not be faithless.'

These verses tell us that God regards divorce so seriously that he will not accept

---

311 For this latter point see *Putting Asunder*, London: SPCK 1966, pp. 33-62 and *Marriage and the Church's' Task*, pp. 123-135.

the sacrificial offerings of the men of Israel who have divorced their wives. Elizabeth Achtemeier comments that:

> Israelites married very early, before the age of twenty, and therefore verse 14 speaks of 'the wife of your youth' (cf. Prov. 2:17). The thought is that these men have spent years of mutual companionship with their spouses—building their homes, raising their children, facing life vicissitudes together—and then they have abandoned their wives for the sake of other women. It is little wonder that the act is called 'violence' (v.16), for it violently injures the well-being, the dreams, the securities of all involved. (The reference to the 'garment' is the man's symbolic act of spreading his garment over the woman as a sign of his choice of her, cf. Ruth 3:9; Ezek. 16:8). Malachi knows all about the desolation that accompanies the breakup of a family.
>
> He is also certain about God's attitude: The Lord hates divorce. It is an attitude that God never gets over, according to the Bible, and yet it is a fact rarely considered by divorcing persons. Usually they ask all the wrong questions. When a couple is considering a separation they are likely to ask, 'Will I be happier?' 'Can I make it on my own?' 'Will it be better for the children?' rather than 'What is God's attitude to the dissolution of this marriage?' Here in this prophetic torah, as the 'messenger of the Lord of Hosts' (2:7), the prophet Malachi furnishes the reply.'[312]

Deuteronomy 24:1-4

Although the Bible thus tells us that God hates divorce, it also recognises that divorce occurs and seeks to limit the damage it causes by regulating it. We can see this in Deuteronomy 24:1-4, which is the key piece of legislation in the Law of Moses regarding the matter since it is the only Old Testament passage that sets out the grounds, procedure, and consequences of divorce.

Deuteronomy 24:1-4 runs as follow:

> When a man takes a wife and marries her, if then she finds no favour in his eyes because he has found some indecency in her, and he writes her a bill of divorce and puts it in her hand and sends her out of his house, and she departs out of his house, and if she goes and becomes another man's wife, and the latter husband dislikes her and writes her a bill of divorce and puts it in her hand and sends her out of his house, or if the latter husband dies, who took her to be his wife, then her former husband, who sent her away,

---

312 Elizabeth Achtemeier, *Nahum-Malachi*, Atlanta: John Knox Press, 1986, pp.182-183.

may not take her again to be his wife, after she has been defiled; for that is an abomination before the LORD, and you shall not bring guilt upon the land which the LORD your God gives you for an inheritance.

John Stott notes that this passage 'neither requires, nor recommends, nor even sanctions divorce.'[313] In technical terms it consists of a *protasis*, or description of conditions, in verses 1-3 and then in verse 4 an *apodosis*, a command that comes into play if these conditions are met. 'If this, then that.'[314] God is not saying that the conditions in verses 1-3 must or should happen, only what must follow if they do.

As Stott says,

The law is not approving divorce; what it is saying is that if a man divorces his wife, and if he gives her a certificate, and if she leaves and remarries, and if her second husband dislikes and divorces her, or dies, then her first husband may not marry her again.[315]

The grounds for divorce referred to in this passage are that a husband finds 'some indecency' in his wife. What this might mean has been widely debated by ancient and modern scholars, but it seems most probable that it refers to some kind of immodest or indecent behaviour which nevertheless fell short of illicit sexual intercourse.[316] If a man divorces his wife on these grounds, the passage says, he then causes her to become 'defiled' (v4) if she marries another man.[317] As Peter Craigie explains, 'the sense is that the woman's remarriage after the first divorce is similar to adultery in that the woman cohabits with another man.'[318] Having caused her to become defiled in this way her husband cannot then marry her again because, to quote Craigie again:

If the woman were then to marry her first husband, after divorcing the second, the analogy with adultery would become even more complete; the woman lives first with one man, then another, and the, finally returns to the first.[319]

This kind of serial quasi-adultery is immoral conduct that will defile the land God is giving to his people. For this reason it is forbidden.

---

313 John Stott, *Issues Facing Christians Today*, Basingstoke: Marshalls, 1984, p.262.
314 See John Murray, *Divorce*, Philadelphia: Prebyterian and Reformed Publishing Company, 1976, pp. 3-8.
315 Stott, *Issues Facing Christians Today*, pp.262-263.
316 S R Driver, *A Critical and Exegetical Commentary on Deuteronomy*, New York: Charles Scribner's Sons, 1902, p.271.
317 The literal translation of the Hebrew is that the woman 'has been caused to defile herself' as a result of the action of her first husband.
318 Peter Craigie, *The Book of Deuteronomy*, Grand Rapids: Eerdmans, 1976, p.305.
319 Ibid, p.305.

The primary purpose of this piece of Mosaic legislation is, as Chris Wright puts it, to stop a woman being 'a kind of marital football, passed back and forth between irresponsible men,'[320] but, as Davidson observes, it also points to the truth highlighted in Malachi 2:16 that divorce is contrary to God's will even when there are grounds for it in the behaviour of a spouse:

> …within the legislation is an internal indicator that such divorce brings about a state tantamount to adultery and therefore ultimately is not in harmony with the divine will. Though not illegal, it is not morally pleasing to God. Already in 24:4 it is indicated that breaking the marriage bond on grounds that are less than illicit sexual intercourse causes the woman to defile herself, that is, commit what is tantamount to adultery. By providing an internal indicator of divine disapproval of divorce, the legislation is pointing back to God's Edenic ideal for permanency in marriage. God's concession to less than ideal situations did not supplant the divine intention set out in Gen 2:24.[321]

Exodus 21:10-11

Exodus 21:10-11 is sometimes cited as another piece of legislation relating to divorce and is seen as showing that divorce is permissible if someone deprives their spouse of food, clothing or other marital rights. However, these verses have to do with the very specific situation of a slave taken as a wife who is then neglected when her husband marries a second wife. In this situation the solution laid down is not divorce, but freedom from slavery. As Doherty says, they thus do not provide 'a general rule for divorce in monogamous marriages.'[322]

What does Jesus say?

Deuteronomy 24:1-4 forms part of the background to Jesus' teaching about divorce. All Jewish schools of thought at the time of Jesus agreed that 'adultery automatically annuls a marriage by creating a new sexual union in its place.'[323] For this reason Jewish law demanded the termination of a marriage if either premarital un-chastity or subsequent adultery was discovered (which is what lies behind Matthew 1:18-19).[324]

---

320 Chris Wright, *Deuteronomy*, Peabody: Hendrickson, 1996, p.255.
321 Davidson, p.397.
322 Doherty, op. cit. p.103. As Davidson argues (op, cit. pp. 191-193) a good argument can also be made that the slave girl in question is not in fact married to her master, which would make the passage even less relevant. The irrelevance of Exodus 21:10-11 undermines the argument of David Instone-Brewer in his book *Divorce and Remarriage* (Milton Keynes: Paternoster, 2011) that the teaching of these verses means that divorce is permissible if there is failure to provide food, clothing, or marital love as well as in cases of infidelity.
323 France, op. cit. p. 123.
324 The Babylonian Talmud, Mishnah *Yebamoth* 2:8, *Sotah* 5:1)

It was also agreed on the basis of Exodus 21:10-11 that divorce could take place if either a husband or wife refused food, clothing or conjugal love.

There was disagreement, however, on how to interpret the meaning of Deuteronomy 24:1, which was understood as a command of God through Moses governing the grounds of divorce. The Rabbinic schools of Shammai and Hillel both agreed that divorce could only rightly happen if a husband found 'some indecency' in his wife, but what did 'some indecency' mean? The school of Shammai held that it referred to some form of sexual offence falling short of adultery. The school of Hillel, on the other hand, held that it could include anything that caused a husband to be displeased with his wife, including burning his dinner, being quarrelsome, or even the husband losing interest in her because he came across another woman who was more beautiful. In fact, for the school of Hillel, 'anything that caused annoyance or embarrassment to a husband was a legitimate ground for a divorce suit.'[325]

In Matthew 5:31-32 and 19:1-9 Jesus addresses the issue in light of this existing Jewish discussion:

'It was also said, 'Whoever divorces his wife, let him give her a certificate of divorce.' But I say to you that everyone who divorces his wife, except on the ground of unchastity, makes her an adulteress; and whoever marries a divorced woman commits adultery. (Matthew 5:31-32)

Now when Jesus had finished these sayings, he went away from Galilee and entered the region of Judea beyond the Jordan; and large crowds followed him, and he healed them there. And Pharisees came up to him and tested him by asking, 'Is it lawful to divorce one's wife for any cause?' He answered, 'Have you not read that he who made them from the beginning made them male and female, and said, 'For this reason a man shall leave his father and mother and be joined to his wife, and the two shall become one flesh'? So they are no longer two but one flesh. What therefore God has joined together, let not man put asunder.' They said to him, 'Why then did Moses command one to give a certificate of divorce, and to put her away?' He said to them, 'For your hardness of heart Moses allowed you to divorce your wives, but from the beginning it was not so. And I say to you: whoever divorces his wife, except for unchastity, and marries another, commits adultery.' (Matthew 19:1-9)

In these passages Jesus makes four points:

---

325 William L Lane, *The Gospel of Mark*, Grand Rapids and London: Eerdmans/Marshall, Morgan and Scott, 1974, p.363.

1. First, he teaches that according to Genesis 2:24 those who are married are joined together by God and it is not right for human beings to dissolve this union: 'What therefore God has joined together, let not man put asunder' (Matthew 19:6).

2. Secondly, following the internal indications in Deuteronomy 24:1-4 that we noted above (and in line with Malachi 2:16), Jesus teaches that even the permission for divorce granted in Deuteronomy is only a divine concession to human sinfulness (Matthew 19:8).

3. Thirdly, developing the implications of the teaching of Deuteronomy 24 about the 'defilement' of the divorced wife who re-marries, he teaches that all forms of divorce and re-marriage result not just in defilement , but adultery since they substitute a new sexual union for the union created by God (Matthew 5:31-32, 19:9).

4. Fourthly, he teaches that the only ground on which divorce is permitted is not the refusal of food, clothing, or conjugal love, or the existence of something in the wife displeasing to the husband, or immodesty or indecent behaviour, but solely sexual intercourse outside the marital union (porneia, 'unchastity' Matthew 19:9). This fourth point is not explicitly made in the record of Jesus' teaching in Mark 10:9-12 and Luke 16:18, but it is implicit in these other texts since any Jewish hearer or reader would have accepted that adultery was a legitimate ground for divorce unless this idea was explicitly ruled out. What Mark 10:12 does imply, however, which Matthew 19:9 does not, is that a wife can divorce her husband as well as a husband his wife.

If we ask how the permission for divorce in Matthew 19:9 fits into Jesus' overall teaching about marriage the answer is helpfully given by Don Carson in his commentary on Matthew. He writes:

> ...sexual sin has a peculiar relation to Jesus' treatment of Genesis 1:27; 2:24 (in Matthew 19:4-6), because the indissolubility of marriage he defends by appealing to those verses from the creation accounts is predicated on sexual union ('one flesh'). Sexual promiscuity is therefore a de facto exception. It may not necessitate divorce; but permission for divorce and remarriage under such circumstances, far from being inconsistent with Jesus' thought, is in perfect harmony with it.[326]

Carson's point that Matthew 19:9 does not necessitate divorce needs to be

---

326 Don Carson, 'Matthew,' in Tremper Longman III and David E Garland (eds), *Expositors Bible Commentary*, vol.9, Grand Rapids: Zondervan, 2010, p.417.

emphasised. As Stott observes, 'Jesus did not teach that the innocent party *must* divorce an unfaithful partner, still less that marital unfaithfulness *ipso facto* dissolves the marriage.' Indeed, Jesus 'did not even encourage or recommend divorce for unfaithfulness... Jesus' purpose was not to encourage divorce for this reason, but to forbid it for every other reason.'[327]

Importantly, Matthew 19:9 permits not only divorce but also remarriage. One tradition of interpretation has held that because the marital union created by God is indissoluble Jesus meant that separation was permissible following adultery, but not re-marriage. However, in the words of Doherty:

> Matthew 19:9 describes remarriage after divorce as adultery except when it follows sexual immorality. The implication is that remarriage after sexual immorality is not adultery, which must mean that the original marriage is truly ended. But most importantly, in Jesus's context, divorce meant by definition that you could marry again. The Jewish divorce certificate said simply, 'You are free to marry any [Jewish] man you wish.' By permitting divorce after adultery, Jesus permitted remarriage too.328

What does St Paul say?

In 1 Corinthians 7:10-16 St Paul begins by quoting the general teaching of Jesus as preserved for us in the Gospels that a wife should not divorce her husband or a husband his wife ('separate' in v.10 means 'divorce.').[329] He then considers an issue which never came up during Jesus' earthly ministry, namely what should happen when a Christian has a spouse who is an unbeliever and that spouse initiates a divorce:

> To the married I give charge, not I but the Lord, that the wife should not separate from her husband (but if she does, let her remain single or else be reconciled to her husband)—and that the husband should not divorce his wife. To the rest I say, not the Lord, that if any brother has a wife who is an unbeliever, and she consents to live with him, he should not divorce her. If any woman has a husband who is an unbeliever, and he consents to live with her, she should not divorce him. For the unbelieving husband is consecrated through his wife, and the unbelieving wife is consecrated through her husband. Otherwise, your children would be unclean, but as

---

327 Stott, *Issues Facing Christian Today*, p.267.
328 Doherty, op.cit, pp. 113-114. For a detailed presentation of the case that Matthew 19:9 permits re-marriage see Murray, op.cit. pp. 33- 43.
329 For the fact that St Paul is drawing on the teaching of Jesus see David Wenham, *Did St Paul Get Jesus Right?*, Oxford: Lion, 2010, pp. 56-6o.

it is they are holy. But if the unbelieving partner desires to separate, let it be so; in such a case the brother or sister is not bound. For God has called us to peace. Wife, how do you know whether you will save your husband? Husband, how do you know whether you will save your wife?

Speaking with the authority of an Apostle,[330] Paul declares that in this situation, 'a Christian should not initiate separation just because they are married to a non-Christian. But if the non-Christian leaves, let them, so that you can live 'at peace' with others. You don't need to try to make them stay. When a non-Christian divorces a Christian, the Christian is 'not enslaved' (v.15).'[331] As Doherty says:

> ...the phrase, 'not enslaved' in 1 Corinthians 7:15 must mean 'free to remarry.' Under Roman law, you obtained the freedom to remarry simply by separating from your previous spouse. This is corroborated by the fact that Paul uses the same word in verses 27 and 39 to say wife and husband are 'bound' together, which he contrasts with being 'free' to marry (see also Rom.7:2-3). Not being bound means being able to marry.[332]

Three principles unite the grounds on which Jesus and Paul allow divorce and remarriage:

1. Both sexual immorality and abandonment by an unbelieving spouse violate one of the two fundamental components of marriage (either the 'leaving and the cleaving' or the 'one flesh' unity).

2. Both sexual immorality and abandonment leave one party without any other option if attempts at reconciliation are spurned.

3. In both cases divorce is therefore a last resort and an admission of defeat.[333]

How should Christians respond to divorce and re-marriage?
Overall the Bible tells us that:

- God intends marriage to be for life. 'His intention was and is that human sexuality will find fulfilment in marriage, and that marriage will be an exclusive, loving and lifelong union.'[334]

---

330 Stott, *Issues facing Christians Today*, p.269.
331 Doherty, op. cit. p.112.
332 Ibid, p. 114. For a detailed study of 1 Corinthians 7:10-16 and why verse 15 allows remarriage see Murray, op cit. ch.3.
333 For these points see Craig Blomberg, *Matthew*, Nashville: Broadman and Holman, 1992, p. 293.
334 Stott, *Issues Facing Christians Today*, p.271.

- Divorce is never either commanded or commended in Scripture. Even when it can be justified 'it remains a sad and sinful declension from the divine ideal'.[335]

- Under the New Testament dispensation there are two legitimate grounds for divorce: (a) when the marital union is broken by extra-marital sexual intercourse, and (b) when a Christian is deserted by their unbelieving spouse.

- When divorce takes place on these grounds then re-marriage can be legitimate.[336]

- Re-marriage in all other circumstances constitutes adultery. In a situation of domestic violence or abuse separation from the perpetrator is justified (and indeed can be argued to be required if there is danger to a spouse or any children involved), but this does not mean that divorce is justified except on the grounds noted above. We are not authorised to exceed the limits for divorce which God has laid down in Scripture.

What all this means is that two opposite positions go against what God has revealed to us and are therefore to be rejected. The first is the Roman Catholic position that says a marriage validly entered into between Christians can never be ended. Although this does allow a marriage between a Christian and a non-Christian to be ended in line with St Paul's teaching in 1 Corinthians 7:15, it goes against the teaching of Jesus in Matthew 19:9 by not allowing for the possibility of ending a marriage between Christians in the case of adultery.

If the Roman Catholic position is too restrictive, then the Church of England position is not restrictive enough. While the Church of England has correctly moved away from an absolute indissolubilist position, it now permits divorce and remarriage on the general ground that the relationship of love in a marriage has died, rather than on the specific biblical grounds that there has been an act of adultery or that a Christian believer has been rejected by their non-Christian spouse.

So, how should Christians act in a way that will 'glorify God in your body' in this area? In general terms we need to bear witness through both teaching and example to what God has laid down concerning marriage and divorce. As Andrew Cornes writes,

---

335 Ibid. p.271.

336 It is sometimes argued that the witness of the Early Fathers shows that the early Church viewed the teaching of the New Testament as prohibiting re-marriage after divorce. However, if we look at the teaching of the earliest Fathers, while they do generally reject the remarriage of wives and guilty male spouses they do not reject all remarriage after divorce in principle (see William Luck, *Divorce and Remarriage*, Biblical Studies Press, 2013 Appendix F). Furthermore, while we need to take their witness seriously it has to be compared with the witness of the Bible itself and set aside if it contradicts it.

Both are necessary. Teaching without example is hollow. If a church teaches about the lifelong nature of marriage, but its members are divorcing in large numbers and its leadership is doing nothing to help marriages in difficulty nor to discipline those who separate contrary to the will of Christ, then that church will have no impact on the attitudes to marriage of the society around it. And example without teaching is ineffective. If a church has a membership whose marriages are largely stable and yet never speaks of Christ's command to man and wife not to separate nor his power to sustain even difficult marriages, society will simply imagine that Christians happen to have good marriages but will remain unaware that Christ's teaching is radically different from their own presuppositions. Teaching and example must therefore be kept together in every church's witness.[337]

In more specific terms we need to:

- Accept and teach that God has ordained that marriage should be for life and that, even when permitted, divorce and re-marriage are a departure from God's intention for his human creatures.

- Practice the Christian calling to exercise forgiveness and seek reconciliation when marriage gets difficult ('Let all bitterness and wrath and anger and clamour and slander be put away from you, with all malice, and be kind to one another, tender hearted, forgiving one another, as God in Christ forgave you', Ephesians 4:31-32) and encourage and support others to do the same. Exercising forgiveness and seeking reconciliation can be extraordinarily hard to do in a marriage that has gone wrong, but it nonetheless needs to be done as part of the pattern of dying to self and living for God which we have seen to be fundamental to what it means to live as a Christian.

- Separate from an abusive spouse if our wellbeing and those of our children requires it, and encourage others to the same, but seek reconciliation if possible and only divorce on the grounds laid down in Scripture.

- Only divorce if the conditions in Matthew 19:9 and 1 Corinthians 7:15 are met through a spouse being adulterous, or an unbelieving spouse wanting a divorce, and then only if there is no realistic possibility of reconciliation.

- When divorced, live a godly life as a single person with the requirement for sexual abstinence that this involves.

---

337 Andrew Cornes, *Divorce and Remarriage*, Tain: Christian Focus, 2012, Kindle edition, Loc.7360. Cornes himself holds that marriage is absolutely indissoluble in all circumstances, but what he says in this passage also applies in the case of the position taken in this chapter.

- Provide friendship and support to those who are single as a result of divorce, particularly when they are facing the challenges of being a single parent.

- Only re-marry if we are free to do so because our former spouse committed adultery before the divorce or has subsequently sundered the marriage bond by entering into a new sexual relationship,[338] or because we have been divorced by a non-Christian spouse.

- Only re-marry in church people who are free to marry under these conditions.

Where re-marriage is possible it still signifies a departure from God's intention that the first marriage of one or both new spouses should have been life-long. There therefore needs to be some way of marking this truth liturgically.

Since neither the *Book of Common Prayer* nor the *Common Worship* rites make provision for this, one way of doing this might be to only allow a service of Prayer and Dedication after a Civil Marriage and to explain to the couple involved the reason for not holding an actual marriage service. What it is not legitimate to do, of course, is to use a service of Prayer and Dedication to bless a new relationship that is in fact adulterous because it exceeds the limits laid down in Matthew 19:9 and 1 Corinthians 7:15.

Finally, should the Church ordain people who are divorced and/or re-married? The requirement in 1 Timothy 3:2 and 12 and Titus 1:6 that those who are ordained should be 'the husband of one wife' means that the person in question should be sexually faithful within marriage. It does not address directly the question of those who are re-married either after divorce or after the death of their spouse. However, the requirement does point to the need for those who are ordained to live in a way that bears public witness to God's standards for marriage. The question that needs to be asked is how 'the concern that the church's leaders live exemplary married lives'[339] should be reflected in our twenty-first century culture? If even the clergy are allowed to divorce and re-marry, this could reinforce the perception that the Church is not really serious about the lifelong nature of marriage. As Cornes says, teaching without example is hollow.

---

338 If adultery makes divorce permissible because it sunders the one flesh marital union then by extension this would be true of a sexual relationship following a divorce. If the marital union was not broken before the divorce it would be at this point.
339 Gordon Fee, *1 and 2 Timothy, Titus*, Peabody: Hendrickson, 1995, p. 81.

Questions for discussion

1. How would you summarise the different positions regarding divorce taken by the Roman Catholic Church and the Church of England?

2. How do these two positions match up to what the Bible has to say about divorce?

3. Is it right for people to divorce and remarry and is it right to remarry divorced people in church?

CHAPTER 10

Birth control and infertility treatment

'And Elkanah knew Hannah his wife, and the Lord remembered her; and in due time Hannah conceived and bore a son, and she called his name Samuel, for she said, 'I have asked him of the Lord.'' (1 Samuel 1: 19-20)

Be fruitful and multiply

Being called to live as people made in God's image and likeness involves obedience to the divine command in Genesis 1:28: 'Be fruitful and multiply, and fill the earth and subdue it; and have dominion over the fish of the sea and over the birds of the air and over every living thing that moves upon the earth.' We saw in chapter three that God created marriage to be the context in which this calling is to be fulfilled by means of sexual intercourse between a husband and wife.

In this chapter we will consider two issues related to the fulfilment of this command. The first is the issue of birth control, that is to say, the issue of whether, and, if so, how, to limit the number of children produced through sexual intercourse. The second is the issue of infertility, more specifically the question of what action can legitimately be taken when it is difficult or impossible to produce children as a result of sexual intercourse.

What did the Church traditionally teach about birth control?

From the time of the Fathers the Church has traditionally taught that avoiding the birth of children through the deliberate prevention of conception is sinful. In *On Marriage and Concupiscence* St Augustine criticises those who engage in sexual intercourse but seek to avoid having children, arguing that such behaviour means that they should no longer be considered husband and wife:

> It is, however, one thing for married persons to have intercourse only for the wish to beget children, which is not sinful: it is another thing for them to de-

sire carnal pleasure in cohabitation, but with the spouse only, which involves venial sin. For although propagation of offspring is not the motive of the intercourse, there is still no attempt to prevent such propagation, either by wrong desire or evil appliance. They who resort to these, although called by the name of spouses, are really not such; they retain no vestige of true matrimony, but pretend the honourable designation as a cloak for criminal conduct. Having also proceeded so far, they are betrayed into exposing their children, which are born against their will. They hate to nourish and retain those whom they were afraid they would beget. This infliction of cruelty on their offspring so reluctantly begotten, unmasks the sin which they had practised in darkness, and drags it clearly into the light of day. The open cruelty reproves the concealed sin. Sometimes, indeed, this lustful cruelty, or, if you please, cruel lust, resorts to such extravagant methods as to use poisonous drugs to secure barrenness; or else, if unsuccessful in this, to destroy the conceived seed by some means previous to birth, preferring that its offspring should rather perish than receive vitality; or if it was advancing to life within the womb, should be slain before it was born. Well, if both parties alike are so flagitious, they are not husband and wife; and if such were their character from the beginning, they have not come together by wedlock but by debauchery. But if the two are not alike in such sin, I boldly declare either that the woman is, so to say, the husband's harlot; or the man the wife's adulterer.[340]

The Protestant Reformers followed Patristic and Medieval tradition in seeing the story of Onan in Genesis 38:7-11 as a specific biblical condemnation of contraception. John Calvin, in his commentary on Genesis, wrote about it:

It is a horrible thing to pour out seed besides the intercourse of man and woman. Deliberately avoiding the intercourse, so that the seed drops on the ground is doubly horrible. For this means that one quenches the hope of his family, and kills the son, which could be expected, before he is born. This wickedness is now as severely as is possible condemned by the Spirit, through Moses, that Onan, as it were, through a violent and untimely birth, tore away the seed of his bother out of the womb, and as cruel as shamefully has thrown on the earth. Moreover he thus has, as much as was in his power, tried to destroy a part of the human race. When a woman in some way drives away the seed out of the womb, though aids, this is rightly seen as an unfor-

---

giveable crime. Onan was guilty of a similar crime, by defiling the earth with his seed, so that Tamar would not receive a future inheritor.[341]

When did Protestant teaching change?

In the first half of the twentieth century non-Roman Catholic churches began to accept that it could be morally legitimate to use contraception. The shift was pioneered by the Anglican Communion. Whereas the Lambeth Conferences of Anglican bishops held in 1908 and 1920 had passed resolutions critical of the use of contraception, the Lambeth Conference of 1930 took a different position. Resolution 15 declared:

> Where there is clearly felt moral obligation to limit or avoid parenthood, the method must be decided on Christian principles. The primary and obvious method is complete abstinence from intercourse (as far as may be necessary) in a life of discipline and self-control lived in the power of the Holy Spirit. Nevertheless in those cases where there is such a clearly felt moral obligation to limit or avoid parenthood, and where there is a morally sound reason for avoiding complete abstinence, the Conference agrees that other methods may be used, provided that this is done in the light of the same Christian principles. The Conference records its strong condemnation of the use of any methods of conception control from motives of selfishness, luxury, or mere convenience.[342]

Where the Anglican Communion led, other non-Roman Catholic churches eventually followed. Today most Christian churches accept that the use of contraception is morally acceptable.

Why does the Roman Catholic Church oppose contraception?

Pope Pius XI responded to the Lambeth Resolution of 1930 in his encyclical *Casti Connubii* published later the same year. He notes the various reasons given for allowing the use of contraception and then responds that contraception must be rejected as being contrary to the natural order established by God:

> But no reason, however grave, may be put forward by which anything intrinsically against nature may become conformable to nature and morally good. Since, therefore, the conjugal act is destined primarily by nature for the begetting of children, those who in exercising it deliberately frustrate its natural power and purpose sin

---

341 *The Complete Biblical Commentary Collection of John Calvin*, Kindle Edition, Loc 20332.
342 Lambeth Conference 1930, Resolution 15, text in Coleman, op. cit. p. 72.

against nature and commit a deed which is shameful and intrinsically vicious.[343]

In a specific response to the Lambeth Resolution, the Pope reiterates Catholic teaching that 'any use whatsoever of matrimony exercised in such a way that the act is deliberately frustrated in its natural power to generate life is an offense against the law of God and of nature, and those who indulge in such are branded with the guilt of a grave sin.'[344]

In the 1960s some people both inside and outside the Roman Catholic Church thought it might move towards the acceptance of contraception as part of the development of the church's teaching and practice following on from the Second Vatican Council, but in 1968 Pope Paul VI restated the Church's opposition. The teaching contained in his encyclical *Humanae Vitae* remains the official Catholic position to this day. In this encyclical the Pope declares that husbands and wives:

> …are not free to act as they choose in the service of transmitting life, as if it were wholly up to them to decide what is the right course to follow. On the contrary, they are bound to ensure that what they do corresponds to the will of God the Creator.[345]

He acknowledges that experience shows:

> … that new life is not the result of each and every act of sexual intercourse. God has wisely ordered laws of nature and the incidence of fertility in such a way that successive births are already naturally spaced through the inherent operation of these laws.[346]

However, he goes on to say that:

> The Church, nevertheless, in urging men to the observance of the precepts of the natural law, which it interprets by its constant doctrine, teaches that each and every marital act must of necessity retain its intrinsic relationship to the procreation of human life.[347]

The reason this is the case is because of the 'inseparable connection, established by God, which man on his own initiative may not break, between the unitive significance and the procreative significance which are both inherent to the

---

343 Pope Pius XI, *Casti Connubii*, 1930, Paragraph 54. Text at https://w2.vatican.va/content/pius-xi/en/encyclicals/documents/hf_p-xi_enc_19301231_casti-connubii.html.

344 Ibid, paragraph 56.

345 Pope Paul VI, *Humanae Vitae*, paragraph 10. Text at http://w2.vatican.va/content/paul-vi/en/encyclicals/documents/hf_p-vi_enc_25071968_humanae-vitae.html.

346 Ibid, paragraph 11.

347 Ibid, paragraph 11.

marriage act.'[348] If there are 'well-grounded reasons for spacing births, arising from the physical or psychological condition of husband or wife, or from external circumstances'[349] the Church teaches that married couples may legitimately:

> ….take advantage of the natural cycles immanent in the reproductive system and engage in marital intercourse only during those times that are infertile, thus controlling birth in a way which does not in the least offend the moral principles which we have just explained.[350]

The Pope notes that the Church is charged with inconsistency when it says that married couples may take advantage of the natural infertile period as means of birth control, but may not use artificial methods such as condoms or the birth control pill 'even if the reasons given for the later practice may appear to be upright and serious.'[351] These actions may appear to be similar, but in reality, he argues, they are completely different:

> In the former the married couple rightly use a faculty provided them by nature. In the later they obstruct the natural development of the generative process. It cannot be denied that in each case the married couple, for acceptable reasons, are both perfectly clear in their intention to avoid children and wish to make sure that none will result. But it is equally true that it is exclusively in the former case that husband and wife are ready to abstain from intercourse during the fertile period as often as for reasonable motives the birth of another child is not desirable. And when the infertile period recurs, they use their married intimacy to express their mutual love and safeguard their fidelity toward one another. In doing this they certainly give proof of a true and authentic love.[352]

Is opposition to contraception theologically valid?

We have to acknowledge that the traditional position of the Christian Church has been to oppose contraception. It is true that much of this opposition was to practices which, in modern terms, were examples of abortion rather than contraception. That is, the Church was opposed to women procuring miscarriages. Nevertheless, there has undoubtedly been opposition to action designed to prevent conception in the first place. St Augustine wrote about people who use 'poisonous drugs to secure barrenness.' The question is whether the reasons given for this opposition are theologically valid.

---

348 Ibid, paragraph 12.
349 Ibid, paragraph 16.
350 Ibid, paragraph 16.
351 Ibid, paragraph 16.
352 Ibid, paragraph 16.

If we look at Augustine's statement quoted at the beginning of this chapter, for example, it depends on the presupposition that sexual intercourse is only legitimate when it takes place in such a way that procreation is at least possible. Augustine never justifies why this should be the case. We have already seen that the way in which human beings have been created, as well as the teaching of Genesis, indicate that God's intention is that marriage, sexual intercourse, and procreation should go together. However, it does not necessarily follow that *every* act of sexual intercourse by a married couple should be intended to carry with it the possibility of procreation.

Arguably, the fact that God created a natural cycle for human fertility which contains large periods of time in which women cannot become pregnant indicates that he did not intend intercourse and procreation to be linked automatically. In the words of Hollinger: 'The fact that God created the natural female reproduction cycle with only a small window in the month in which conception can occur, demonstrates that sex is for far more than procreation.'[353]

Turning to Calvin's comments on the actions of Onan, we find that Calvin was correct to see what Onan did as something deeply sinful. After all, Genesis 38:10 tells us that 'what he did was displeasing in the sight of the Lord, and he slew him for it.' However, as Davidson comments, the real issue in the context of Genesis 38 is not so much Onan's desire to avoid having children in the abstract but the deceit involved in his pretending to have full sexual intercourse with Tamar and thus appearing to perform his responsibility to provide offspring for his dead brother whilst actually refusing to try to make her pregnant:

> Most likely what brought upon Onan the divine judgement was his pretending to perform the levirate responsibility when in fact he did not consummate the sex act and thus did not give Tamar the chance to have progeny, since the progeny would one day deprive Onan of his brother's inheritance and of the opportunity for the family life to pass through him. By his act of subterfuge, Onan was in effect causing the extinction of his brother's entire line of descendants (i.e., the line that would be reckoned to his brother). By pretending but not in fact performing the levirate duty, he also deprived Tamar of her right to be free and marry someone else (of close kin) who would give her children as heirs to her first husband.[354]

If this reading of Genesis 38 is correct (and it is supported by the way in which issues of deception and failure to perform the levirate responsibility are the themes

---

353 Hollinger, op.cit. p. 166.
354 Davidson, op.cit. p.465.

of the rest of the chapter) it follow that it would be a mistake to think that the condemnation of Onan is a condemnation of birth control as such. That is simply not what the text is about and nowhere else in Scripture is birth control itself described as sinful.

When we consider the contemporary Roman Catholic opposition to contraception set out in *Humanae Vitae*, we find there are three problems with it. The first problem lies in its insistence that 'each and every marital act must of necessity retain its intrinsic relationship to the procreation of human life.' In other words, procreation must be in view every time a husband and wife make love. The problem with this position, as Oliver O'Donovan notes, is that it wrongly atomises the relationship between a husband and wife. This violates:

> the principle that the sexual life of a married couple should be viewed as a whole, not in terms of its distinct acts of intercourse. Fornication may take the form of a series of one-night stands (for that is its moral corruption, that the sexual act never leads beyond the occasion to establish a permanent bond of loyalty), but married love is entirely different. To break marriage down into a series of disconnected sexual acts is to falsify its true nature. As a whole, then, the married love of any couple should (barring serious reasons to the contrary) be both relationship-building and procreative; the two ends of marriage are held together in the life of sexual partnership which the couple live together. But it is artificial to insists, as Humane Vitae did, that 'each and every marriage act' must express the two goods equally.[355]

The second problem is that, in spite of the argument of Pope Paul VI to the contrary, the argument of *Human Vitae* is inconsistent. It asserts that 'each and every' act of sexual intercourse between a husband and wife should be open to procreation, whilst also maintaining that it is right for married couples to control the number of children they have by only having sex outside the wife's fertile period. Both cannot be logically maintained simultaneously. *Humane Vitae* does not, in fact, advocate no birth control, but, rather, a specific way of achieving birth control. It accepts the twentieth century Christian consensus that birth control is legitimate for Christians, but differs from the position taken by other churches in holding that the only method that should be used is the so-called Natural Family Planning method of abstaining from intercourse during a wife's fertile period.

The third problem is that *Humane Vitae* does not explain why it is wrong to

---

355 O'Donovan, *Begotten or Made?* .p. 77.

use artificial contraception to 'obstruct the natural development of the generative process.' Human beings obstruct nature all the time, as for example when we divert a river to power a water mill or take action to prevent people being infected by malaria. It is generally accepted that it is legitimate to obstruct nature providing this action is taken for a good end. Why should this not also be the case in the regulation of human fertility?

To quote Hollinger again, God has given human beings the responsibility of acting as stewards of nature (see Genesis 2:15-20) and:

> …within this framework of stewardship we can accept contraception, not in order to negate the procreative character of sex, but to steward the gifts and resources that God grants to us. We can utilize non-natural means of contraception just as we steward many dimensions of natural life through technology and human knowledge.[356]

As he goes on to say, however, stewardship is not without limits:

> Such stewardship cannot utilize unethical means that harm or destroy human life, and this can never transpire out of an ethos of total control or a 'right over my own body.' This is inconsistent with the nature of life, divine providence and human stewardship. Stewardship is not an attempt at human autonomy or self-centredness, but is a response to the sovereignty of God who lovingly invites us to share in the care of his creation. Out of a framework of human stewardship in which we care for human life and for the natural world, contraceptives can be used in order to plan our families so that we can better serve them, Christ's kingdom, and the world to which God calls us.[357]

How should Christians assess different methods of birth control?

If it is legitimate for Christians to practice birth control, and also legitimate in principle to use artificial technology as a means of doing so, this still leaves us

---

356 Hollinger, op.cit. p. 165.
357 Ibid, p.165. As Matthew Leavering notes (op.cit. p.223) part of the human calling to act as responsible stewards involves taking seriously the environmental impact of population growth. On the other hand, begetting children to live in God's kingdom is also an important good. His conclusion is that:
The charitable married couple…will be loath not to share the gift of existence. Yet, for the sake of other important goods (including the common good of the ecosystems of the earth), a charitable married couple may prudently abstain from procreation. Given the greatness of the potential good involved—a child of God—there must be an important good that motivates the couple's abstinence. The blessing of life is the greatest blessing a married couple can share, and so having children is the charitable norm, and marriage involves the commitment to having children when it becomes prudently possible.

with the challenge of deciding whether every means of birth control is legitimate. Perhaps some should not be used because they are morally objectionable.

It is difficult to see any moral objection at all to the use of Natural Family Planning. This method of birth control simply uses the natural cycle of human fertility which God has created. If we accept that is legitimate to use artificial means of birth control it is also difficult to see any moral objection to barrier methods such as condoms, diaphragms, cervical caps or spermicidal sponges. If there are morally justifiable reasons for preventing pregnancy entirely (such as a permanent threat to the woman's life if she becomes pregnant) then it is also difficult to see any moral objections to permanent sterilisation.

Where moral problems do arise, however, is with methods of contraception that result (or can result) in the destruction of an embryo. This is true of the abortion pill (RU 146) which is specifically designed to abort an existing embryo. It is also potentially true of hormonal contraceptives such as the birth control pill, intrauterine devices (IUDs) using copper, and emergency contraception (the so-called 'morning after' pill). These latter forms of contraception are primarily designed to prevent ovulation (that is the release of eggs from a woman's ovaries). However, it is also suggested that they can have a secondary effect of decreasing the thickness of the endometrial lining of the womb thus lessening the chance of an embryo implanting successfully (and therefore potentially causing embryos to perish).

Forms of contraception which are designed to destroy the embryo, or may do so as a secondary effect of their operation, are morally problematic because there is a good case that human life beginning at the point of fertilisation. In the words of Doherty:

> Fertilisation is when a new human life begins physically. A fertilised egg is not a part of the father or the mother in the way that the sperm or the egg were—something new has begun. No new beginning takes place after this: all that ensues is the natural development of the new life that has already begun.[358]

If human life begins at fertilisation then the deliberate destruction of the embryo through the use of the abortion pill is certainly morally unacceptable since and the use of devices that that may prevent implantation of the embryo also raise moral questions. It would be necessary to decide whether the risk of preventing implantation, even if it were very small, was a risk worth taking given that the destruction of a human life would be involved.[359]

---

358 Doherty, op.cit. p. 13.
359 For an up to date guide to the moral issues around the use of different types of contra-

It is important to recognise that even if one is not entirely certain when human life begins, if the point of fertilisation is a possibility, then one would have an obligation to act as if it did begin at that point (in the same way that one would have to act on the possibility that someone was trapped in a burning building).[360] The same moral issues therefore apply.

Forms of infertility treatment

The debate about contraception concerns whether, and, if so, how, it would be right to prevent birth taking place. However, as the biblical stories of Abraham and Sarah (Genesis 15 – 21), Elkanah and Hannah (1 Samuel 1) and Zechariah and Elizabeth (Luke 1 – 2) remind us, a very large number of couples have problems with conceiving any children at all. This is a situation which causes great pain to the people involved and can often place a great strain on their marriages.

Due to advances in medical technology there are now a range of treatments on offer to people who have problems conceiving naturally. The debate about infertility treatment is about which of these treatments it might be right for infertile couples to use in order to fulfil the command to 'be fruitful and multiply'. Christians have a responsibility to understanding the moral issues involved in such treatments in order to make right decisions themselves and to help others to do so.

There is general agreement among Christian ethicists over the legitimacy of medical intervention to allow a couple to conceive through sexual intercourse. This would include surgery to clear a blockage in a man's testicles or a woman's fallopian tubes, the use of drugs to aid or stimulate ovulation, or even a womb transplant. In all these cases the aim is to try to counteract a disorder resulting from the Fall in order to allow conception to take place in the normal course of events.

There is continuing debate, however, about whether it is morally right to use techniques that go beyond enabling people to conceive through normal sexual intercourse. The techniques involved can be listed as follows:

- Intrauterine insemination (IUI) in which sperm from a husband is inserted artificially into a woman's uterus rather than through sexual intercourse.

- Donor insemination (DI) in which the insemination is performed using sperm from someone other than the husband.

---

ception see Rick Thomas, Contraception: a guide to ethical use, London Christian Medical Fellowship, 2017.

360 See Robert Song, 'To be willing to kill what for all one knows is a person is to be willing to kill a person' in Brent Waters and Ronald Cole Turner (eds.), *God and the Embryo: Religious Voices on Stem Cells and Cloning*, Washington DC: Georgetown University Press, 2003, pp. 98-107.

- Egg donation in which eggs from a female donor are used and then fertilised using a husband's sperm though either gamete intrafallopian transfer or in vitro fertilisation.

- Gamete intrafallopian transfer (GIFT) in which eggs from a woman or a donor are placed with sperm from the husband inside a woman's fallopian tubes.

- Zygote intrafallopian transfer (ZIFT) in which embryos are implanted in a woman's fallopian tubes.

- In vitro fertilisation (IVF) in which fertilisation between eggs and sperm takes place in a petri dish with an embryo or embryos being implanted in the woman's uterus in the hope of implantation.

- Surrogate motherhood arrangements involving either *genetic surrogacy* in which a woman conceives using sperm donated from someone else's husband with the resulting child being then given to that husband and his wife or *gestational surrogacy* in which embryos produced through IVF are implanted into a woman's womb with the resulting baby being given to the couple from whom the embryos came.

- Intracytoplasmic sperm injection (ICSI) in which a single sperm is injected in an egg to produce an embryo.[361]

Are Roman Catholic objections to fertility treatment valid?

The Roman Catholic Church officially rejects all these forms of fertility treatment. Two fundamental objections are set out in the teaching document *Donum Vitae* which was issued by the Congregation for the Doctrine of the Faith in 1987. They are summarised as follows in the *Catechism of the Catholic Church*:

> Techniques that entail the dissociation of husband and wife, by the intrusion of a person other than the couple (donation of sperm or ovum, surrogate uterus), are gravely immoral. These techniques (heterologous artificial insemination and fertilization) infringe the child's right to be born of a father and mother known to him and bound to each other by marriage. They betray the spouses' 'right to become a father and a mother only through each other.'

> Techniques involving only the married couple (homologous artificial insemination and fertilization) are perhaps less reprehensible, yet remain morally unacceptable. They dissociate the sexual act from the procreative act. The act which brings the child into existence is no longer an act by which two persons

---

361 This list is from Scott B. Rae, *Moral Choices, An Introduction to Ethics*, Grand Rapids: Zondervan, 2009, Kindle edition, Loc.3284-3324.

give themselves to one another, but one that 'entrusts the life and identity of the embryo into the power of doctors and biologists and establishes the domination of technology over the origin and destiny of the human person. Such a relationship of domination is in itself contrary to the dignity and equality that must be common to parents and children.[362]

From a Roman Catholic perspective, therefore, the two fundamental objections to the use of medical techniques to achieve fertility are that (a) they introduce a third person into the conception or gestation of a child and (b) that they separate conception from the act of sexual intercourse.

The first of these two objections must be granted. It is wrong to introduce a third party, such as a donor, into the begetting of a child. As we have seen, according to the creation narratives in Genesis, God has so created the human race that children are meant to come into existence as the fruit of the exclusive love between husband and wife expressed through sexual intercourse. As O'Donovan puts it, 'This is a knot tied by God, which men should not untie.'[363]

It might be argued that because the donor of eggs, sperm, or womb, 'has no sexual relationship with the opposite partner in the marriage' it therefore follows that the sexual bond between husband and wife 'remains un-breached by any alien presence.'[364] To put it simply, there has been no extra-marital sexual intercourse, and therefore no adultery, and so everything is OK. However, as O'Donovan goes on to say, everything is not OK. If we go down this road we replace the begetting of children through marital love with making children as an act of the will by means of medical technology:

> …when we narrow our concern for the exclusiveness of marriage to the area of sexual relations, leaving a wide-open field for third party intervention in procreation, we have taken a fundamental and decisive step to 'making' our children. We have done it by taking the procreative good of marriage away from its natural root in the exclusive sexual bond of husband and wife. That bond is allowed to go its own way, un-encumbered by procreative implications, while we have made a project of the will out of producing children.[365]

O'Donovan is also critical of the argument that the separation between sexual intercourse and having children has already been accepted in the case of adoption. As he sees it, this argument is based on a misunderstanding of adoption:

---

362 *Catechism of Catholic Church* p.509 quoting Donum Vitae II.1 and II.5.
363 O'Donovan, *Begotten or Made?* p.17.
364 Ibid. p.38.
365 Ibid. p.40.

Adoption is not procreation, and does not fulfil the procreative good of marriage. It is a charitable vocation indicated to childless couples by the personal tragedy of their deprivation in this area. And although it may richly compensate for the sorrow and satisfy the desire to nurture and educate children, it is still a substitute for procreation rather than a form of procreation. This is not to belittle or demean the adoptive relationship. Indeed, it might be said to praise it on altogether a higher level, inasmuch as it points beyond the natural goods of marriage to the supernatural good of charity. But adoption cannot be taken as a precedent for interpreting procreation as a simple enterprise of the will.[366]

Furthermore, the reason why adoption is only considered when all possibilities for a child to be raised by its natural parents have been exhausted is precisely because it is recognised that a child's well-being is best met if it knows and is raised by its biological parents. As Doherty comments,

> It seems odd, therefore, that we would deliberately create a child whom we already know will not be raised by one or both of their genetic parents. Put more bluntly, this shows that gamete donation exists to serve the interests of the parent not the child.[367]

While we should accept the Roman Catholic objection to forms of infertility treatment involving third party donation, we need not accept their objection to forms of treatment using eggs or sperm provided by a husband or wife. Here again O'Donovan is helpful. He questions the Roman Catholic claim that forms of aided conception necessarily disassociate the procreative from the sexual act:

> If they are indeed independent (and not subordinate to the couple's quest for fruitfulness in their sexual embrace) then they are certainly offensive. But that point cannot be settled simply by asserting that they are distinct. The question remains: is there a moral unity which holds together what happens at the hospital with what happens at home in bed? Can these procedures be understood appropriately as the couple's search for help within their sexual union (the total-life union of their bodies, that is, not a single sexual act)? And I have to confess that I do not see why not. News reports tell us that some IVF practitioners advise their Roman Catholic patients to have sexual intercourse following embryo replacement, in order to respect the teaching of their church. It would seem to me that such advice might well be given to all patients, in order

366 Ibid, p.40.
367 Doherty, op.cit. p.49.

to help them form a correct view of what is, or should be, meant by the technique: not the making of a baby apart from the sexual embrace, but the aiding of the sexual embrace to achieve its proper goal of fruitfulness.[368]

Seen in this light, the second Roman Catholic objection falls away. What this means is that there is no overall moral objection to assisted conception providing that it does not involve either donations of eggs or sperm from a third party.

What moral issues are raised by gestational surrogacy and *in vitro* fertilisation?

The fact that there is no overall moral objection to assisted conception does not mean that all such forms of assisted conception are morally acceptable. Two forms in particular raise serious moral issues. The first is gestational surrogacy. Here there are two issues:

1. In order for the child to flourish in the womb the surrogate mother needs to bond emotionally with the child she is carrying, a child which is then taken away from her. What this means is that emotional distress for the surrogate is a necessary part of the process.

2. In addition, in commercial forms of gestational surrogacy, even if women are not being exploited (which they very often are), there is still the problem of the commercialisation of the womb 'which is a sacred space reserved for the beginning and development of human life.'[369]

The second is *in vitro* fertilisation. Here the problem is not with the basic concept of bringing together the egg and the sperm in a petri dish. The problem is that IVF techniques produce more embryos than are normally implanted in the prospective mother thus leaving a surplus of embryos which are destroyed or frozen. If we accept that an embryo is a human being this deeply troubling because it means that people are being destroyed or neglected by being left in freezers. There are possible ways around this problem, such as using all the embryos that are produced, using the GIFT procedure in which sperm and eggs are placed in the fallopian tube, or using frozen eggs rather than frozen embryos, but anyone considering IVF techniques does need to bear the status of the embryo in mind when agreeing to forms of treatment. What would be morally wrong would be to take part knowingly in forms of treatment that one knew or believed would lead to the destruction or neglect of a person created in God's image and likeness.[370]

---

368 O'Donovan, *Begotten or Made?*, pp.78.
369 Hollinger, op.cit. p.214.
370 See Doherty, *op.cit.* pp. 50-56 and Hollinger, *op.cit*, pp. 206-27.

What about 'designer babies'?

Since it is possible to decide which sperm and embryos to use in assisted conception, there is the potential for seeking to produce babies that have a particular sex, particular physical characteristics (e.g., tall, blond-haired, blue-eyed), or will have a high IQ. There is also the possibility of producing 'saviour siblings' who will supply suitable transplant tissue for an existing child who is critically ill or dying. Conversely, it is possible to reject embryos who will be handicapped, or who will be carriers of a genetic disease.

As Hollinger explains, the problem with all attempts to produce designer babies, even when it is done for good reasons, as in the case of saviour siblings, is that they go against the basic Christian idea that children are a gift from God:

> We do not manufacture or possess our children, they belong to God. They come to us not by our designs to achieve something for ourselves, but by our joyful and reverent entrance into the ongoing drama of life in which children are a fruit of our love and unity. To design our children, even for so-called good causes, is to lose sight of the mystery which accepts whatever may come from the sexual union of husband and wife. Their covenant love in a fallen world means 'for better or worse' even in the challenges that may come with the gift.

> The one-flesh covenant of love ensures that the least among us in IQ, physical capabilities, or appearance will be embraced and loved unconditionally for that is a moral responsibility that a sexual relationship requires. Designing babies to fit our needs is a sin against our children, a sin against the very nature of marital sex, and a sin against a holy God who calls us to accept the gift as a given part of marital union.[371]

What does all this mean in practice?

Christians always have a responsibility to act within the framework for human life which God has given. This means accepting God's general call to be fruitful and multiply, respecting the moral status of a human being from the moment of conception, and begetting babies as the fruit of the marital union between husband and wife. Where birth control and infertility treatment are live personal issues, we need to accept that we cannot simply use whichever techniques are most convenient or that seem most likely to achieve our desired goals. As in all the areas we have examined in this study, techniques for birth control and assisted conception

---

371 Hollinger pp.211-212.

have to be assessed in the light of God's created framework and only those that are consistent with it should be utilised.

If we are supporting someone who is dealing with these issues we should listen to their hopes and concerns, support them as they wrestle with the moral, emotional and physical challenges involved, share in their happiness if new life does come ('rejoice with those who rejoice, mourn with those who mourn' Romans 12:15) and finally be willing to act as their conscience, reminding them of their need to walk in the way that God has laid down.

Finally, we need to address the public debate about birth control and infertility treatment, reminding people that we cannot simply do what we want and is now technologically possible, but only that which accords with God's will by respecting God's call to be fruitful and multiply, the God given dignity of all human life from the moment it comes into existence and the God given link between procreation and the sexual union between husband and wife in marriage.[372]

Questions for discussion

1. Is it right to seek to limit the number of children we have?

2. If it is right to seek to do this, what form, or forms, of family planning is it legitimate to use?

3. How should Christians decide what kind of fertility treatment they should be willing to undergo?

---

372 The God-given link between procreation and sexual intercourse between men and women in marriage means that it is wrong from a Christian point of view for single people or same-sex couples to seek to have babies through the use of fertility techniques such as egg or sperm donation or surrogacy. To do this is to separate procreation from sexual intercourse, marriage, and parenthood, which God created to go together.

PART III

Conclusion

CHAPTER 11

Conclusion— Glorify God in your body

This chapter summarises the argument developed in the course of this study. We will use a series of questions and answers to take the reader step-by-step through the key points.

Question 1: What is a human being?

Human beings are creatures with rational souls and bodies. We are divided into two sexes, male and female, according to the biology of our bodies and we are designed to reproduce by means of sexual intercourse between these two sexes.

Question 2: Why do human beings exist?

Contrary to the claims of atheist writers like Bertrand Russell, Lewis Wolpert and Richard Dawkins, human beings do not exist as the accidental result of the operation of material forces which had no understanding of what they were doing.

Human beings exist because we are created and preserved in existence by the infinitely powerful, wise and good God who is Father, Son and Holy Spirit, the creator of heaven and earth. Since humans are created by this immaterial God, we have an immaterial element to our being, namely our souls, and have an ineradicable sense that there is a difference between good and evil and that good is better than evil.

Question 3: What is the purpose of human existence?

Human beings exist to know, love, and serve God both in this world and the world to come and, as those made in God's image and likeness, to love and care for the people and the world that he has made.

Question 4: How do we live rightly before God?

We live rightly before God when we fulfil the purpose for which we were made.

The grace of God means that we have the freedom to do this because we have been liberated from the power of sin, death, and the devil by the death and resurrection of Jesus Christ and because the Holy Spirit has been poured into our hearts to make us holy people who live according to God's will.

Because of the continuing activity of the Devil and the continuing influence of our old natures, we shall not in this life ever live perfectly rightly before God. However, when we do fail God offers us forgiveness and a new start.

Question 5: What does it mean to love?

To love someone or something is to discern its nature, delight in its existence, and act towards it in accordance with its existence.

To love God is therefore to discern who God is, to delight in who he is, and to respond to him in ways that accord with who he is. Because we discern that God is our all-wise and all-loving king, we love him by submitting to his authority, accepting his love, and allowing ourselves to be guided by his instruction.

To love other human beings is likewise to discern who they are, delight in who they are, and respond to them accordingly. Because all human beings are made by God to know, love, and serve him, we show love to them when we behave towards them in ways that help them to achieve this purpose.

Question 6: How do we receive God's instruction about how to live?

Although God can instruct us through visions and prophecies, we normally receive God's instruction in two ways:

1. Through the way that he has made us and the world as a whole (so called 'natural revelation').

2. Through the Bible, which supplements natural revelation by telling us about how God has created us, how he has acted in the history of Israel and through Jesus Christ to rescue us and all creation from sin and death, and how he will act in future so that we can share life with him forever in a new heaven and a new earth.

Through these two sources we learn who God is, who we are, and how we should behave in consequence.

The teaching of the Early Fathers and the Church of England's historic formularies help us to understand the teaching given to us in the Bible and how it applies to our lives.

Question 7: What is sex?

Sex means two things. First, it means the biological distinction between male and female human beings. Secondly, it is short hand for sexual activity, which is the penetration of the female vagina by the male penis and other forms of bodily activity that are intended to accompany or lead to such penetration, or to simulate the physical pleasure produced by it.

Question 8: Is it possible to live outside the 'gender binary?'

The 'gender binary' is the term that is used nowadays to refer to the belief that human beings are either male or female and should relate to each other as such. Some people are now seeking to live outside the gender binary by claiming to be neither male nor female, or by seeking to live as women though they are biologically male, or as men though they are biologically female.

From a Christian perspective it is impossible really to live outside the gender binary for two reasons. First, natural revelation teaches us that almost all human beings are clearly either male or female, even when psychologically they find this something that is hard to accept. Secondly, even the tiny minority of people who are genuinely intersex do not have bodies that are neither male nor female, but rather bodies that contain elements of both. This means that in spite of the disorder in their sexual development they too bear witness to God's creation of humanity as a sexually dimorphic species.

In addition, the Bible teaches us that to reject our sex is to be disobedient to God by choosing not to live as the person he has created us to be.

Question 9: What is the God given context for sexual activity?

The Bible teaches that the God-given context for sexual activity is marriage, which is an exclusive, lifelong, relationship between one man and one woman. Within marriage sexual activity has two purposes: to express and deepen the loving union between husband and wife and to be the means through which children are conceived.

Question 10: What are the goods of marriage?

There are three goods of marriage:

1. It is a relationship of friendship in which a man and a woman are able to provide each other with 'mutual society, help and comfort' as they journey together towards God's eternal kingdom.

2. It is a relationship that bears witness to God's faithful love for his people and

its future consummation in the communion between God and his people in the coming kingdom.

3. It is a relationship that provides the best context for the conception of children and their nurture as people who will love and serve God in their turn.

God calls men and women to live together in marriage in an ordered form of mutual submission. The husband submits his own desires to the well-being of his wife and family by providing them with servant leadership modelled on Christ's care for his people. The wife supports him in this role and is willing to obey him when he exercises it, not because he is better or smarter than she is, but out of reverence for Christ and as a witness to the Church's need to submit to him.

Question 11: Is it right for married couples to use birth control and infertility treatment?

It is legitimate for married couples to seek to plan the number and spacing of their children and to use methods of birth control for this purpose. However, birth control methods that result in the destruction of embryos are morally problematic since embryos are people.

It is likewise legitimate for married couples to use medical technology to assist conception where this is proving difficult. However forms of infertility treatment that involve the use of third party (as in egg or sperm donation or surrogacy) are morally problematic, as are those that result in the destruction or freezing of embryos.

Question 12: Is it ever right for those who are married to divorce and re-marry?

God's intention is that marriage should be for life, so divorce is always contrary to God's perfect will. However, the New Testament permits divorce where the marriage bond has been broken through adultery and where a non-Christian spouse seeks to end the marriage. In these instances divorce is permitted (although not mandatory) and re-marriage may then follow because the first marriage has ended.

Question 13: Is everyone called to be married?

No, God does not call everyone be married. Many people are called to be single either at particular points in their lives, or for the whole of their lives.

Like marriage, singleness has its own goods. Single people are able to offer God wholehearted dedication to his service without the need to care for a family as well (as in the case of Jesus and St Paul). Single people also point to the truth that marriage is not the final form of human existence, but that in the world to come marriage as we know it will not exist, but will be transcended in a life of perfect communion with God and with all of God's people.

Like married people, those who are called to a life of singleness need the opportunity to experience deep relationships of friendship with people of both sexes. Churches need to take responsibility for enabling this to happen.

Question 14: What is chastity?

Chastity is living in obedience to God by being sexually abstinent outside marriage and sexually faithful within it. Chastity is not only a matter of refraining from sexual activity outside marriage, but seeking to control the existence of sexually immoral thoughts by avoiding situations and activities that will lead to them.

Question 15: What is *porneia* and why should it be avoided?

Porneia is the catch-all term used in the New Testament for all forms of sexual activity outside marriage. Among other things, the first Christians were distinctive because they regarded all forms of *porneia* as off-limits for both men and women because of the command that Christians should 'glorify God in your body' by living lives of chastity. Christians today have to regard *porneia* as off-limits for the same reason, as well as because of the physical, emotional and psychological damage that extra-marital sexual activity brings in its wake.

According to the Bible, a relationship between two people of the same sex can never be marriage (even if the law describes it as such) because God created marriage as a relationship between two people of the opposite sex. In consequence, all same-sex sexual relationships are *porneia* in that they are a form of extra-marital sexual activity.

Question 16: How should Christians (including those who are same-sex attracted themselves) respond to others who are sexually attracted to those of the same sex? How should Christians (including those who suffer from gender dysphoria) respond to others who find it difficult to accept the sex into which they were born?

a. Christians are called to treat all people with value and dignity, including everyone with same-sex attraction and gender dysphoria, as those created in God's image and likeness and for whom Christ died. Christians should also understand that this is not a matter of 'them' and 'us'. There are Christians who experience same-sex attraction and Christians who find it difficult to accept the sex into which they were born.

b. Christians should offer unconditional friendship and seek to understand the particular challenges faced in living in obedience to God in these areas. It is wrong to think that anyone is intrinsically less godly because of the desires they experience or the struggles they have about their sexual identity.

c. If anyone is not already living in accordance with God's will, Christians should be willing, when the time is right, to explain to them why they believe it is not right to have sex with people of the same sex, or to reject the sex into which you were born.

d. Christians should be willing to stand by those who are struggling and offer prayer, encouragement, and emotional, psychological and practical support to help believers to live in obedience to God.

e. Christians should also challenge (and when necessary discipline) those who are Christians but who claim that they do not need to live in accordance with God's will in these areas, and nobody should be ordained who is not living in ways that offer a 'wholesome pattern and example' to the Church and to the wider world.

Question 17: What is the Church called to do in the present situation?

The teaching about marriage and sexuality that has been outlined in this study and summarised above involves a call to an ascetic lifestyle, as Christopher Roberts suggests in his book *Creation and Covenant*. That is to say, it involves a call to renounce things that we desire to do for the sake of God and his kingdom. Furthermore, as Roberts goes on to say,

> If the church wants to commend such asceticism as regards sex, it will be credible if the church is a community wherein a life of celibacy and singleness is plausible and attractive. If sexual difference is to be an occasion of freedom, an arena in which men and women seek together a social ecology to mock and rival the ways of concupiscence, then very few aspects of contemporary church life will remain unscathed. The early patristic confidence that ecclesial social life should be visibly different from pagan life, in particular at the sexual level, would need to be reclaimed. How would the church respond to youth culture if it genuinely believed that the dynamic of the sexes is grounded in the imago

Dei and not in romance? How might courtship habits and living arrangements need to be reconfigured if lay celibacy were a bona fide response to sexuality? What new tone of voice would need to be adopted of Christians who realized that everyone who has ever lusted selfishly is judged by the tradition's teleology for sexual difference and not just the homosexually inclined? Reclaiming the theological tradition about sexual difference would entail not only a chastening word to the revisionist theologians but also a thoroughgoing revolution for almost all Christians.[373]

It follows that the challenge facing anyone in the Church of England who wishes to remain faithful to God in the areas of sexuality and family life is not just to stop the Church of England changing its teaching and practice—important though that is—and not just to persuade politicians to allow a space for traditional Christian teaching and practice in the public square. First and foremost it is a challenge to allow God to enable us to live lives that are distinctive and attractive, and show why living in God's way is a good idea. We need to allow God to make us people who live in such a way that those watching us stop and say 'I want some of that.'

Of course, we need to be realistic about the fact that, even if we live in this way, we may not achieve immediate and obvious success. The Church remained a tiny and despised minority in the Roman Empire for many centuries. During the Nazi rise to power in both the German state and church, Dietrich Bonhoeffer reminded his listeners in a sermon on Matthew 16:13-18 that Christians must accept that it is Christ's prerogative to build his Church as and when he wills, and our lesser job is to remain faithful and to bear witness to him, confident that he knows what he is doing:

It is a great comfort which Christ gives to his church: you confess, preach, bear witness to me, and I alone will build where it pleases me. Do not meddle in what is my province. Church, do what is given to you to do well and you have done enough. But do it well. Pay no heed to views and opinions, don't ask for judgements, don't always be calculating what will happen, don't always be on the look-out for another refuge! Church, stay a church! But Church confess, confess, confess! Christ alone is your Lord, from his grace alone can you live as you are. Christ builds.

And the gates of hell shall not prevail against thee. Death, the greatest inheritance of everything that has existence, here meets its end. Close by the prec-

---

373 Christopher Roberts, *Creation and Covenant*, London and New York: T&T Clark, 2007, p.p.245-246.

ipice of the valley of death the church is founded, the church which makes confession of Christ its life. The church possesses eternal life just where death seeks to take hold of her; and he seeks to take hold of her because she has possession of eternal life. The Confessing Church is the eternal church because Christ protects her. Her eternity is not visible in this world. She remains despite the attack of this world. The waves pass right over her and sometimes she seems to be completely covered and lost. But the victory is hers, because Christ her Lord is by her side and he has overcome the world of death. Do not ask to see the victory; believe in the victory and it is yours.[374]

---

374 Dietrich Bonhoeffer, *No Rusty Swords*, London: Fontana, 1970, pp.212-213.

APPENDIX 1

St Andrews Day Statement

Introduction

Faced with practical questions which arouse strong and conflicting passions, the church has only one recourse: to find in the Gospel a starting-point of common faith from which those who differ can agree to proceed in their discussions. Such a question now before the Church of England is how we should respond to those, including clergy, seeking to live in quasi-marital relations with a partner of the same sex. The purpose of the following statement is to provide some definition of the theological ground upon which the issue should be addressed and from which any fruitful discussion between those who disagree may proceed. By defining its fundamental agreements more clearly, the church may lighten the weight which is at present laid upon a practical question not without importance in its own right but in danger of being over-freighted with symbolic resonances. This in turn may create a context for principled pastoral care which is more responsive to particular individual circumstances and less to political meanings that can be read into them. That the issue should have become so highly dramatised calls for repentance on the part of all members of the church. It suggests that the Gospel has not been directing the acts, words and thoughts of Christians on this subject.

To emphasise its purpose the statement is in two parts, the first an affirmation of credal principles, the second an application of these principles to the question of homosexuality as it presents itself to the church today. It is not intended to cover every issue that must be considered in this context, and nothing should be inferred from what the statement does not say. If its assertions prove susceptible of being accommodated within more than one interpretation of present disputes, that will be an advantage, since it hopes to include all who do not intend a decisive break with orthodox Christianity. Of those who, nevertheless, find that they cannot agree, it is asked only that they should be precise about their disagreements, so that the extent of common ground available to the church may become clear.

Principles

I

Jesus Christ is the one Word of God. He came in human flesh, died for our sins and was raised for our justification. In the flesh he lived for us a life of obedience to the will of God; on the Cross he bore God's judgement on our sin; and in his resurrection our human nature was made new. In him we know both God and human nature as they truly are. In his life, death and resurrection we are adopted as children of God and called to follow in the way of the cross. His promise and his call are for every human being: that we should trust in him, abandon every self-justification, and rejoice in the good news of our redemption.

II

The Spirit of Jesus Christ bears witness to the Gospel in Holy Scripture and in the ministry of the people of God. He directs us in the task of understanding all human life and experience through the Scriptures. And so, guided by the Spirit of God to interpret the times, the church proclaims the Word of God to the needs of each new age, and declares Christ's redeeming power and forgiveness in mutual encouragement and exhortation to holiness.

III

The Father of Jesus Christ restores broken creation in him. For he himself is its fulfilment: in him the church learns by its life and witness to attest to the goodness and hope of creation. The Spirit gives us strength and confidence to live as men and women within the created order, finding peace and reconciliation and awaiting the final revelation of the children of God.

Application

I

"In him"—and in him alone—"we know both God and human nature as they truly are"; and so in him alone we know ourselves as we truly are. There can be no description of human reality, in general or in particular, outside the reality in Christ. We must be on guard, therefore, against constructing any other ground for our identities than the redeemed humanity given us in him. Those who understand themselves as homosexuals, no more and no less than those who do not, are liable to false understandings based on personal or family histories, emotional dispositions, social settings, and solidarities formed by common experiences or ambitions. Our sexual affections can no more define who we are than can our class, race or nationality. At the deepest ontological level, therefore, there is no such thing as "a" homosexual or "a" heterosexual; there are human beings, male and female, called to redeemed humanity in Christ, endowed with a complex variety of emotional potentialities and threatened by a complex variety of forms of alienation. "Adopted as children of God and called to follow in the way of the cross", we all are summoned to various forms of self-denial. The struggle against disordered desires, or the misdirection of innocent desires, is part of every Christian's life, consciously undertaken in baptism. In any individual case, the form which this struggle takes may be determined by circumstances (wealth or poverty, illness or health, educational success or failure). Often these are not open to choice, but are given to us as a situation in which we are to live faithfully. We are not promised that the struggle will be quickly and triumphantly resolved, nor even that it will be successful at every point along the way; only that it will be crowned at last by a character formed through patience to be like Christ's.

II

The interpretation of homosexual emotion and behaviour is a Christian "task", still inadequately addressed. "Guided by God's Spirit", the church must be open to empirical observation and governed by the authority of the apostolic testimony. According to this testimony the rebellion of humankind against God darkens our mind and subverts our understanding of God and creation (Acts 26.18; Romans 1.19-32; Ephesians 4.17-19). For the biblical writers the phenomena of homosexual behaviour are not addressed solely as wilfully perverse acts but in generalised terms, and are located within the broader context of human idolatry (Romans 1.26-27 with 1.19-32; 1 Cor. 6.9-10 with 6.12-20). Many competing interpretations of the phenomena can be found in contemporary discussion, none of them with an unchallengeable basis in scientific data. The church has no need to espouse any one theory, but may learn from many. To every theory, however, it must put the question whether it is adequate to the understanding of human nature and its redemption that the Gospel proclaims. Theories which fail this test can only imprison the imagination by foreclosing the recognition of emotional variety and development. To "interpret the times" in the midst of this theoretical confusion, the church must avoid being lulled by the vague idea that there is a transparent and necessary progress of thought working itself out in history, with which it has only somehow to keep abreast. It must search for conceptual and theological clarification. Without this there are dangers in a wide-ranging programme of discussions which, with insufficient support from the church's teaching, may serve merely to amplify the Babel of confused tongues. The primary pastoral task of the church in relation to all its members, whatever their self-understanding and mode of life, is to re-affirm the good news of salvation in Christ, forgiveness of sins, transformation of life and incorporation into the holy fellowship of the church. In addressing those who understand themselves as homosexual, the church does not cease to speak as the bearer of this good news. It assists all its members to a life of faithful witness in chastity and holiness, recognising two forms or vocations in which that life can be lived: marriage and singleness (Genesis 2.24; Matthew 19. 4-6; 1 Cor. 7 *passim*). There is no place for the church to confer legitimacy upon alternatives to these.

Pastoral care, however, needs a certain flexibility, taking note of the circumstances which make each individual case different from every other, and discerning ways in which the Gospel touches people in different situations. The church, then, will give constant encouragement in following Christ not only to those who conform to one of these two vocations, but to all who seriously intend discipleship in fellowship with the body of the church. It is in this sense that the Bishops' Statement (Issues in Human Sexuality, 1991) is to be understood when it speaks of "respecting the integrity" (cf. 5.21) of those who conscientiously dissent from the biblical teaching as the church understands it. While this teaching applies to all-for the priesthood of believers consecrates all Christians to a life of holiness-the Bishops have Scripture on their side in arguing that special considerations affect the behaviour of the clergy, who have a particular commission to expound and exemplify the teachings of the church (cf. 1 Tim. 3.1-13; 4.12-13; 5.19-20; Tit. 1.5-9; Jas. 3.1; 2 Pet. 2.2).

III

The "fulfilment" of all creation is found in Christ (Eph. 1.23; Col. 1.15-19). Our own fulfilment, then, is not merely a private one but a communal, even a cosmic one. Both marriage and singleness in their different ways point forward to this fulfilment in the fellowship of God with his redeemed creation. In neither vocation, then, does fulfilment require or allow the exercise of every power or the satisfaction of every desire that any individual may reasonably have: a life may be fulfilled without occasion to employ the power of sexual expression, just as it may without occasion to exploit the potential for education, parenthood or mobility. Both vocations in their different ways give equal expression to the blessing of human friendship, which is sanctified by Christ who calls us his friends (John 15.13-15; cf. Isa. 41.8) and elevated in him to become the "fellowship of the Holy Spirit" (2 Cor. 13.14). Every aspect of our common life in Christ, friendship included, has a properly exploratory character: understanding our humanity in him, we are freed from human constructs to search out and discover the richness of creation that is opened to us by God's redeeming work.

This search finds its fulfilment as it is directed by the hope for the final appearing of Jesus, the Son obedient to the Father who will put all things in subjection to him.

For the grace of God has appeared, bringing salvation to all, training us to renounce impiety and worldly passions, and in the present age to live lives that are self-controlled, upright, and godly, while we wait for the blessed hope and the manifestation of the glory of our great God and Saviour, Jesus Christ. He it is who gave himself for us that he might redeem us from all iniquity and purify for himself a people of his own who are zealous for good deeds. Declare these things; exhort and reprove with all authority. Let no one look down on you. Titus 2.11-15

Michael Banner,
F.D Maurice Professor of Moral & Social Theology, King's College, London;

Markus Bockmuehl,
University Lecturer in Divinity and Fellow of Fitzwilliam College, Cambridge;

Timothy Bradshaw (chairman),
Dean of Regent's Park College, Oxford;

Oliver O'Donovan,
Regius Professor of Moral and Pastoral Theology, Oxford;

Ann Holt,
Director of Care for Education;

William Persson, *F*
ormerly Bishop of Doncaster;

David Wright,
Senior Lecturer in Ecclesiastical History, Edinburgh;

St Andrew's Day 1995.

APPENDIX 2

St Matthias Day Statement

On the 30th November 1995, as the world celebrated St Andrew's Day, under the aegis of the CEEC, a group of British Biblical and moral theologians published a significant and widely welcomed contribution to the then debate on homosexuality within the church. It was received by many as a thoughtful, cogently argued and pastorally sensitive contribution to the discussions, and has been broadly referenced, read and re-read in the seventeen years since it was first published.

The church's conversation on the theology and ethics of same sex relationships continues unabated. Sometimes good thinking has been marred by insensitive and occasionally homophobic attitudes. Other times, genuinely compassionate and inclusive attitudes have been weakened by a lack of biblical rigour, and a consequent misreading of the revealed mind of God.

Since 1995 social change, relational practice and ethical thinking within the church have undergone a notable transformation away from orthodox biblical thinking. Parallel to this is an increasingly comprehensive public avowal of homosexual practice greater than in any other time in our church and nation's history. Now that the government has called for a public debate on same sex marriage, effectively involving a redefinition of marriage itself, the urgency of thoughtful, biblical discussion set in the context of the Anglican formularies, their commitments and hermeneutic is especially pressing.

The Church of England Evangelical Council offers this irenic, finely argued, biblically articulate monograph, set as it is in the rich context of foundational Anglican thinking, to engage all in our church of whatever persuasion. Like its predecessor it is notable for both its rigour and sensitivity, and for this we are deeply thankful for its authors' humanity and outstanding scholarship. Of course there are other important matters such as equality and human rights that also require thorough biblical thinking and analysis; but before we address such issues, we believe it is important to restate and reaffirm classic, foundational Anglican teaching on this matter.

As a council we pray that engagement with this material will lead to deeper biblical discussion on an issue of great concern to God, and therefore for his church too. For that reason, and in the expectation and prayer for his Spirit's enablement, we offer to the Anglican Church with its many constituencies, this St Matthias Day Statement.

Michael Lawson *St Matthias Day 14 May 2012*

St Matthias Day Statement 2012

Introduction

The following short statement seeks to help Anglicans understand our church's teaching in the area of marriage and sexual relationships and its relevance today.

It does so by providing a five-fold summary of that teaching based in Scripture and Anglican tradition. This teaching should be our guide if we are to remain faithful in our pastoral, prophetic and missional responsibilities and in our inter-Anglican and ecumenical relationships.

The Church must, like Christ, welcome, love and respect all, particularly those who feel excluded and marginalised such as those who identify as sexual minorities. It must also, like Christ, bear witness to God's good purposes for humanity and call for repentance, assisting a return to God's will whenever we depart from these purposes.

Why is this statement of Anglican teaching necessary?

The Church of England's teaching about marriage and sexual relationships other than marriage currently faces a number of challenges:

Within British society, attitudes to sexual relationships have changed in recent decades and there are plans to redefine marriage.

Within the Anglican Communion, some dioceses and provinces are changing their teaching and practice.

Ecumenically, some of our sister churches, notably among the Porvoo churches, are also revising their doctrine and marriage liturgies.

What is the basis of this statement of Anglican teaching?

In the words of the Declaration of Assent, "The Church of England is part of the One, Holy, Catholic and Apostolic Church, worshipping the one true God, Father, Son and Holy Spirit. It professes the faith uniquely revealed in the Holy Scriptures and set forth in the catholic creeds, which faith the Church is called upon to proclaim afresh in each generation. Led by the Holy Spirit, it has borne witness to Christian truth in its historic formularies, the Thirty-nine Articles of Religion, The Book of Common Prayer and the Ordering of Bishops, Priests and Deacons".

Therefore, basing itself on Scripture and these formularies, the statement draws out their significance in this area if in the Church of England we are to express our "loyalty to this inheritance of faith" as "our inspiration and guidance under God" and bring "the grace and truth of Christ to this generation" **by making Him known.**

What does this statement seek to achieve?

The statement seeks to express Anglican teaching in a way that

- those committed to that teaching will welcome it as a guide and reference as they seek to teach it and live it out,

- those uncertain about that teaching will find it informative and persuasive and

- those seeking to revise that teaching will be able to dialogue with it constructively in order to clarify the nature and depth of our differences.

1. God's love and call to love

Dear friends, let us love one another, for love comes from God. Everyone who loves has been born of God and knows God. (1 John 4:7)

O Lord, who hast taught us that all our doings without charity are nothing worth: Send thy Holy Ghost, and pour into our hearts that most excellent gift of charity, the very bond of peace and of all virtues, without which whosoever liveth is counted dead before thee. Grant this for thine only Son Jesus Christ's sake. Amen. (Collect for Quinquagesima Sunday in the Book of Common Prayer)

    1a.   Empowered by the Holy Spirit, all Christians are called by God to practise Christian love (or 'charity'). Although God has called us to love all people everywhere, he has also given us certain key forms of relationship in which we can learn what it means to give and to receive love.

1b. These God-given forms of relationship include relationships between believers, marriage and other family relationships, and committed loving friendships.

1c. The Church is therefore called to affirm and support the value of all such God- given relationships. In a culture which overemphasises sexual relationships and wrongly implies that love and sexual activity necessarily belong together, we must particularly commend the importance of intimate, committed friendships that remain chaste.

2. God's Word and Church

The grass withers and the flowers fall, but the word of our God endures forever. (Isaiah 40:8)

The Church hath power to decree rites or ceremonies and authority in controversies of faith; and yet it is not lawful for the Church to ordain anything contrary to God's word written, neither may it so expound one place of Scripture, that it be repugnant to another. (Article XX).

2a. The authority of the Church to decide its own actions is limited by the word of God in Holy Scripture.

2b. The Church is not free to use certain parts of the Bible, such as the commandment to love our neighbours, as a justification for setting aside teaching contained in other parts of the Bible, such as the rejection of same-sex sexual activity.

2c. The Church therefore does not have the authority to introduce any form of marriage that differs from the form of marriage authorised and commended in Holy Scripture or to commend sexual behaviour forbidden by Holy Scripture.

3. God's gift of marriage

"Haven't you read," he replied, "that at the beginning the Creator 'made them male and female,' and said, 'For this reason a man will leave his father and mother and be united to his wife, and the two will become one flesh'? (Matthew 19:4-5)

For be ye well assured, that so many as are coupled together otherwise than God's Word doth allow are not joined together by God; neither is their matrimony lawful. (BCP Solemnization of Matrimony)

3a. Marriage as created by God is an exclusive relationship between one man and one woman that is entered into for life and that is intended in normal circumstances to result in the gift of children who are to be brought up to love and serve God. It is given to us by God both as a created institution which benefits all in society (Genesis 2.18-24) and as a relationship which images the relationship between Christ and His Church (Ephesians 5.21-32).

3b. Because marriage is instituted by God, neither the Church nor the state is authorised to re-define it.

3c. A relationship between two men or two women cannot therefore be a marriage and neither the state nor the Church should describe it as such.

4. God's grace and call to holiness

As the body without the spirit is dead, so faith without deeds is dead. (James 2:26)

Albeit that good works, which are the fruits of faith and follow after justification, cannot put away our sins and endure the severity of God's judgement, yet are they pleasing and acceptable to God in Christ, and do spring out necessarily of a true and lively faith, insomuch that by them a lively faith may be as evidently known as a tree discerned by the fruit. (Article XII)

4a. The Church is not only called to proclaim the justifying grace of God in Jesus Christ, but also to teach clearly that true faith expresses itself in holy behaviour.

4b. This holiness includes holiness in the area of sexual behaviour: faithfulness within marriage between a man and a woman and abstinence outside marriage.

4c. The Church is therefore not free to affirm or bless any form of sexual activity or sexual relationship outside marriage but should welcome those in such relationships with pastoral care, a call to repentance, and the good news that God gives us the gift of the Holy Spirit to enable us to flourish by living lives that are in accordance with His call to holiness.

5. God's people united in and by God's word

They devoted themselves to the apostles' teaching and to fellowship, to the breaking of bread and to prayer. (Acts 2:42)

The visible Church of Christ is a congregation of faithful men, in which the pure word of God is preached and the sacraments be duly ministered according to Christ's ordinance in all those things that of necessity are requisite to the same. (Article XIX)

5a. The visible Church of Christ is a place where the life-giving and life-changing word of God is faithfully proclaimed.

5b. Redefining marriage to include same-sex relationships or affirming or blessing sexual activity outside marriage is contrary to God's word.

5c. When a church does either of these things it therefore becomes difficult to recognise it as part of the visible Church of Christ. Consequently such matters fall outside the scope of acceptable ecumenical diversity and are a legitimate ground for division between churches.

Conclusion

Make every effort to live in peace with everyone and to be holy; without holiness no one will see the Lord. (Hebrews 12.14)

We offer this five part statement to Anglican Christians in the hope that, guided and nourished by Scripture and tradition, we may be led together into the way of peace and holiness as we seek to bear faithful witness to the grace and truth of Christ in society and the wider church.

We do so aware that as individuals and as a church we constantly fall short in our understanding and in our obedience.

In this and every area of our discipleship and mission we must, therefore, be constant in prayer, seeking the grace of God

O God the strength of all them that put their trust in thee, mercifully accept our prayers; and because through the weakness of our mortal nature we can do no good thing without thee, grant us the help of thy grace, that in keeping thy commandments we may please thee both in will and deed; through Jesus Christ our Lord. Amen. (Collect for the First Sunday after Trinity BCP)

APPENDIX 3

Gospel, Church & Marriage
Preserving Apostolic Faith and Life

As members of the Church of England Evangelical Council ("CEEC") within the Church of England and the one, holy, catholic and apostolic Church, we offer this reflection out of our deep love for the Church of England, the wider Anglican Communion, and the world we want to serve.

As we face many changes in British society and forceful challenges within the Church of England on matters of human sexuality and marriage, we believe it is important not simply to focus on these contentious areas of disagreement but to set them within a wider and deeper theological vision. Our desire is for the Church's teaching and practice to offer a vision of human flourishing which is faithful to Scripture.

This vision begins with God's good purposes for us all as human beings and His plan to bring these purposes to birth in His world through the gospel of His forgiveness and grace, revealed in Jesus Christ and proclaimed in the power of the Spirit by Christ's apostles. This good news creates and shapes a holy people who are called to believe it, live it, guard it, and share it with others. Together, we are called to worship the Triune God, *the source of grace* who 'has created all things, and us in His own image' and from whom comes 'all life, truth, holiness and beauty'

Scripture reveals that the Creator's passionate longing is for human flourishing and the good of all. He works to bless all nations through His people (Genesis 12:3). The laws God gave to Israel were His gracious gift ('for your good': Deuteronomy 10:13) designed to create a healthy society that would reflect God's holiness and goodness, His justice and compassion. The prophets called Israel back to this way of life in obedience to God and away from idolatry, injustice and immorality so that she could be 'a light to the nations' (Isa. 42:1-6). Likewise the Church, rooted in the apostles' teaching, is called by Jesus to be 'salt and light' in the world (Matt. 5:13-16). The Gospel shines into the darkness of our fallen hearts and cultures, and gives us the transforming knowledge of God's mercy and grace in the face of Jesus Christ.

We long for all to hear and believe this message—of God's unmerited grace and mercy shown to us all as sinful people through the atoning death and resurrection of Jesus Christ, our Lord (1 John 4:10; Ephesians 2:1-10)—and, in particular, for the people of England to come under the loving rule of Christ and so to discover the life-changing goodness of this 'amazing grace' for themselves.

The presenting divisive issues in the Church surrounding marriage and sex, and our society's movement away from Christian teaching in this area, must not distract us from working towards that goal. Yet neither can they be ignored or treated as having no bearing on how this is achieved. In order to discern how to respond to these specific matters, we must first recall and re-commit ourselves to the gospel and its purpose as revealed in Scripture:

i.   Through His Son and by His Spirit, God is working within human history and across all cultures to rescue His creation from sin and to transform the lives of Jesus' followers so that we embody His positive, life-enhancing purposes for all people.

ii.   The Church is God's gift, sign and instrument of the restoration of His creation, and is the foretaste of His new creation that is breaking in. This in turn requires us to consider what it means for the Church to have integrity as the body of Christ by remaining rooted in God's grace and being shaped by the biblical story of creation, fall, redemption and future hope.

iii.   In awaiting the final judgment and the fulfilment of God's good purposes, the Church must—at all times and in all places—faithfully obey the apostles' teaching on the pattern of faith and life that we are called to in Christ. This includes their teaching on marriage and singleness.

Only when we have received what the apostles have to say to us in each of these three areas and uncovered the deeper biblical truths that are at stake in this debate can we draw conclusions as to the necessary shape of apostolic faith and life today and what that means for our way forward as Anglicans within the one, holy, catholic and apostolic Church.

A. Apostolic Insistence on the Gospel's Purpose

As God's grace and truth prepare us for Christ's return as the *triumph of grace* over all the effects of sin, His will is that all who come under Christ's rule should turn from sin and be sanctified (1 Thess. 4:3). In this way, the true nature of God's holy purposes in the gospel are revealed to the world.

The apostolic gospel proclaimed the *work of grace*: that God, revealing His glory in human form, demonstrated His holy love and His opposition to all sin by redeeming His creation and rescuing humanity through Christ and His atoning death and glorious resurrection (Gal. 1:4; 1 John 4:10; Rom. 3:21-26). Christ had thus 'given himself' in dying on the cross with the express purpose 'to purify for himself a people, eager to do what is good' (Titus 2:14, *cf.* Rom 7:4). The gospel, as proclaimed by the apostles, had the goal and purpose—as well as the power—to transform people's lives into the likeness of Christ (Eph. 2:8-10; 1 Jn. 3:2-10; Rom. 8:29).

The apostles proclaimed that the 'grace of God has appeared', not only to affirm and redeem our created humanity and bring us forgiveness but also to 'train us to say "No" to all ungodliness' (Titus. 2:11). Such transforming grace draws us all to repentance and empowers all of us for the 'obedience of faith'. We give ourselves to God and walk by His Spirit in the path of costly grace in every sphere of our lives (Rom. 1:5; 8:12-17; 16:26).

In establishing Christian communities the apostles therefore did not teach doctrine without discipleship, faith without formation, or grace without godliness. Rather, they called believers to 'live lives worthy of the gospel', insisting 'in the Lord' that they abandon their 'former way of life' and embrace 'the new humanity', 'putting on Christ' and living His new life (Eph. 4:17-24; *cf.* Rom. 6:1-14; 1 Pet. 1:14-15; 2:11).

Moreover, the apostles consistently taught that the baptised were, by the Spirit, to pursue godliness and combat sin by putting to death the 'works of the flesh' (*e.g.* Gal. 5:16-21; 1 John 2:15-17). In founding and teaching communities of disciples who would offer this good news of God's grace to all, the apostles therefore repeatedly issued a serious call to holiness which embraced all areas of human life including sexual conduct (1 Cor. 6:9-11; 1 Tim. 1:8-10; Heb. 12:14-16; Jude 4; Rev. 2:14).

B. Apostolic Commitment to the Church's Integrity

In its ministry of *stewarding God's grace* so as to offer it to the world, the Church, being 'built on the foundation of the apostles and prophets' (Eph. 2:20) must in every age follow the apostles' example. Its teaching and discipline must remain centred on Christ and within the boundaries of essential apostolic teaching.

The apostles' preaching established *communities of grace* who confessed 'Jesus is Lord'. These 'apostolic congregations' were marked by believers' devoted submission to apostolic teaching (Acts 2:42; Rom. 6:17; Eph. 4:20). Building on the one foundation of Jesus himself (1 Cor. 3:11; Eph. 2:20), who had 'loved the Church' as His bride and had 'given himself up for her to make her holy' (Eph. 5:25-26), the apostles could not compromise the holiness of the Church. Instead they saw that, as God had called Israel to be 'holy', 'set apart' as distinct 'amongst the nations', so now the Church was to be a 'holy temple' and a 'holy nation' (Eph. 2:19-22; 1 Pet. 2:4-9; *cf.* Exod. 19:3-6; Lev. 18:3-5; 19:2; Deut. 4:5-8; Isa. 42:6-7). They thus sought to build a united body drawn from the nations ('one' and 'catholic') which was the 'pillar and foundation of the truth' (1 Tim. 3.15) and which, through obedience to apostolic teaching (Rom. 15:18; Phil. 2:12-13; 1 Pet. 1:22), conveyed and embodied that teaching in the wider world with clarity and consistency (Eph. 3:10; 4:4-17).

In order, then, for the Church to witness to the gospel with integrity and to embody the gospel's purpose, the apostles had to guard the Church's distinctive boundaries on matters of both doctrine and ethics, including sexual morality. This is evident in their use of appropriate loving discipline to ensure obedience to apostolic teaching (1 Cor. 4:14-5:5; 2 Cor. 2:5-11; Rev. 2:20), their appointment of local teachers to teach the truth (Tit. 1:9; 2 Tim. 2:2), and their warnings against harmful false teachers (*e.g.* Acts 20:29-31; 2 Pet. 2:1-3; 1 John 2:18-23).

This is why, as part of the 'one, holy, catholic and apostolic' church, the Church of England rightly orders its common life so that there are 'shepherds of Christ's flock and guardians of the faith of the apostles' who, in 'proclaiming the gospel of God's kingdom and leading His people in mission', vow to 'refute error' (Common Worship: Ordination & and Consecration of a Bishop) and are called to 'banish and drive away all erroneous and strange opinions' (Canon C18).

C. Apostolic Teaching about Marriage and Singleness

The Bible as the *revelation of grace* clearly teaches that God made humanity in His image and likeness—embodied as male and female—and gave the gifts of marriage and singleness for our benefit. This apostolic teaching about marriage and singleness is part of God's gracious call and purposes for human flourishing and is good news for all.

On Jesus' authority (*e.g.* Matt. 19:4-6, based on Gen. 2:24), the Church of England bears witness to this teaching by affirming that 'marriage is in its nature a union permanent and lifelong, for better for worse, till death them do part, of one man with one woman, to the exclusion of all others on either side' (Canon B30). Moreover, like the sacraments, marriage is a gift of God and a *sign of grace* in which His faithful and sacrificial covenant-love for us is made visible in and through our created human bodies (Eph. 5:31-2). As 'a gift of God in creation', marriage enables human flourishing and serves the common good by being 'the foundation of family life in which children are [born and] nurtured and in which each member of the family, in good times and in bad, may find strength, companionship and comfort, and grow to maturity in love' (Preface to Marriage Service).

Jesus' own understanding of the importance of marriage is underlined by His radical teaching on adultery and divorce (Matt. 5:27-32), which went to the heart of the Old Testament prohibitions in these areas. His reputation as a 'friend of sinners' was never won at the cost of watering down such ethical teachings or advocating 'cheap grace'. He rather held together grace and truth (John 1:14) in His teaching and pastoral practice — a model which the Church should always aim to follow.

Jesus, in His own experience and express teaching (Matt. 19:12), also affirmed singleness, equally, as a gracious gift from God—as did Paul (1 Cor. 7:7, 32-35); it is an opportunity for faithful and sacrificial dedication to 'the Lord's affairs' and for demonstrating an embodied longing for the ultimate marital union of Christ to His Church (Rev. 19:6-9).

In keeping with this understanding, rooted in the teaching of the Old Testament (*e.g.* Exod. 20:14; Prov. 5:15-23) and reaffirmed by Jesus himself, the apostles taught that any sex outside marriage has the character of sin (*e.g.* Matt. 5:27-29; 1 Thess. 4:3-8; Heb. 13:4). Thus, as the House of Bishops recently reaffirmed, sexual relations are 'properly conducted only within heterosexual marriage' (GS 2055, para 54). Sex is not a personal 'right' to be grasped or demanded. It is a gracious gift ordained by our Creator—tied to His gift of marriage—which is to be 'received with thanksgiving' (1 Tim. 4:4), but only within the limits He has laid down.

Application: Apostolic Faith and Life Today
In the light of this wider theological vision and apostolic teaching on the gospel's purpose, the church's integrity, and marriage and singleness, we therefore commit

ourselves to the following five conclusions and commend them to the Church of England as it considers these complex issues of human sexuality and marriage:

1. We, in the church of Jesus Christ, are called to welcome, and offer God's saving grace to, everyone—whatever their sexual history, identity or behaviour—thus manifesting the radical inclusivity of the gospel by which 'God our Saviour wants *all* people to be saved' (1 Tim. 2:3).

- Knowing that God's created intent for human sexuality has been spoilt by sin in all people and all societies, we acknowledge our own need, following conversion, to keep turning to God for forgiveness and transformation.

- We confess that to be the *community of grace* the Church itself needs forgiveness and transformation. We long for all to hear and receive the gospel message of grace and truth, rather than to fear that we, as Christians, will cast the first stone. So we receive Jesus' words as also applying to us and to all: 'Neither do I condemn you … Go now and leave your life of sin' (John 8:11). We want the church to be a community of love, warmth, hospitality, vulnerability, covenant friendship, appropriate touch, mutual support, and to be a family unit which is far bigger than some small, inward-looking heterosexual pairing.

- We therefore repent of our many failures in this area, seeking God's grace afresh to welcome, listen to, and provide pastoral support and care for all.

- Together, we will seek to honour the gift of our embodied sexual differentiation; to express life-long faithful love in marriage; and to nurture love and intimacy while abstaining from sex in all our relationships other than marriage.

2. We recognise that some fellow Christians no longer accept the Church's teaching on marriage, singleness and sex but, because it is an integral part of our calling to be holy, we cannot treat this teaching as an 'optional extra' (or *adiaphora*).

- We believe this teaching is both apostolic and essential to the gospel's transforming purpose and thus must be compassionately and clearly proclaimed and explained in and by the Church.

- This area is therefore of a higher order than other divisive matters, often viewed as 'secondary' (for example, the ordination of women), because it calls for faithful obedience to the unambiguous and authoritative teaching of Scripture concerning godly living and human flourishing.

- Thus, the upholding of this teaching, rooted in our creedal confession of God as Creator, and the enabling of Christians to live it with joy and confidence, is an essential aspect of biblical faithfulness—especially when, as in our day, these matters are being so hotly contested.

3. We believe that the Church of England, being defined by adherence to essential apostolic truth, should not accept teaching or affirm behaviour—whether implicitly or explicitly—which contradicts or undermines the boundaries laid down by apostolic teaching and practice

- Although other actions may also amount to such affirmation, we hold, on the basis of our Anglican understanding of our prayers expressing what we believe ('*lex orandi, lex credendi*') and of a Church that is ordered by its liturgy, formularies and legal provisions, that any changes in our liturgy or canons which seek to express, authorise or commend a divergence from these distinctive boundaries would be seen as a departure from the apostolic faith.

4. We further believe that, as we have sadly witnessed in recent years among Anglicans, the affirmation of non-apostolic teaching and behaviour necessarily 'tears the fabric of our Communion at its deepest level' (Primates' Communiqué, Oct. 2003) and creates 'significant distance' (Primates' Communiqué, Jan. 2016) between those who are following the apostles' teaching and those departing from it. Such affirmation by the Church of England would have a similar distancing effect on our ecumenical relationships with the Roman Catholic, Orthodox and most Protestant and Pentecostal churches, which have not changed their doctrine in this vital area.

- These consequences inevitably arise because—for those who wish to follow the apostles' practice—such significant departure from apostolic teaching regrettably requires in response some degree of visible differentiation, in order formally to acknowledge and mark this distance. Moving away from 'apostolic' and 'catholic' teaching concerning what it means to be 'holy' will tragically mean we are less visibly 'one'.

- The potential forms and extent of such differentiation are varied and they must never lose sight of the goal of restored unity in apostolic truth. Nevertheless, such acts of differentiation become a necessary component of biblical faithfulness if they are the only means to ensure the continued preservation of a cohesive 'apostolic' community, clearly defined and publicly distinguished by apostolic truth and thus able to offer a faithful and coherent witness to a confused and needy world.

5. We do not wish for this differentiation, but recognise that it may become a tragic necessity. Our submission to apostolic teaching and practice means that, as apostolic Anglicans, we are deeply committed to being members of Church of England provinces which are similarly submissive and so communicating and clearly upholding—both *de facto* and *de jure*—the pattern of teaching and discipline handed down to us by the apostles.

- We therefore pray that the Church of England does not turn away from its teaching on marriage, singleness and sex—entrusted to it by Christ and His apostles—or abandon its goal of empowering Christians to live lives worthy of the gospel of grace.

- We believe this teaching remains good news for society today, where many struggle to form wholesome and life-giving intimate friendships, lack good models of loving, faithful marriage and parenting, and face confusing choices of identity and gender.

- And so we commit ourselves to working within our local congregations and networks in order that they too may walk compassionately in obedience to the apostles' teaching. We also commit to praying for the people of England that these biblical truths will increasingly come to be recognized for their long-established and proven benefit.

Conclusion

In offering this reflection we place ourselves afresh under the grace of God and the authority of Scripture, and we consecrate ourselves to Jesus as Lord, rededicating ourselves to obey the teaching of His apostles. And we do so in a spirit of repentance for the ways we daily fail to practise the grace and truth that Jesus both preached and lived.

Our hope and prayer is that it will provide clarity in a time of confusion, encourage and bring together those who share its vision, and enable those with a different vision to understand the nature and depth of our concerns and disagreement. Going forward, we need to consider together the implications of our differences for our life together. We do this with the positive hope that in due course we might come again as Anglicans to 'experience that unity in truth and love we have in Christ especially through confession of the apostolic faith'.

'*Now to Him who is able to do immeasurably more than all we ask or imagine, to Him be glory in the Church and in Christ Jesus for ever and ever*' (Eph. 3:20-21).

Almighty God, who built your Church upon the foundation of the apostles and prophets, with Jesus Christ himself as the chief corner-stone: so join us together in unity of spirit by their doctrine, that we may be made a holy temple acceptable to you; through Jesus Christ your Son our Lord, who is alive and reigns with you, in the unity of the Holy Spirit, one God, now and for ever. *Amen.*

SCRIPTURE INDEX

Genesis 1:26	25, 45, 46, 47, 49, 50	Malachi 2:13-16	169
Genesis 1:26-31	45, 46, 50	Malachi 2:16	172, 174
Genesis 1:27	111, 174		
Genesis 2:15	51, 188	Matthew 1:23	54
Genesis 2:18	50, 51, 106	Matthew 5:27-30	137
Genesis 2:18-25	50	Matthew 5:31-32	173, 174
Genesis 2:24	52, 53, 62, 74, 78, 92,	Matthew 11:27	99
	103, 169, 174	Matthew 12:46-50	99
Genesis 2.24	210	Matthew 15:19	134
Genesis 2:25	54	Matthew 19:1-9	174
Genesis 3:7-11	54	Matthew 19:3-6	45, 54
Genesis 4:1	54	Matthew 19:4-5	70
Genesis 5:1-2	46	Matthew 19:4-6	174
Genesis 29:30-31	99	Matthew 19: 5-6	163
Genesis 38:7-11	182	Matthew 19:8	174
		Matthew 19:12	99, 101, 133
Exodus 19:10-11	92	Matthew 22:23-33	58
Exodus 20:12	20	Matthew 22:30	57, 101
Exodus 20:13	20	Matthew 25:1-36	66
Exodus 20:14	137		
Exodus 21:10-11	172, 173		
		Mark 2:15-17	143
Leviticus 19:18	38	Mark 7:21	134
		Mark 10:2-9	45, 54
Deuteronomy 5:18	137	Mark 10:6	43
Deuteronomy 6:4-5	38	Mark 10:12	174
Deuteronomy 21:15-17	99	Mark 12:18-17	58
Deuteronomy 24:1-4	170, 172, 174	Mark 12:29-31	38
		Mark 12:30	106
1 Samuel 1: 19-20	181		
1 Samuel 20:41	107		
1 Samuel 21:4-7	92	Luke 7:36-50	143
		Luke 20:27-40	58
Psalm 19:1	25	Luke 20:35	62
Psalm 119:105	29	Luke 24:36-42	62
Psalm 139:13	43		
		John 3:27-30	64
Proverbs 2:17	91	John 15:12-17	104
Proverbs 9:10	15	John 15:16	95
Proverbs 27:2	105		
		Acts 1:9-11	62
Isaiah 54:6	64	Acts 2:28	37
Isaiah 65:17	57	Acts 26.18	209
Ezekiel 16:8	64	Romans 1.19-32	209
		Romans 1:20	25
Hosea 2:19-20	64	Romans 2:14-15	25
		Romans 8:1-11	37

Romans 8:18-25   36
Romans 8:29   59
Romans 12:3-6   105
Romans 12:15   196
Romans 15:14   105
Romans 16:16   107

1 Corinthians 6   11, 37, 74, 96,
    102, 135, 136, 141, 154, 155, 159
1 Corinthians 6.9-11   159
1 Corinthians 6:12-20   74, 135, 136
1 Corinthians 6:15-20   141
1 Corinthians 6:20   37
1 Corinthians 7:3-5   74
1 Corinthians 7:7   101
1 Corinthians 7:10-16   175, 176
1 Corinthians 7:15   164, 176, 177, 178, 179
1 Corinthians 7:32-35   100
1 Corinthians 7:38   101
1 Corinthians 8   52
1 Corinthians 11:8-9   51
1 Corinthians 12:13   37
1 Corinthians 15   61, 62, 136
1 Corinthians 15:23   62
1 Corinthians 15:44   61
1 Corinthians 15:52-54   62

2 Corinthians 4:17   40, 162
2 Corinthians 5:10   66
2 Corinthians 11:2   64

Galatians 3:28-29   73
Galatians 5:13-24   68
Galatians 5:16-24   38
Galatians 5:19-21   134
Galatians 6:2   105

Ephesians 4:13   59
Ephesians 4.17-19   209
Ephesians 4:31-32   178
Ephesians 4:32   106
Ephesians 5:19   105
Ephesians 5:21   64, 67, 75, 76, 90
Ephesians 5:21-33   64, 75, 76, 90
Ephesians 5:22   76, 83, 85

Philippians 4:14   105

Colossians 3:16   105
Colossians 3:18-19   75, 76

1 Thessalonians 4:4   74
1 Thessalonians 5:11, 14-15   105

1 Timothy 2:11-14   51
1 Timothy 2:13   52
1 Timothy 5:9   74

Titus 2:4-5   75

Hebrews 3:13   106
Hebrews 13:4   134
Hebrews 13:16   105

James 5:16   105

1 Peter 3:1-7   75, 76, 79
1 Peter 4:3   135

1 John 1:8   39
1 John 4:16   104

Revelation 12:17   39
Revelation 19:6-9   64
Revelation 20:11-15   66
Revelation 21   57, 65
Revelation 21:1   57

The Church of England Evangelical Council

CEEC was first created by John Stott in 1960 to provide a "collective" evangelical voice within the Church of England.

There is much more diversity among Anglican Evangelicals today than at that time. In recent years a number of new networks have been established, all with different emphases and objectives. At the same time local groups of evangelicals from different networks, sometimes known as Diocesan Evangelical Fellowships, need a national body to which they can affiliate. CEEC exists to provide for the continuing need for an overarching group to which the networks can belong, based on common understandings of the Christian faith and its Anglican expression, and united by a common vision to promote and maintain orthodox evangelical theology and ethics at the heart of the Church of England.

CEEC is particularly concerned to encourage evangelism, bible-based and Christ-centred formation of discipleship, evangelical leadership within the Church of England, and evangelical unity within and outside Anglicanism.

The Council consists of representatives from the College of Bishops, theological colleges, mission societies, General Synod, networks and local associations, all of whom have signed agreement with the Basis of Faith and its additional declarations. CEEC is also the representative body for EFAC, the Evangelical Fellowship in the Anglican Communion.

The entire Council meets residentially once a year, and then the out-working and implemening of policy is delegated to a Working Group.

CEEC

Church of England Evangelical Council